D1718240

THE ETHICS OF BANKING

Issues in Business Ethics

VOLUME 30

For further volumes:
http://www.springer.com/series/6077

The Ethics of Banking

Conclusions from the Financial Crisis

by

PETER KOSLOWSKI

VU University Amsterdam, The Netherlands

Translated from German by

DEBORAH SHANNON

 Springer

Prof. Dr. Peter Koslowski
VU University Amsterdam
Department of Philosophy
De Boelelaan 1105
1081 HV Amsterdam
Netherlands
P.Koslowski@ph.vu.nl

Translator

Deborah Shannon
Norwich, United Kingdom
shannon@academictranslation.co.uk

The English translation has been made possible thanks to financial support from the Department of Philosophy, VU University Amsterdam, The Netherlands; *Bank für Kirche und Caritas* (Bank for Church and Charitable Works Caritas) Paderborn, Germany; and Springer Science+Business Media.

German Original: *Ethik der Banken. Folgerungen aus der Finanzkrise*, München (Wilhelm Fink Verlag) 2009.

ISSN 0925-6733
ISBN 978-94-007-0655-2   e-ISBN 978-94-007-0656-9
DOI 10.1007/978-94-007-0656-9
Springer Dordrecht Heidelberg London New York

Library of Congress Control Number: 2011924352

Printed on acid-free paper

Springer is part of Springer Science+Business Media (www.springer.com)

Preface

The crisis in the financial markets unexpectedly turned a spotlight on the ethical aspects of financial markets and financial institutions as a topic of considerable interest to the wider public. At the same time, it unleashed a debate about the future of capitalism which throws down the gauntlet to philosophers and economists. The financial crisis is not only a crisis of the economic system, but also a crisis of ethics for financial intermediaries, whose conduct threatened to turn the financial industry into a field of unmitigated self-enrichment. In that light, although this book was originally intended as the second edition of a volume published in 1997, in the event it was necessary to write an entirely new work.

The author is grateful to the institutions which have given him the opportunity to pursue his research: the Department of Philosophy at the Vrije Universiteit Amsterdam (VU University Amsterdam), Netherlands, where he has worked since 2004; the International Center for Economic Research, Turin, Italy, where he worked the year 2003–2004 and spent shorter research visits in 2005, 2006 and 2009; and Liberty Fund Inc., Indianapolis, Indiana, USA where he served as visiting scholar in residence for the year 2002–2003. Working with Liberty Fund gave the author a unique opportunity to become acquainted with the USA, not least by taking part in numerous Liberty Fund Conferences in all parts of the country. He hopes that his experience in America has made a beneficial contribution to the substance of this book.

Finally, the author thanks the members of the two working groups that he chairs, the Working Group for Economic Ethics and Economic Culture, German Philosophical Association, and the Working Group on Compliance and Ethics in Financial Institutions, German Business Ethics Network, for valuable discussions.

For the financial support of the translation of this book into English, the author thanks the Department of Philosophy, VU University Amsterdam, Netherlands, the *Bank für Kirche und Caritas* (Bank for Church and Charitable Works Caritas), Paderborn, Germany, and Springer Publishers.

Amsterdam   Peter Koslowski
September 2010

Introduction: Is the Finance Industry Ethically Irrelevant?

In the years before the crisis in the financial markets, banks and other financial institutions seemed to assume that nothing about their business was ethically relevant. The only principles it followed were the laws of financial mathematics. Shareholder value and return on investment were concepts that defied ethical relevance and appeared to be immanent to finance alone. The shareholder approach ousted ethical relevance to some place beyond the bounds of the financial system. The finance department of the firm maximizes shareholder value on condition that everyone in the firm abides by the firm's contracts. According to the "financial theory of the firm", the market ensures that these contracts are ethically sound since it only permits contracts that are ethically unobjectionable.

Banks in particular need not be aligned to ethical criteria like fairness because, thanks to the total rationality of market participants and "full disclosure" of contractual conditions, these standards are enforced anyway by the market.

Completely rational market participants were thus face to face with completely rational banks, and neither party could fool the other. That being the case, neither party had to ask itself whether what it was doing and contractually agreeing was ethically justifiable. Given the extraordinary rationality of market participants, the question just seemed irrelevant. What is more, some other glaringly irresponsible assumptions were made, like the belief that the market could never be wrong because, after all, it produces perfect information.

In reality, even before the financial crisis, numerous studies had shown that the market is full of hidden perils. There is contagion, the infectious over- or underestimation of stock market values; there is herding, the instinct to follow those who seem to have attracted the most followers; adverse selection, the choice not of the best but of the most loudly asserted value; moral hazard, the way that being insured against risks makes them seem less risky, and so on. Let us take herding: if the first people in a herd have rational reasons for following an opinion leader, then it can be rational to fall in behind them. For the next wave of people who follow these followers, it is already harder to say whether they are acting rationally or following people who follow other rational actors. They may equally be following other people who only followed the crowd without having rational reasons for doing so.

Following people who are following other people is a maxim that is neither rational nor ethical, because it does not question the reasons for following. But it is frequently a maxim of the stock exchange. Never following others as a matter of principle is another maxim that is neither rational nor ethical, because it is not rational never to follow others and because the "following" syndrome is also relevant to the stock market value of securities. It can therefore be rational to follow the herd instinct. Here we see a first insight of ethics, an insight of wisdom: it is not always right to follow others, nor is it always right not to follow others. But it is always right, and a dictate of wisdom, to obtain as much information as can possibly be acquired at reasonable cost about the motives of others, and to act autonomously based on this information and one's own evaluation of the other people's behavior.

The ethics of wisdom implies skepticism about one's own and other people's knowledge, caution about exaggerations, and verification of the objective situation and the quality of the service or product. Practical wisdom or *phronesis*, as it is known in Greek – particularly Aristotelian – ethics, is not the whole of ethics but an important part of it.

How can a wise person think that creating a "structured product" like a collateralized debt obligation (CDO) by packaging together three bad mortgage loans will result in something good? How can the international banking system place so much faith in magic or financial alchemy as to make such incredible losses, when alchemy and magic have been branded as charlatanism and discredited for centuries?

An argument that is dangerous but quite clever is, of course, the argument that nobody had ever dared to create structured products in the credit industry before, so there is always a chance that it might work. We can never rule out a priori the possibility that something will work if it has never previously been attempted. Nobody could rule out the possibility that Columbus would discover India on his route westwards, even though it is located to the east of Europe. When Morgan Stanley introduced collateralized debt obligations (CDOs) for the first time in the history of the financial system in order to be able to issue more loans, why shouldn't it have worked?

Alchemy is bound up with magic, the power of the mind to exert a direct influence over matter and its aggregate states. As the philosopher Ludwig Wittgenstein put it, ironically alluding to Lewis Carroll's *Alice in Wonderland*: in magic, the mind works directly on matter. Reading aloud an especially dry poem will make the washing on the line dry especially quickly. With less dry or dull poems, it will dry more slowly. The banker puts his well-paid mind to work on the matter of the "structured products", and transmutes three relatively poor-quality loans into a single package of good credit.

An old regulation says that the farmer or grain dealer must not sell false wheat ("cheat") but true wheat. Even as a student of economic ethics, the author used to wonder what this false wheat could be; it had to be a kind of wheat with little grain in the ears. It seems easy enough to tell true wheat from cheat. Yet traditional economic ethics is full of admonitions of this nature. The butchers' guild of Cologne used to punish members who had put too much water in their wurst by forcing them to drink Rhine-water in front of all the guild members, which was naturally rather humiliating. The guild members did this because they were aware that a maker of watered-down wurst brought not just the guild but all butchers into disrepute and undermined confidence in their product. They knew it would harm the whole trade, because customers could choose substitute products – fish pâté, fruit preserves, vegetable spread, and so on – or simply eat less meat and wurst.

It was with diluted products like collateralized debt obligations that the financial sector brought itself into disrepute. The damage done will be immense and long-lasting.[1] The customers will find substitutes for commercial bank loans. Cooperative banks, building society loans, equity interests in place of loans, saving under the mattress instead of in a bank account, loans from state banks, etc. will shrink the volume of commercial bank loans. The demutualization of the banking sector in favor of the retail banks will be reversed into remutualization in favor of the cooperative banks, mutual savings funds, and so on.

Where do ethics come into this? It is difficult for us as human beings to make an objective mental representation of reality because we are endowed with intellect, creativity and imagination. The more endowed with them we are, the more we run the risk of not recognizing what is real and mistaking our own phantasm for reality. Who would not like to be able to turn three bad things into one that is good? The Greeks called it *"Metabasis eis allo genos"*, a shift to another genus, when a false conclusion was drawn from one species about another. To start with, ethics here means simply holding fast to reality as something real to stave off the temptations of our own phantasms. A great enemy of the real is value, because value comes between the real and the imaginary. What is the true value of the collateral for a loan? It might have a book value, a market value, a tax value; the multiplicity of possible valuations is an indication of how easily value can elude the valuer. An American suburb that was built only 5 years ago can plummet, within the space of a year, to the residual value of the land it is built on – and even that won't be worth much any more. When more than one-third of the houses are standing empty, nobody wants to live in the other two-thirds. The whole town begins to decay. On the other hand, we have no choice but to make valuations – it is unavoidable. A wise Swiss banker at a major bank in Basel, which was in the process of being taken over, once told the author that the most important thing he ever learned in his banking career was to view the money business in the same way as the potato business: soberly, skeptically, realistically and unostentatiously.[2]

Potatoes lack the propensity to inspire alchemy and magic, whereas money has it in spades. To deal with money without succumbing to phantasms, we have to view

---

[1] Cf. on the history and chronology of the crisis in the financial markets, the bank losses and collateral damage, see the well-researched history of the crisis in: BEAT BALZLI et al.: "Der Bankraub" [The bank robbery], in: *Der Spiegel*, 17.11.2008, no. 47, pp. 44–73, online: http://www.spiegel.de/spiegel/0,1518,590656,00.html and its precise chronology in HANS-WERNER SINN: *Kasino-Kapitalismus. Wie es zur Finanzkrise kam, und was jetzt zu tun ist* [Casino capitalism. How the finance crisis happened and what to do next], Berlin (ECON) 1st edn. 2009, 2nd edn. 2009.

[2] The investment banker who sells IPOs or shares is a retailer and has the duty to sell only goods that fulfill the normal quality standards of the goods in question. Cf. LOUIS D. BRANDEIS: *Other People's Money and How the Bankers Use It* (1914), Boston, New York (Bedford/St. Martin's) 1995, p. 98: "The investment banker has the responsibility of the ordinary retailer to sell only that merchandise which is good of its kind."

it as if it were potatoes. Sobriety, skepticism and realism keep in check our own wishful overestimation of value. The result will be cautious valuation, fair pricing and realistic profit expectations. These are the sober goals of an ethics of practical wisdom for the financial system. But financial values are manifestly not potatoes. In the financial system, it is all the more difficult to heed an ethics of wisdom because the phantasm is in constant danger of inveigling its way between the financial instrument and our valuation of it, and clouding our view of reality. Hence, the financial economy is ultimately more ethically relevant and in more ethical peril than the real economy, in which the reality of the product is easier to recognize and to value.[3]

Because banks play a part in a sovereign state function – the creation of money – when they create money by lending, the financial industry is more ethically relevant than the industries of the real economy. Nevertheless, at its root – as in the real economy – is freedom of action: commercial freedom and freedom of contract. The financial economy has the right to act in and of itself, not a license to act granted by the state. The state is not the entity that gives the banks and financial institutions license to act, or withdraws it – even during and after a financial crisis. Even if a few banks made big mistakes, it is untenable to deprive all citizens of the right to found and operate banks. To say that companies are given a "social license to operate" is the wrong expression. Private autonomy and freedom of contract are not something granted by the state but principles on which the state is founded. They must therefore be unassailable by the state. The state does not grant freedom, but it guarantees it. Contractual and commercial freedom in the banking sector, then, is not something that the state exceptionally authorizes, but something that it must guarantee.

Banks may do business by accepting deposits and issuing loans as long as the business partners have the capacity to form contracts, and these are performed reliably in accordance with the terms of contract. Even in a crisis, the state has no right to prohibit or drastically curtail these contracts unless the law has clearly been broken. Instead, the opportunity to exchange banking services in a market must be guaranteed unconditionally. The state has the duty, in banking as in other sectors, to enable business interaction on the principle of private autonomy and not to inhibit or restrict it by giving inappropriate advantages to banks in state ownership.

---

[3]It is interesting to note that in the discussion about money trust and financial monopolization during the anti-trust movement in the United States prior to World War I, the term "bank ethics" described the informal rule that a bank should not deal with a customer who is already doing business with another bank. Bank ethics, at that time, meant the dividing up of the market, and collusion. Cf. Brandeis (1914), p. 68: "Bankers . . . invented recently that precious rule of so-called 'Ethics', by which it is declared unprofessional to come to the financial relief of any corporation which is already the prey of another 'reputable' banker." Cf. also the Pujo Report of 1913, House of Representatives: *Report of the Committee Appointed Pursuant to House Resolutions 429 and 504 to Investigate the Concentration of Control of Money and Credit, Submitted by Mr. Pujo, February 28, 1913*, Washington (Government Printing Office) 1913, p. 131: "[W]hat virtually amounts to an understanding not to compete . . . is defended as a principle of 'banking ethics'." – Needless to say, the term "ethics of banking" used in this book has nothing in common with the use of the term at the beginning of the 20th century.

Contents

Part I
Foundations of Business and Finance Ethics

A developed money, loan and capital market which supplies the economy with the financial resources that are necessary for economic transactions and economic growth is the hallmark of a high degree of economic development. Banks play a central role as financial intermediaries in the markets for money, credit, capital and derivatives. They broker the money supply, mediating in the money market between the central bank and the economy. They broker loans, mediating between the demand for credit and the supply of credit in the form of savings, and finally, they assume the function of the intermediary between industry's demand for capital and listed bonds and the supply of capital that is made available by industry, the financial institutions and private individuals. Banks are therefore the brokers, the financial intermediaries, par excellence.

The financial sector's brokering or intermediary function has grown in recent decades. In the US economy in the year 2000, 7% of gross national product was spent on financial intermediation, more than twice as much as four decades earlier.[1] A modern national economy has a capital-output ratio of 1:3. That means that an increase in the efficiency of capital allocation by 2% creates an economic yield equivalent to a 6% rise in gross national product.[2] These figures give an indication of the significance of the financial sector in normal times. For the years following the 2008 financial crisis, however, they suggest that the misallocation of capital by the financial market crisis can be expected to have an equally severe negative multiplier effect, and a commensurately sizeable contraction of the real economy.

In a universal banking system, the banks are not just the brokers of capital for investment but also the final arbiters on investments and the alternative options for investing capital as well as on the creditworthiness of their customers in the credit

---

[1] L. H. SUMMERS: "International Financial Crises: Causes, Prevention, and Cures", *American Economic Review*, 90 (2000), Issue 2, pp. 1–16. — Summers is the director of the National Economic Council of the United States (until the end of 2010).

[2] Ibid., p. 2f. — The thesis of the enormous multiplier effect of finance has been doubted, e.g. in: ANDREW HALDANE, ADAIR TURNER, MARTIN WOLF: "What is the Contribution of the Financial Sector: Miracle or Mirage?", in: *The Future of Finance*, LSE Report, 2010, downloadable at http://harr123et.files.wordpress.com/2010/07/futureoffinance1.pdf.

market. They not only mediate between parties but constantly evaluate risks and creditworthiness.

Moreover, banks operate as investors on their own account on the stock exchange, but also give advice to institutional and private investors on how they should invest their capital in the capital market. Their roles as valuers and judges in the credit market, and as investors and advisors to other investors in the capital market, make them highly influential factors in the economic process, whose influence extends far beyond their function as intermediaries between savings and investments.[3]

---

[3]Cf. also on finance ethics J. R. BOATRIGHT: *Ethics in Finance*, Malden, MA and Oxford (Blackwell) 1999 (Foundations of Business Ethics), and A. ARGANDOÑA (ed.): *The Ethical Dimension of Financial Institutions and Markets*, Berlin, New York, NY, Tokyo (Springer) 1995 (Studies in Economic Ethics and Philosophy, Vol. 7).

Chapter 1
Ethical Economy, Economic Ethics, Business Ethics: Foundations of Finance Ethics

Where there is a great measure of influence and power, there must also be a great measure of conscientiousness and moral awareness, because power itself is a moral or ethical phenomenon. Every powerful action must be morally responsible and defensible. An ethical code of conduct for banking and stock trading would therefore seem to be an obvious requirement. If we consider the current discourse in the discipline of economics, however, the literature yields up precious few titles that engage with the ethics of banking or financial ethics.[1]

Purely Economic Economics Versus Ethical Economy

The reason for this phenomenon can be sought in the separation of economic and ethical analysis that was induced by the dominance of the theory of general equilibrium in neoclassical economics. In the theory of general equilibrium, the economic good, i.e. efficiency, is determined independently of the ethical good, morality. Owing to the assumption of the general equilibrium theory that preferences are what they are (the theory of revealed preferences), and that they are coordinated for the sake of economic efficiency purely by economic but not ethical adaptation, no room exists for ethical criteria. Considerations relating to the justifiability of preferences, or indeed the original distribution of property rights and the resulting allocation of production factors, goods and services, have no place in the theory of general equilibrium.

---

[1]For the German debate cf. K. ANDREAS: "Denkansätze für eine Ethik im Bankwesen" [Philosophical approaches to banking ethics], in: P. KOSLOWSKI (ed.): *Neuere Entwicklungen in der Wirtschaftsethik und Wirtschaftsphilosophie*, Berlin, Heidelberg, New York, Tokyo (Springer) 1992 (= Studies in Economic Ethics and Philosophy Vol. 2), pp. 177–193; A.-F. JACOB (ed.): *Bankenmacht und Ethik* [Bank power and ethics], Stuttgart (Poeschel) 1990; A.-F. JACOB (ed.): *Eine Standesethik für den internationalen Finanzmanager?* [A code of professional ethics for the international finance manager?], Stuttgart (Poeschel) 1992; HANS-BALZ PETER, HANS RUH, RUDOLF HÖHN: *Schweizer Bankwesen und Sozialethik* [Swiss banking and social ethics]. Teil I: Einleitung. Sozialethische Erwägungen und Folgerungen, Teil II, Bern and Lausanne 1981, Vol. II, Ch. 2: "Bankwesen und Wirtschaftsethik", pp. 88–121.

P. Koslowski, *The Ethics of Banking*, Issues in Business Ethics 30,
DOI 10.1007/978-94-007-0656-9_1, © Springer Science+Business Media B.V. 2011

Since the stock exchange is usually viewed as a perfect market, which almost completely realizes the conditions of perfect competition, within the framework of the general equilibrium theory there appears to be no necessity for an ethics of the capital market. In the capital market – according to the assumptions of general equilibrium theory – more than in any other market, the general equilibrium is achieved without any reference to ethics.

This book will demonstrate that this assumption is mistaken, and that the features by which the capital market and stock exchange approximate to a perfect market do not effectively exempt the stock exchange from the need for a specific finance ethics. On the contrary, the credit and capital markets are far more in need of business ethics than other markets, firstly because their business – finance – is abstract and intangible in nature, and secondly because their goods – money and capital – are substitutable (fungible), non-physical and hence equally intangible in character.

The purely economic theory of the economy starts out from the assumption that markets in which actors are motivated by self-interest lead to optimality, even without recourse to ethical motivation. It makes the further assumption that, out of self-interest, the actors will fulfill their obligations and will not breach contracts if more advantageous alternatives come to light than those already contractually agreed.

Purely economic economics further assumes that asymmetries of information make no significant difference or can be overcome by market participants. The problem of the divergence of self-interest and corporate interest is not seen as a serious one, since it can be overcome by means of incentives and the process of incentivization with the promise of suitable rewards. The assumption is even made that incentivization with the promise of sufficiently large economic rewards can lead to hyper-motivation of actors. More than most, the financial institutions that are the subject of this book made intensive use of monetary incentives like bonuses and share options.

Yet another assumption of purely economic economics is that increasing enlargement of the market will diminish, rather than magnify, all the problems mentioned. In other words, on the one hand it will diminish false self-interest or the divergence of the manager's self-interest from corporate interests, but also the divergence between corporate and customer interests through the greater competitive pressure of the enlarged market. In reality, the opposite can also occur: the divergences between self- and corporate or industry interest can potentially be exacerbated by the growing size of the market.

Finally, purely economic theory assumes that the increasing commercialization and shareholder-value orientation of banks, together with the dismantling of their specific professionalization, their traditions and their norms as a profession, has not reduced but actually increased the rationality of the banking sector, because archaic traditions and profession-specific norms have been superseded by the competitive pressures of globalized banking.

Ethical economy, a theory that recognizes ethics as one of the optimization conditions of the market economy, takes up the opposing position on all the points mentioned. It assumes that markets in which actors are motivated by self-interest alone do not produce an optimum without recourse to ethical motivation. It makes the further assumption that out of self-interest, actors tend not to fulfill their obligations, and breach contracts when more advantageous alternatives than those already agreed in the contracts become apparent, and that the sanctions of law, i.e. civil action and conviction before a civil court, are ineffective because breach of contract is barely justiciable, especially in cases of imperfect contracts and on complex matters where proof is impossible.

The theory of ethical economy also assumes that asymmetries of information make a substantial difference, specifically in the finance industry, and can only be overcome with great difficulty by market participants, particularly non-professional investors and bank customers. Ethical economy does view the problem of the divergence of self-interest and corporate interest as a serious one, since this divergence cannot be completely overcome even with incentives and in the process of incentivization, and can only be alleviated by means of suitable incentives, although not by means of perverse incentives. The assumption that incentivization by means of sufficiently high economic rewards leads to hyper-motivation of actors is viewed as problematic, since financial motivation and intrinsic or professional motivation are not always in harmony. Principally the financial institutions made excessive use of monetary incentives, which led to a dominance of the bank's interests over the customer's interests.

Ethical economy theory also assumes that as the size of the market increases, all the problems cited tend not to diminish but to grow, because false self-interest or the divergence of the manager's self-interest and corporate interests, on the one hand, but also the divergence between corporate and customers' interests due to the pressure of competition in the enlarged market, is only diminished if the bank customers can rely on greater transparency in the financial market, which is not the case if the regional rootedness of the banking business based on the tenet that "Every business is local" is in decline.

Finally, ethical economy theory has grounds for the assumption that the increasing commercialization of banks results in the dismantling of their specific professionalization, their traditions and their norms as a profession, and has thus reduced the rationality of the banking sector because competitive pressure and the profit opportunities of globalized banking have ousted the traditions and profession-specific norms without having created any new equivalents to take their place.

The Justification of Ethical Duties from the Nature of the Matter

The ethics of the financial industry is aimed, firstly, at the ethical analysis and the norms of the institutional framework in this sector, at the legislation and the informal rules of custom and practice; and secondly, at the ethical analysis of individual and interpersonal action within these rules and institutions.

Which rules should apply in the finance industry and in finance companies? With reference to which rules and values do financial institutions set their own rules, statutes and corporate policies?

The problem of how appropriate norms of an institutional domain can be derived, once it is deemed to be in need of norm-setting, brings us on to the purpose or the function of the institutional domain. As long as a domain succeeds in operating without state norms and laws and mediates the private autonomy of individuals itself, no state norms are necessary and the legislator should refrain from intervention in the form of laws. If norms become an irrefutable necessity, however, the question arises as to which criteria the legislator should base decisions on. Even with a democratic legislator, this question cannot be answered solely by pointing to the consensus principle or a simple majority. Even the legislator – parliament, in the case of a democracy – together with the initiator of law, the executive, must orientate their legal decision-making towards objective aspects. They cannot make parliamentary consensus or a parliamentary majority double up as a criterion of legislation without getting into a loop in which the consensus or the majority is itself justified by consensus or majority.

In the financial sector as in other social and economic domains, the norms and criteria of right decision-making and action stem from material appropriateness, from the nature of the matter at issue – in the case of insider knowledge, for instance, from the nature of the matter of the fiduciary relationship of shareholders and financial intermediaries, which excludes financial intermediaries from using insider knowledge for their own personal enrichment. Or, in the case of banking secrecy, it stems from the nature of the matter at issue and from the task of the banks, which is to provide secure and discreet custodianship of value for customers.

The principle that the obligation arises out of the nature and the purpose of the institutional domain applies both to law and to ethics. For law, the content of the statute derives from the purpose and the nature of the matter at issue; for ethics, the ethical personal norm derives from the purpose and the nature of the matter at issue.

The principle that the obligation derives from the nature and purpose of the subject domain breaks down into three further sub-principles: a duty or an obligation is derived firstly from the purpose or the teleology of the institution or the operative domain at issue, secondly from the idea of justice as equality under the law, and thirdly from the demands of legal certainty. Admittedly, the principle of legal certainty overlaps more obviously with business law than with economic ethics, but nevertheless, legal certainty is an element of material appropriateness, and thus it is an ethical demand as well.

The purpose or purposes of the cultural domains and legal domains of the financial institutions and financial markets determine the norms that apply within them.

The idea of justice is the second principle which – particularly as formal justice – demands that all those who work in a domain should be equal under the law.

The third principle of legal certainty, finally, demands that those working in these domains can form constant expectations in relation to the stability of the law and the continuity of judicial rulings. Unless there is some constancy of expectations regarding legal norms, it is impossible to have a free and efficient economy. If economic subjects have to assume that the norms underlying the economic domain are constantly changing, they cannot make long-term plans or form long-term expectations about the regulatory setting in which they operate and the operative strategies of their trading partners in the market.

The ethical line of inquiry is not a special perspective but the central perspective on what is broadly considered "good". Therefore the inquiry into economic ethics is not primarily an additional aspect that intrudes from some extraneous domain and joins the economic, sociological and political aspects of economic activity. Ethics is rather the integrating assessment of the totality of arguments by which we judge human action. For example, we cannot say, "This action is morally bad but, in other regards, economically or technically good." The moral verdict overrides other subordinate aspects of the good. And, therefore, it must only be applied with caution.

In the assessment of an action, morality is not one aspect among others but a way to assess the perspectives and arguments of the sciences, to order and evaluate them and make them useful for human action. Ethics, as has been shown, not only has to be morally cogent but also appropriate to the matter, i.e. it has to do justice to all the characteristics of a matter.

The question of financial ethics is therefore:

What institutional framework and what norms and rules of the financial sector correspond to the nature of the matter at issue, i.e. the function and the purpose of the financial industry, and are therefore materially appropriate?

It is the principle of ethics in the Natural Law tradition that moral obligation springs from the nature of the matter at issue. Ethics also contributes to material appropriateness and is defined by congruence with the matter at issue. Ethics in conjunction with the individual sciences defines the materially appropriate norms. The ethical is not the antithesis of the efficient and the expedient, but is the integration of both these aspects of the economic to arrive at ends that are "efficient" and "good". Ethics is the integrating judgment according to the totality of criteria by which we guide human action. Obligation arises from the nature of the matter at issue, from the purpose and the functional laws of the domain in which we are operating.

The principle of justifying economic ethical obligation from the nature of the matter follows the theory of legal justification, as developed in Radbruch's legal philosophy and followed by the German Federal Constitutional Court in its justification of norms, for the concrete case of economic ethics, for the concrete ethics of financial institutions. According to Radbruch, the idea of law arises from the ultimate purpose of legal regulation, from the principle of formal justice, and from the principle of legal certainty.[2] The idea of law is meant in the sense of the idea prescribing the ideal norm for the domain in question, as the lodestar for legislation and for individual choices of action.

The law, it is well known, only gives general norms but cannot decide each individual case optimally. The application of law to the individual case makes demands

---

[2]GUSTAV RADBRUCH: *Rechtsphilosophie* [Legal philosophy], Stuttgart (Koehler) 8th edn. 1973, p. 114.

upon the ethical quality of the individual. The personal aspiration, within the bounds of what is legally permissible also to realize that which is good, is the essence of ethics and means that ethics goes above and beyond law. Essentially, however, this is only in the sense of an added requirement and not in the sense of something antithetical to law. Ethics consists not only of legal duties but also of moral duties; economic ethics therefore comprises not only a theory of duties in the sense of legal duties constituting a legal ethical minimum, but also makes demands over and above economic law in the direction of a moral theory of the attitudes and practices of actors in the economic domain that can be qualified as good.

To take material appropriateness as the principle of a concrete ethics of social domains is to reject the idea that, beside the purpose and nature of the matter at issue, there might be particular superordinate principles that do not derive from the material domain. Examples of this kind of normativism decoupled from material appropriateness are the theory of the republican public as the metasubject of a discourse about rules in Peter Ulrich and Ulrich Thielemann[3] or the theory of a consensus of an ideal discourse community as in Jürgen Habermas. Ulrich in his model of economic ethics largely follows the discourse theory of Habermas and Karl Otto Apel. These are circular theories, because in its application to concrete norms the ideal consensus is, in turn, only justified by the factual consensus; in other words, the method is also a criterion of the method. Or they achieve no concretization of the norm because they do not engage with the material problems and the norms arising from the purpose of the material domains.

In the following, in contrast to such theories the norms of the financial institutions will be developed out of their purpose or dedicated end. The normativism of the ought, which Hegel called "the precociousness or the pseudo-cleverness of the ought", will be avoided in favor of the normativity of the real, the ought that derives from the nature of the matter at issue.

In order to clarify what a right decision and action means in the domain of financial ethics, it is first necessary to establish what the valid norms in these domains are and should be, whether they are well founded, and what the purpose of these legal norms is.

What, for example, is the purpose of the law against the use of insider knowledge, particularly in the form of insider trading on the stock exchange? The use of insider knowledge means that someone exploits their knowledge of facts divulged to them in confidence for their own advantage and for financial gain. The Swiss Penal Code expresses this further substantive element of insider knowledge very precisely in Article 161, entitled "Misuse of knowledge of confidential facts" ("*Ausnützen der Kenntnis vertraulicher Tatsachen*").[4] Insider trading on the stock exchange is

---

[3]ULRICH THIELEMANN, PETER ULRICH: *Brennpunkt Bankenethik. Der Finanzplatz Schweiz in wirtschaftsethischer Perspektive* [The focal issue of banking ethics. A business ethics perspective on Switzerland as a financial center], Bern (Paul Haupt) 2003.

[4]Cf. NIKLAUS SCHMID: *Schweizerisches Insiderstrafrecht. Ein Kommentar zu Art. 161 des Strafgesetzbuches: Ausnützen der Kenntnis vertraulicher Tatsachen* [Insider trading in Swiss criminal law. A commentary on Art. 161 of the penal code], Bern (Stämpfli) 1988.

just the best known and perhaps most spectacular exploitation of insider knowledge because large sums of money on the stock market are at stake.

The misuse of insider knowledge is not confined to the stock exchange and financial institutions, however. It is a problem that affects all fields of economic decision-making and action, in the private and in the public sector. In all branches of industry and all domains of economic activity, the agents pursue knowledge that only they have and that only they, as proprietors of this information, can exploit for the accumulation of wealth. It can therefore be said that the pursuit of a certain level of insider knowledge is perfectly legitimate. The entrepreneur must pursue the knowledge that only he has, e.g. the manufacturing method, the patent, the brand name, that only he possesses and has the right to, and of which only he possesses insider knowledge. It is far from easy, and therefore all the more necessary, to draw the line between legitimate practices and the unethical and unlawful or illegal pursuit and misuse of insider knowledge.

How difficult this can turn out to be in grey areas in specific instances is illustrated by the absence of any clear consensus, within the disciplines of law and economics, on the question of whether insider trading, i.e. the misuse of privileged information on the stock exchange, is economically harmful or – even – useful. There are economists who believe that insider trading ought to be allowed because of its economically important function of disseminating information.

As we see, this is a case of dissent among the subject disciplines as to which legal norm should be valid at all in the operative domain of the stock exchange. What can be done to throw light on academic dissent about a legal norm? If economists and jurists cannot even agree on the justification of law, how should the individual entrepreneur or banker draw the line between what is correct business practice and what must be deemed unethical and illegal?

In economic ethics there is no evading the question of norm justification. In order to shed light on ambiguous domains of economic ethical decision-making, it is necessary to identify which norm applies to these domains and what the intention of the norm is, so that the economic agents, as entrepreneurs and managers, as employees and trustees, endorse the purpose and intention of the law and can refer to it as the lodestar of their action.

Business Ethics and the Fiduciary Duties of the Manager

Applied business ethics comprises both the analysis of institutions and the rules of action of the branch of industry, in this case the social or institutional ethics of the financial sector, as well as the analysis of individual actions of individual managers, their attitudes toward themselves, and the analysis of interpersonal communication and interaction of members of the firm with others, with staff and customers.[5]

---

[5]On corporate ethics, cf.: F. NEIL BRADY: *Ethical Managing: Rules and Results*, Upper Saddle River, NJ (Prentice Hall) 1989; R. E. FREEMAN, D. L. GILBERT: *Unternehmensstrategie,*

Because firms are central institutions and actors of the economy, it can be helpful to group the norms of the firm's legal structure and the norms governing action within the institutions known as "firms" or "corporations" under the umbrella term of "corporate ethics".

Ethical economy is the general integration of economic theory and ethical theory, and is thus the foundation of economic ethics and corporate ethics. It lays the groundwork for business ethics in the sense of "economic ethics" (*Wirtschaftsethik*), meaning the institutional ethics of the economy and of the economic system as well as its constitutional framework and implications, and the legal norms of an industry and of corporate law. It also provides the basis for business ethics in the sense of "corporate ethics" (*Unternehmensethik*), meaning the applied ethics of the firm's management. If a purely economic theory of the economy were valid, there would be no place for business ethics because mere self-interest would bring about market equilibrium or the economic optimum, even without recourse to ethics, by virtue of the invisible hand of the market. In a purely economic model, ethics would be utterly superfluous. Ethical economy theory can show that this assumption is incorrect because a market with ethically-oriented market participants, e.g. with a will to honor contracts regardless of whether they are reinforced with sanctions, leads to a better market outcome than a market without any ethical orientation, since it creates space for the possibility of an applied ethical theory of the economy and of corporate management.

The firm or the organization of the firm is a possible subject and object of corporate ethics, and the economy as a whole or its industries are the subject and object

---

Ethik und persönliche Verantwortung [Corporate strategy, ethics and personal responsibility], Frankfurt a. M. (Campus) 1991; ROBERT C. SOLOMON: *Ethics and Excellence: Cooperation and Integrity in Business*, New York (McGraw Hill) 1993; HORST STEINMANN, ALBERT LÖHR: "Einleitung: Grundfragen und Problembestände einer Unternehmensethik," [Introduction: Fundamental questions and problems in corporate ethics] in: HORST STEINMANN, ALBERT LÖHR:. (eds.): *Unternehmensethik* [Corporate ethics], Stuttgart (Poeschel) 2nd edn. 1991, pp. 3–32. HORST STEINMANN, ALBERT LÖHR: *Grundlagen der Unternehmensethik* [Foundations of corporate ethics]. Stuttgart: (Poeschel) 1991, 2nd edn. 1994; PATRICIA PEILL-SCHOELLER: *Interkulturelles Management* [Intercultural management], Berlin, New York (Springer) 1994; KLAUS M. LEISINGER: *Unternehmensethik. Globale Verantwortung und modernes Management* [Corporate ethics. Global responsibility and modern management], Munich (C. H. Beck) 1997; ANNETTE KLEINFELD: *Persona oeconomica: Personalität als Ansatz der Unternehmensethik* [Personality as an approach in corporate ethics], Heidelberg (Physica) 1998; SONJA GRABNER-KRÄUTER: *Die Ethisierung des Unternehmens: ein Beitrag zum wirtschaftsethischen Diskurs* [The ethicalization of the firm: A contribution to the business ethics discourse], Wiesbaden (Th. Gabler) 1998; BETTINA PALAZZO: *Interkulturelle Unternehmensethik: deutsche und amerikansiche Modelle im Vergleich* [Intercultural corporate ethics: German and American models compared], Wiesbaden (Th. Gabler) 2000, repr. 2001; JOSEPH F. JOHNSTON: "Natural Law and the Fiduciary Duties of Business Managers"; and P. KOSLOWSKI: "The Common Good of the Firm as the Fiduciary Duty of the Manager", both in: NICHOLAS CAPALDI (ed.): *Business and Religion: A Clash of Civilizations?*, Salem, MA (M&M Scrivener Press) 2005, pp. 279–300 and 301–312; LAURA P. HARTMAN: *Perspectives in Business Ethics*, New York (McGraw Hill) 2004; MANUEL G. VELASQUEZ: *Business Ethics. Concepts and Cases*, Upper Saddle River, NJ (Prentice Hall) 6th edn. 2005.

of business ethics (or economic ethics), because organizational failure, meaning the failure of institutional norms and control mechanisms, is found both in corporations, in industries, and in the economy as a whole. Organizational failure fosters individual, personal failure on the part of members of the organization, which cannot therefore be ascribed solely to the individual organization member who engages in unethical conduct. The installation of codes of ethics and compliance officers (responsible for adherence to legal and ethical rules) in an industry and a firm are designed for the prevention of ethical organizational failure, as was made mandatory after the Enron scandal by the Sarbanes-Oxley Act in the USA, with repercussions for all large international corporations.

Corporate ethics addresses the ethical duties, values and virtues of commercial, profit-making and firm-like organizations, and of not-for-profit organizations for the public benefit. The essential starting point for corporate ethics is the firm's management, because this exerts the greatest influence on the firm due to its leadership function. Because the management function is not confined only to commercial firms, corporate ethics is equally relevant to other, non-commercial organizations.

Compliance with and the ongoing refinement of rules in complex organizations are tasks that firms themselves must perform, because the legislator and the courts can only enforce and develop adequate rules for the rapidly changing economy and its technology in collaboration with firms and branches of industry. This affords an important role to business ethics in the law-making process for economic and business law.

Corporate ethics and corporate compliance are a means of risk management. The risks that arise from unethical or even delinquent conduct of members of the organization consist of damage to the firm's reputation and brand, and potentially also the payment of fines and damages. The firm must minimize the risk of non-compliance with the rules of business ethics and business law through the implementation and sanctioning of corporate policies which make the organization's ethical principles clear to all its members. Business ethics is also part and parcel of corporate risk management.

The duties of the manager are determined by his position as managing director of the firm, appointed by the owners. He is, however, not only the agent of the owners (the principals) but managing director of the entire corporation. He has an obligation to the corporation as a whole and its collective well-being. The manager of a large corporation is therefore not only the agent of the owners or shareholders but their fiduciary, and the fiduciary of those who work under his leadership. As such, it is his fiduciary duty to act as a trustee ("fiduciary") to the shareholders (or "principals") and the entire corporation.

As a concept in business ethics, fiduciary duty consists of the following particular obligations: the duties of good faith, loyalty, diligence and prudence, and the duty to avoid or disclose possible conflicts of interest. In fulfilling these duties, managers are not free to pursue their own interest at the firm's expense. The trustee relationship implies a kind of self-commitment on the part of the owners and the managers which transcends the naked self-interest of shareholders and managers as well as the idea of the manager's position as a mere agent of the shareholders.

The duty of loyalty inherent in the fiduciary duties obliges the manager to undivided and unselfish loyalty to the firm, not just the shareholders. It is more than just a contract between the manager and the owners who appoint him; it is an obligation towards the firm as a whole. The duty of diligence and prudence obliges the manager to act with diligence and prudence in the interests of the firm and not just in his own interests. The duty of disclosure obliges the manager not to take advantage of facts that become known to him in confidence in the course of his work or information divulged to him by the firm's owners. His fiduciary duty of disclosure rules out the use of this knowledge as insider knowledge in order to carry out insider trading in the course of performing his management role or as a private individual. The prohibition on the use of insider knowledge, or the duty of disclosure, follows from the fiduciary role of the manager towards the firm as a whole, not just from an agent role vis à vis the owners. This is also reinforced by the fact that the ban on insider trading applies even where the owner might authorize the manager to use insider knowledge. The overall interest of the firm and the right of all shareholders to the inside knowledge prohibit the use of insider knowledge by the manager even where the owner or principal shareholder releases him from his duty to refrain from insider trading.

The duties that arise from a fiduciary relationship are valid for all fiduciary relationships: for the relationship of bank clerks and financial consultants to their consultancy clients, for the employee as an administrator, for the doctor in relation to the patient, for the architect in relation to the home-builder, and so on.

The definition of the relationship between the firm and the manager solely according to the principal/agent relationship and the almost exclusive remuneration of the manager according to improvement in the firm's stock market value leads to the neglect of success criteria other than stock market price development. What results is a hit-and-run mentality. It is the task of business ethics to ask whether the right incentives are set, since there are also such things as perverse incentives which counteract the firm's objectives. It is not just a matter of setting economic incentives but also of setting economically and ethically sound incentives to stimulate the right contributions within the firm.

Through movements like Global Compact and the Global Reporting Initiative, state coercion as an element of efforts to reduce environmental pollution and to respect the rights of future generations is replaced by voluntary self-commitments in the form of voluntary undertakings by the companies. Respecting natural capital is reputation-enhancing for companies, a fact that is acknowledged by investors and viewed positively in the valuation of firms. Investors – within the scope of institutionalized ethical investment or outside it – are more and more frequently prepared to pay a price-premium for firms which possess a higher reputation for respecting ethical principles like the rights of nature and future generations.

Similarly, showing the corporation's environmental and social audits in the annual accounts on the triple bottom line accounting principle according to economic performance indicators, environmental performance indicators and social performance indicators, effects a greater inclusion of ethical criteria and corporate social responsibility in the overall valuation of corporate success. These criteria encompass services of the corporation for its social and natural environment, respect for intergenerational justice, etc. The new weight of the ethical, environmental and social indicators, in turn, compels management and shareholders, by force of competition for investors, consumers and workers, to take account of these indicators of corporate success in their management decisions.

Part II
The Ethical Economy and Finance Ethics of the Markets for Credit, Capital, Corporate Control, and Derivatives

Chapter 2
The Ethical Economy of the Credit Market

Banks are suppliers of payment-processing and lending services, and operate in the market for these services, where they as suppliers meet the individuals as well as firms which are the demanders and consumers of credit. Banking should be described in terms of the market for credit and payment-processing services, and not in terms of a quasi-state, official "credit-granting" function. Once upon a time, the banking sector and the supply of loans were referred to in terms of quasi-state administration and the granting of loans to applicants. During the recent decades of credit expansion and easy money, credit – especially consumer credit and lending for share purchases – has come to be seen as a type of consumer good that requires no deeper ethical norm-setting than any other consumer good.

The financial crisis has shown both positions to be untenable. Credit is neither a sovereign act of credit-granting, nor is it a consumer good like any other. Banks and financial institutions must be mindful of the special character of their service without lapsing into the mode of sovereign officialdom. An element of trust and faith in the customer plays a far more significant part in the supply of credit than in other markets. Hence, a purely commercial and profit-oriented interpretation of the credit industry, which does not fully reflect its quasi-sovereign function of money-creation through lending, is found equally wanting. The bank also has to carry out monitoring of the debtor's continuing creditworthiness over the term of the loan, and verify this within an ongoing bank-customer relationship. If it fails to do so or attempts, as in the example of the collateralized debt obligations, to divest the duty of monitoring to others, who in turn are not sufficiently able to perform this function, the debtor-risk drifts about in the financial system, lacking the safe anchorage of an enduring bank-debtor relationship and diligent monitoring.

Purpose and Task of the Credit Market

Given the economic association between the credit market and the capital market, it seems advisable to define the banking system in terms of the market for credit. According to the portfolio theory of investment, investors invest their savings in investments in different risk classes with varying exposures to risk. Savers

P. Koslowski, *The Ethics of Banking*, Issues in Business Ethics 30,
DOI 10.1007/978-94-007-0656-9_2, © Springer Science+Business Media B.V. 2011

and investors can choose between investing their own savings in an instant access account with the facility to make withdrawals at any time, investing them in a deposit account which stipulates a notice period for withdrawals, investing in debt securities (bonds) or investing in shares (in corporate stock) in the capital market. These choices depend on investors' attitudes to risk and their preferences regarding the accessibility of the sum invested over the course of time, i.e. their liquidity preferences.[1] The providers of savings optimize their portfolios between the different allocations of their savings, which they invest either in the credit market in short- or long-term bank accounts or debt-based securities, or in the capital market in ownership-based securities or shares.[2]

Banks therefore compete for the financial assets or savings of their customers, especially those who are current-account holders. Of course, they are competing to attract these assets as deposits in their accounts, not only among themselves but also against all the alternative possible deployments of savings in fixed-interest securities or in shares.

The Purpose of the Bank for Deposit Customers, as the Bank's Creditors

Account holders hand over their money to banks, thereby investing in the various types of bank accounts, for three reasons. They invest money in current accounts for the sake of easier payment transactions and in order to hold their cash in a form that is liquid at all times. They invest their savings in interest-bearing bank accounts with fixed notice periods, as the part of their portfolio which carries a low risk and ensures a small profit. Customers who maintain a current account at a bank expect the bank to reduce or even completely bear the risks of their payments, and to serve as a place of value-custodianship for their liquid funds and financial investments.

---

[1]Cf. B. M. FRIEDMAN: Article on "Capital, Credit and Money Markets", in: *The New Palgrave. A Dictionary of Economics*, London (Macmillan), New York (Stockton), Tokyo (Maruzen) 1987, Vol. 1, pp. 320–327.

[2]Different definitions of the credit market and the capital market exist, based on different distinctions. In the German discourse, the capital market is defined as the market for long-term financial resources or long-term loans, according to E. TUCHTFELDT: Article on "Kapitalmarkt", in: *Handwörterbuch der Wirtschaftswissenschaft*, Stuttgart, New York (G. Fischer), Tübingen (Mohr Siebeck), Göttingen (Vandenhoeck & Ruprecht) 1978, Vol. 4, p. 433. In the Anglo-American discourse, in contrast, the capital market is defined in line with the portfolio theory of investment as the market for risk-bearing financial investments, as in FRIEDMAN (1987), p. 320f. By the latter definition, listed bonds belong to the market for credit, whereas by the former, they belong to the capital market. Since listed bonds are long-term investments for the investor and carry a certain price-risk, though not the risk of total loss or bankruptcy, they fall somewhere between bank loans and corporate shares. Listed bonds will not be dealt with in the present book. The definition of the capital market used here is that of the market for risk-bearing investments, as per the portfolio theory of investment.

The first duty of banks to the customers who entrust their money to them, therefore, follows logically from the nature of the matter at issue, i.e. from banking, from the essential task of the banking business to reduce risks for their on-demand deposit customers. Their first duty towards customers with on-demand deposits is therefore reliability and management security in the administration of these customer accounts, and the first virtue of the banker is reliability and risk aversion. To this can be added discretion and the preservation of banking secrecy.

The tasks of the banks in their relationships with current-account customers can therefore be summarized as follows:

(1) Banks facilitate and coordinate payment transactions.
(2) They provide safe value-custodianship for liquid funds under conditions that preserve liquidity.
(3) Banks create opportunities for the investment of capital, which is invested without risk whilst ostensibly assuring (modest) rates of return.

The Purpose of the Bank for Credit Customers, as the Bank's Debtors

Banks are faced with quite different expectations on the part of their debtors. Private and industrial debtors or borrowers expect their bank to offer them funds at an affordable price even for projects that carry risk. In the market for loans to industrial customers, banks for their part are in competition with the capital market and whatever alternative means firms have at their disposal for financing their investments. Firms can introduce capital by issuing bonds or shares in the capital market, or generate their own finance by converting profits into equity capital, otherwise known as self-financing. Banks have to compete for debtors and hence for profitable lending business, both among themselves and against the capital market and the various forms of corporate self-financing.

The first duty of banks towards those customers who demand loans therefore stems from the nature of the matter at issue, i.e. lending, from the essential task of the banking business to make financial resources available for the risk-bearing enterprises of their credit customers.

The first duty of banks towards their credit customers is therefore to maintain objectivity whilst having the courage, seasoned with rational skepticism, to issue loans to good investment projects. The first virtue of bankers towards their credit customers is objectivity and a rationally robust attitude to risk.

Task of the Bank: Intermediating Between Its Creditors and Debtors

It is obvious that the duties and virtues on the assets side of the bank's balance sheet and those on the liabilities side are not in harmony with each other but in conflict. In their actions and attitudes towards customers who are holders of current accounts or on-demand deposits, the bank must be risk-averse and cautious; in relation to industrial borrowers, however, it must be risk-embracing and courageous. The bank must therefore find a way to reconcile the different duties and virtues of risk-reduction and risk-assumption. It must intermediate between its deposit customers' expectations of avoiding risk and its borrowers' expectations of taking some risk.

Considered on the level of an ethics of banking, the tension between the two role expectations and virtues of banking activity, and the necessity to strike a balance between them, mirrors the bank's task of mediating between the supply of and demand for financial resources, between saving and investing or, to be even more precise, mediating between the supply of financial resources for low-risk investments and the demand for financial resources for high-risk investments. They also reflect the fact that the bank is simultaneously debtor and creditor, borrower and lender. It is the debtor of its deposit customers, and the creditor of its credit customers. It stands between two opposing obligations.

The bank's task of fulfilling both its roles, as the deposit customers' debtor and the credit customers' creditor, is not always easy. There are times when it is necessary – and a requirement of commercial law – to erect firewalls between departments of a bank that are bound to adhere to different norms, so that no insider trading occurs between them. Such a wall must be instituted between the department advising the customer on stock purchases and the department working on an initial public offering (IPO), the introduction of a firm to the capital market. The divergent expectations of these two departments' customers must not be reconciled by means of an insider deal. The bank's IPO department is interested in selling the IPO to the bank's investment consulting department. This part of the bank, however, should not be put into a conflict of interest between the need for objectivity and the bank's interest to sell an IPO.

Not all contradictions end up being resolved by trading between the departments of a bank. Accordingly, a difference must prevail between the department of the investment bank that administers deposits and the department that makes lending decisions. It is the conflict of interest between the interests of the deposit customers and the credit customers that has to be considered and reconciled here.

The effectiveness of firewalls is constrained by the fact that the board of every corporation must be informed about all events within the corporation, and in this respect a bank is no different from any other type of corporation. For the bank's board, then, firewalls have to be permeable. The board must always be informed about all events within the bank, irrespective of firewalls. Only the constraints of financial ethics prevent the board from taking advantage of its position as an insider with cross-firewall access.

It is obvious from the present analysis that banks cannot merely be brokers between the supply of financial resources for low-risk investments and the demand for financial resources for high-risk investments, because the supply and demand for financial resources are not congruent and compatible. In point of fact, these two factors must first be made compatible. This is accomplished through the banks' task of pooling the funds deposited at low risk, and transforming them into financial resources available at normal or high risk for their lending business. Banks must mediate risk on behalf of their deposit customers who are their indirect lenders-, and they must mediate risk on behalf of their credit customers, their debtors or borrowers.

Schuldverhältnisse: *Relationships of* Schuld, *of Guilt, Debt, or Obligation. Excursus with Reference to an Equivocation in the German Language*

In contrast to the English language, German uses the same word for guilt, debt, and obligation. All are denoted by *Schuld*. In German, the law of obligations is called the *"Recht der Schuldverhältnisse"* ("law of relationships of guilt, debt, obligation"). The fact that *Schuld* is synonymous with guilt, debt, and obligation causes some interesting equivocations in the German language.

An obligation refers to every legal relationship or relationship of exchange that entitles a party – the creditor, the vendor, the child or parent and ultimately the state, to demand performance – which may also take the form of an act of omission – from the other party – the debtor, purchaser, parent or child, and ultimately the citizen. Obligations arise from relationships of exchange. Entry into a relationship of exchange and the voluntary consent to an exchange thereby given are the basis of an obligation, be it legally formalized or not.

Legal obligations (or *Schuldverhältnisse*, relationships of guilt, debt, obligation,) are the basis for a certain class of obligations, namely those which are adjudicable or justiciable, meaning enforceable through the courts. According to the German Civil Code (*Bürgerliches Gesetzbuch*, BGB), obligations in German civil law arise from legal transactions, torts or special provisions (Section 241 BGB). The law of obligations formalizes the law governing such relationships and comprises the legal provisions regulating the formation, the detailed terms and conditions, and the fulfillment of obligations between parties. In *German* law, the law of obligations is contained in Book II of the Civil Code (Sections 241, 853) and is distinct from property law and from family law and the law of inheritance. The freedom of those involved to conclude and arrange their relationships of obligation, or the contractual freedom of the contracting parties, forms the foundation of the law of obligations.

Austrian law regulates the law of obligations as "personal property law" (*persönliches Sachenrecht*; Sections 859 & 1341 ABGB), whereas in German law, property law governing ownership and possession is separated from the law of obligations as personal law. *Swiss* law in contrast to German and Austrian law does not use the term *Schuldverhältnisse* but *Obligationen* and deals with the law on obligations under the Swiss Code of Obligations.[3] The Swiss legal terminology is distinctive in

---

[3]Cf. articles on "Schuldrecht (Recht der Schuldverhältnisse)" [Law of obligations] and "Schuldverhältnis" [Obligation], "Schuld" [Guilt], and "Verschulden" [Fault], in: *Der Brockhaus*, computer version, Mannheim (Bibliographisches Institut & F.A. Brockhaus) 2002.

making use of the concept of *Obligation* for the obligation or duty arising from a legal transaction, probably reflecting the stronger influence from French civil law, rather than the concept of *Schuld* used in Germany and Austria, which can also be morally laden.

The German and Austrian legal tradition follows a blanket concept of *Schuld* without a phonetic distinction between the sense of debt or *dette* (French for debt) on the one hand, and guilt or *culpabilité* (French for guilt) on the other, and applies the category of *Schuld* not only to civil law but also to criminal law and morality. Likewise, there is no distinction in Italian and Latin between *debito/debitum* as an obligation or as a debt; nevertheless, these languages clearly differentiate between obligation as debt, *debito/debitum* on the one hand, and moral culpability, *colpa/culpa* on the other.

The broadness of the *Schuld* concept in German has implications for the definition of the term in the German discourse. *Schuld* is 1) in civil law, the bindingness of the obligee's commitment to render some service (by doing something or by refraining from doing something) based on a relationship of obligation; 2) in penal law and in ethics, reproachability as an evaluation of human behavior (fault). Of course, a *Schuld/dette/*debt in civil law can also entail *Schuld/culpabilité/*guilt in penal law. By the same token, *Schuld/culpabilité/*guilt in penal law may be associated with a civil law *Schuld/dette/*debt by way of a compensation payment. The civil law *Schuld* or obligation and the penal law and moral *Schuld* or culpability are linked, linguistically and materially, but are not identical. A legal subject is accountable for an obligation because he or she is the cause of it; furthermore, the legal subject is guilty if he or she is not merely a neutral cause but if some reproach also attaches to this causal status because the subject's causative action comes into the category of morally and legally reproachable actions. Debts are not morally reproachable in themselves. In economic terms, to enlarge the actor's scope for action as an investor they are not only useful but frequently imperative. Only in the event of over-indebtedness, when the debtor can no longer bear the burden of interest and can no longer service or repay the debt, do they become a legal or a moral problem.

The *Verschulden* (fault) in the sense of the cause of the exchange that leads to an obligation, and the *Schuldverhältnis* (obligation) that arises from that fault, are not just linguistically associated. The linguistic relationship between *Verschulden* as fault, *Schuld* as culpability and *Schulden* as debt, the outcome of a loan transaction, is also a material one. Not every fault and every debt is a basis for culpability, but culpability always has some connection with fault, and all debts are caused by an act of becoming indebted. The heir who takes over debts with an inheritance consents to becoming indebted by accepting the inheritance. This is also a possible explanation for the underlying assumption of the Christian doctrine of original sin: the transmission of ancestral culpability by inheritance. In assenting to existence by the very act of living, we accept both the good and the bad parts of this inheritance as joint debtors.

Culpability, debt and forgiveness are pivotal concepts of Christianity. According to Margaret Atwood, "The whole Theology of Christianity rests on the notion of spiritual debts and what must be done to repay them, and how you get out of paying by having someone else pay instead."[4] A passage found in the writings of Augustine of Hippo declares that God not only grants remission of debts but makes himself the debtor.[5] Nietzsche takes up this idea: in Christianity, the creditor sacrifices himself for the debtor, "God sacrificing himself for man's debt, none other than God paying himself back, God as the only one able to redeem man from what, to man himself, has become irredeemable, the creditor sacrificing himself for his debtor, out of love (would you credit it?), out of *love* for his debtor!. . ."[6] Phenomena like the economic relief of debt, the remission of payments to a later date and debt relief rituals, according to Waldenfels, are the "extraordinary fringe" that surrounds normality.[7]

Task of the Bank: Transforming Time Periods and Bearing Risk

The pooling of risks by the bank is simultaneously a pooling of investment time horizons. The transformation of financial resources that are made available for low-risk investment and over very disparate time horizons into investments carrying high risks, also over disparate time periods, makes it necessary for banks to perform a dual task of transformation:

In order to transform deposits into loans, banks must

(1) transform disparate and sometimes very short-term deposit periods into short-term and long-term loans, and they must also
(2) transform the different attitudes to risk by mediating the risk on both sides of their balance sheet. They must mediate the different attitudes to risk both among their deposit customers or creditors and between their borrowers or debtors.[8]

---

[4]Quoted after NICK PAUMGARTEN: "The Death of Kings. Notes from a Meltdown," *The New Yorker*, May 18, 2009, (Annals of Finance), pp. 40–57, here p. 49. Paumgarten refers to MARGARET ATWOOD: *Payback. Debt as Metaphor and the Shadow Side of Wealth*, London (Bloomsbury) 2008. – The author has shown this connection between obligations and debt relief with reference to the "satisfaction theory of redemption", a theory of the assumption of debt by a third party for the satisfaction of the creditor. Cf. P. KOSLOWSKI: "Schuldverhältnisse", in: MARCO M. OLIVETTI (ed.): *Le don et la dette*, Padova (CEDAM e Biblioteca dell'«Archivio di filosofia») 2005, pp. 421–436, and PETER KOSLOWSKI, FRIEDRICH HERMANNI (eds.): *Endangst und Erlösung 1. Untergang, ewiges Leben und Vollendung der Geschichte in Philosophie und Theologie*, Munich (W. Fink) 2009, and PETER KOSLOWSKI (ed.): *Endangst und Erlösung 2. Rechtfertigung, Vergeltung, Vergebung in Philosophie und Theologie*, Munich (W. Fink), in preparation 2010. – Paumgarten concludes his article with the statement: "Capitalism without bankruptcy is like Christianity without Hell." (ibid., p. 57).

[5]AUGUSTINE OF HIPPO, *Confessiones* V, 9, 17.

[6]NIETZSCHE, Genealogie der Moral, 2. Abhandlung, § 21, KSA 5, 331. Saint Augustine and Nietzsche cited after: BERNHARD WALDENFELS: "Geschenkte und geschuldete Aufmerksamkeit", in: MARCO M. OLIVETTI (ed.): *Le don et la dette*, Padova (CEDAM e Biblioteca dell'«Archivio di filosofia») 2005, p. 301; quotation from Nietzsche's second essay after: FRIEDRICH NIETZSCHE, *On the Genealogy of Morality*, ed. Keith Ansell-Pearson, trans. Carol Diethe, CUP 1994/2007, p. 63.

[7]Ibid., p. 303.

[8]Cf. also NIKLAS LUHMANN: "Kapitalismus und Utopie", *Merkur*, 48 (1994), H. 3, p. 191.

In the modern market economy, it is rational behavior for anyone to supplement their own capital with external capital, i.e. with loans, because they would miss out on too many business opportunities if they were solely dependent on their own ability to build long-term savings. In this respect also, loans have the function of transforming the time interval between payments.

The difference between the compensation for the transformation of time periods that borrowers pay to the bank as lender, and the compensation paid by the bank as borrower to its deposit customers as its creditors, forms part of the bank's profits.

Banks operate with the differential between two payment promises: on one side, they lend money from their on-demand deposit customers, and promise them that their deposits will be kept liquid at all times; on the other side, meanwhile, they lend money to their borrowers, who promise the banks in return that these loans will be repaid.

From the functions of banking, from the nature of the matter at issue, we are able to infer the potentially ethically sensitive areas and the corresponding ethical duties and virtues of banking. The obligations and duties of people who work in banking can be established from the nature of their task within the economy as a whole. These duties are established by conducting a critical interpretation or hermeneutic inquiry into the functions and institutional tasks of the banks.

From this, it transpires, many of the ethical duties of banking coincide with the legal obligations that are formulated in banking laws and regulations. The laws of banking can only articulate legal duties, however, and not any duties concerning the intentions and virtues of economic action. The law cannot oblige anyone to espouse the intention of the law as their own intention, and it can only define and demand an ethical minimum of obedience to the rules of the law. It cannot impose a binding obligation on anyone to embrace obedience to the law as a personal intention.

Duties of Banks Arising from the Nature of Their Tasks to Facilitate Payments and to Enable Credit

The task of facilitating payment transactions is not, in itself, ethically sensitive but it does throw up certain ethical questions.

Duties Arising from the Bank's Task to Facilitate Payments and Safeguard Liquid Funds

Bank customers often complain about the delay in processing credit transfers into accounts, whereas debits are deducted from customers' accounts immediately. This is a criticism of the banks' value-dating practice. In applying uneven value-dating practices, banks not only save interest payments on bank deposits with credit balances but also earn a little extra interest when customers' accounts go briefly overdrawn and incur interest charges on overdrawings that only arise because of this delay in crediting the value of incoming payments. So the banks make an additional profit, over and above their fees for payment transactions and the interest they earn from the use of bank deposits for loans. In the case of those customers who are in the red, the opportunity costs for the customer also include the interest incurred for any overdrawing of their accounts that they would have avoided if the value had been credited more immediately.

When German consumer groups investigated the time-span required for the transfer of monies to German banks, they found that these payment transactions are often no quicker today than in the era of the Fugger Bank in the sixteenth century. Slowest and costliest are transactions with foreign accounts, although EU legislation has speeded up money transfers between EU countries. These delays are not caused by real problems of transport or telecommunications. Due to modern electronic communication systems, the international finance world is in a position to transfer substantial sums of money around the globe in practically no time at all. The practice of delayed value-dating and the delay of payment transactions cannot therefore be justified on the basis of technical problems, but is a means used by the credit institutions to make additional profit.

A problem arises here of justice in exchange between customers whose deposit accounts are in the red and who therefore pay debit interest on sums credited to their accounts which would reduce their debts, whilst those whose accounts are in credit lose a very much lower rate of credit interest on their balance. This value-dating practice therefore harms the less wealthy, or at least those whose accounts are in debit, more than those who are wealthy and keep their accounts in credit. This value-dating practice is not neutral in relation to the criterion of distribution. The banks' value-dating practice fulfills neither the criterion of justice in exchange nor that of distributive neutrality.

Since customers deposit part of their savings in on-demand accounts in order to have liquid funds available, it is one of the main duties of the bank to ensure that these are indeed liquid at any given moment.[9] The legal regulation of the liquidity reserve is aimed at ensuring the banks' liquidity. Situations are conceivable, however, in which even the legally defined liquidity reserves are not adequate. The bank therefore has the duty to fulfill its legal obligations and, at the same time, to exceed the liquidity-reserve compliance target, if this is required by the nature of their business, namely unusually high withdrawals of cash by their customers. Here, the duty of the economic ethics of banking exceeds the ethical minimum of the legal duty.

This observation can also be extended to the money market. The money supply in the economy is created by cooperation between the central bank and the commercial banks. The ethics of banking obliges the commercial banks to cooperate with the central bank to secure the right quantity of money and to avoid inflation, which

---

[9]JOHANNES MESSNER: *Ethik. Kompendium der Gesamtethik* [Ethics. Compendium of general ethics], Innsbruck, Vienna, Munich (Tyrolia) 1955, *Book VII: Wirtschaftsethik* [Economic/business ethics], p. 431, calls the liquidity principle the first principle of the ethics of banking.

is caused by an oversupply of money, and deflation, which is triggered by an inadequate supply of money. Here again, the banks cannot withdraw to the minimum position defined by legal provisions. They must make the common good of price stability into their own interest or particular good, and support or, where necessary, criticize the policy of the central bank.

Duties Arising from the Task of the Bank to Transform Deposits into Loans

It is the duty of banks on the part of their deposit customers to satisfy the task and the expectation of reducing the risk for their customers with savings invested in on-demand deposits, and at the same time it is their duty to meet the expectation of their credit customers to make capital available for risky enterprises. The bank must strike a balance between these two contradictory role expectations which arise from these two functions. The balance between their two business functions and role expectations must inform the definition of ethically and legally appropriate business practices, attitudes and virtues, rules and duties of the banks.

Material appropriateness of the banking system calls for a synthesis of risk-aversion and willingness to embrace risk, of sober risk-control and bold openness to risk-capital and risky investments. Now in the universal banking system, there is always a danger of shifting this balance too far in one direction, either giving undue prominence to the deposit customers' interests in risk-free investments since they are the ones who provide the bank's capital, or making too many concessions to the interests of borrowers in easy (credit) money at the cost of limiting risk for the deposit customers.

With regard to the first imbalance in risk assessment, in the past the large banks were often accused of refusing loans to entrepreneurs, however trustworthy they were as individuals and however promising their projects, because they were simply unable to furnish the required securities. Large banks have the duty of counteracting the tendency inherent to all large bureaucratic institutions, namely following immovable general rules which fail to do justice to the individual case. Branches of the large banks are often in danger of following their head office's rules too rigidly and unimaginatively, leading them to refuse personal credit to the promising entrepreneur, who might have received support in the form of credit from a personal private bank. The large banks tend to devote too little attention to unsecured personal credit. This practice is an obstacle for venture capital and often prevents promising projects from being realized.[10]

In the decades before the crisis in the financial markets of 2008, on the other hand, there was a distinct impression that the policy of easy money unilaterally

---

[10]Cf. GÜNTHER ENGEL: "Zur Problematik eines gesetzlichen Verbots von Insider-Geschäften" [On the problems of a statutory ban on insider trading], *Jahrbuch für Sozialwissenschaft*, 42 (1991), pp. 388–407.

focused interest on cheap credit at the expense of safeguarding deposits. It is unethical not to stick to the institutional rules of lending, most notably the obligatory ratio of equity to balance sheet total for lending, and moreover – via the sale of synthetic CDOs – to breach the limit set by this ratio, even when this policy of easy money is in the borrower's interest, because the policy of lending by the banks infringes on the protection interests of deposit customers. Nor can one replace the institutional criteria of lending with personal trust in the person of a borrower.

People are given credit when it is believed that they will be in a position to pay their debts. They are trusted to be capable, by virtue of their economic abilities, to repay the loan they have been given. In the case of investment credit, this presupposes a promising business plan and securities; in the case of a mortgage, a certain proportion of own savings and the security of the property for which the mortgage is lent. The own-savings ratio in mortgage lending can vary. In the Netherlands until recently, mortgages of up to 120% of the market value of the property they were secured against were available; in Germany the ratio is generally limited to 80%. This difference does not imply that the Dutch banks trust Dutch customers more than German banks trust German customers. The Dutch banks have more trust in their own financial system than the German banks and the German legislator have in Germany's. There is greater institutional trust among the Dutch banks.

Institutional trust is mostly the opposite of personal trust. Institutions transform uncertainty about the individual contractual partner, or mistrust of the individual customer, with a set of procedures which permit them to know more about the other party and therefore reduce uncertainty about the customer and the risk, and make it unnecessary to resort to personal trust.

Very often the ethics of banking does not require new rules to be introduced, only the implementation and enforcement of those that already exist. It requires ensuring that the rules – which are often very simple – are taken seriously. One example is the German financial crisis surrounding the Schneider real estate bankruptcy. This was a case in which the banks made the mistake of not applying the most rudimentary control regulations. They did not take a look in the land register to verify the register of mortgages, nor did they make a site visit to the buildings on which they lent to convince themselves personally that the size of the living and office accommodation stated in the mortgage applications actually coincided with their true size.[11]

The simple rule of verifying with one's own eyes whether every property on the plot coincides with the borrower's description was disregarded – partly because of a tendency that is peculiar to all repeat-business relationships: normally, once a sound business relationship has been maintained with a partner over a long period of time, a lender will not check every property with the same diligence as it would for a first-time customer.

The evaluation of investment projects falls within the free decision-making scope of the credit institution, and is therefore, like any other free decision, subject also

---

[11]Cf. SPIEGEL magazine cover story: "Der Pleite-König. Millarden-Versagen der Banken" [The bankruptcy king. Banks lose billions], *Der Spiegel*, No. 16, 18 April 1994, pp. 22–30.

to the considerations of moral responsibility. Banks unavoidably have the power to decide whether a project that depends on external capital is creditworthy or not, and therefore whether it will be realized or not. In its decision-making process the bank must apply the criteria of economic efficiency and justice both in exchange and in price equity, although these can only be formalized to a very limited extent. Nor can the impacts of such a decision ever be completely anticipated in experiment or by scientific methods. The assessment of future outcomes of investments always implies a high degree of freedom of judgment.

Banks must treat everyone who applies for credit fairly, i.e. they must treat equivalent situations equally and non-equivalent situations unequally. They must follow the principle of rule equality and the principle of objectivity and universality. The interest rates for all customer loans must follow the market interest rate. Preferential treatment in the evaluation of creditworthiness must be excluded, along with special favors in the granting of credit to customers or unjustified discounts or premiums on credit costs.

The same principle of equitable price and equitable interest rate also applies to the bank's relationships with current and deposit account holders. Here, too, the market price and market interest rate must form the guideline for individual pricing and the setting of interest rates. The ethics of banking requires that banks practice neither preferential treatment of wealthier clients nor undue stringency or leniency towards less wealthy customers.

The duty of impartiality[12] and objectivity is further underscored by the fact that banks often command a natural monopoly in local contexts where the market is not sufficiently large to bear numerous competing local branches of different banks. These local monopolies of banks in small towns or villages are problematic from the viewpoint of ensuring competition and consumer freedom of choice. There is a certain justification for them, however, in that their personal knowledge of their customers and the local community can enable them to manage personal credit more efficiently than anonymous banks.

In their credit decisions, banks must strike a balance between sympathy and stringency. On the one hand, they must be prepared to countenance certain risks in order to facilitate innovations; on the other hand, they are duty bound to ensure that they do not invest in economically unsound projects. Credit institutions are not lending their own money but the deposits of their customers. It is in this dialectical union of creative entrepreneurial imagination and a sense of reality, objectivity and thrift that the duty and the virtue of efficient and fair banking practice reside.

Banks are often criticized for undue bias in their decisions on lending to industrial companies towards the aspects of profitability and security. Criteria that transcend economic efficiency in the narrower sense, such as assessment of the investment's

---

[12]Cf. F. N. BRADY.: "Impartiality and Particularity in Business Ethics", in: P. KOSLOWSKI, Y. SHIONOYA (eds.): *The Good and the Economical. Ethical Choices in Economics and Management*, Berlin, Heidelberg, New York, Tokyo (Springer) 1993, pp. 175–194.

environmental effects or the impacts on public welfare, are not sufficiently considered, the accusation goes. Banks usually reply that the profit expectation from the loan given to private or industrial customers coincides with the profit expectation for the bank and hence the maximization of shareholder value of the bank's shares, and constitutes the control principle of banking, which should not be weakened by introducing other principles into the objective function of the bank.

Two objections can be raised against this argument. First, an increasing number of shareholders and customers prefer banks to pursue a broader objective function than that pursued by banks oriented purely to shareholder value, although these banks need not lose sight of the necessity of making a profit. Many bank deposit customers expect their bank to take certain ethical criteria into account in its decisions regarding the extension of loans to others. The emergence of "ethical funds" or "environmental funds" as well as alternative banks confirm this development. It is possible that it will be more profitable for the commercial banks to broaden and deepen the criteria for lending, in order to attract more discerning customers, than to cling to the narrow principle of maximizing shareholder value or profit.

The second objection to the "only profit counts" criterion is a logical one: if positive profit is the necessary condition for the continuation of a firm or a bank in business, it does not follow that positive profit is also the sufficient condition for its business. Nothing prevents a bank from supplementing the control principle of profit with additional principles. These principles should not reduce profits in the long term, however, because any such decline in profit would indicate shortcomings in the efficiency of the bank's activity.

Chapter 3
The Ethical Economy of the Capital Market

The need for capital and thus financial resources to finance firms and projects creates its own market in which capital, in its most abstract form, is bought and sold as a securitized, exchange-tradable share of a firm. This established market begets norms of practice and trade in this market, norms of exchange and norms of advice on trading, which arise in the interplay between the capital market's factual development and the normative rules of ethics and of legislation.

The Globalization of the Capital Market

The capital market has entered a new phase since the beginning of the 1990s as a result of globalization. It has itself been globalized, which means it has become a single global market for capital. This market not only sells capital internationally but also "produces" it globally. In the past, internationalization meant that goods were produced nationally and sold internationally on global markets. Globalization implies that even the products – and not just sales – are now produced globally in a number of different countries. The precondition for globalization is the integration of the single global market by means of the Internet.

Globalization Extends the Simultaneity of Space and Compresses the Non-Simultaneous Nature of Human Time

Space, says Leibniz, is the ordering of all things that are simultaneous; time is the ordering of all things that are not simultaneous. Space and time order all things. Those things that are simultaneous are ordered by space, those that are not simultaneous, by time. All things are ordered in space and in time, i.e. spatially and temporally.

The Internet and new technologies alter the fundamental relations that order human experience, space and time, and thus alter the simultaneity and non-simultaneity of things for people. Leibniz's definition describes absolute space and

P. Koslowski, *The Ethics of Banking*, Issues in Business Ethics 30,
DOI 10.1007/978-94-007-0656-9_3, © Springer Science+Business Media B.V. 2011

absolute time, not human space and time. Even for human space and time, however, the definition is valid that human space is the ordering of things that are simultaneous for us and time is the ordering of things which are non-simultaneous for us. Human space is stretched by those things that a human being can access simultaneously. Human time is defined by what is not simultaneous for us. Time is things in their succession; space, things in their simultaneity. The Internet brings about a shift in the relations of simultaneity and succession and the relationship of center and periphery. It renders even distant places simultaneous that were never simultaneous for us in the past. Transactions and information over great distances, which used to be non-simultaneous and outside the decision-making scope of the individual, are becoming simultaneous and entering our decision-making scope. Transactions that could once only be executed with long time delays and did not therefore belong to the space of the human being, to our space of simultaneity, become simultaneous and grow into our decision-making space. The individual's decision-making and action space is growing because the control of large spaces in simultaneity becomes possible.

Financial investments always comprise the element of corporate decision-making and corporate control. To the extent that effective control becomes possible across large distances, investments take on a growing spatial range and potential for control. With the help of online brokerage, an equities portfolio can be controlled from any place on Earth without high transaction costs.

The process of globalization in the 1990s led to the expansion of financial investments into territories which were not previously targets for such investments, mainly the countries of the former Eastern bloc as well as China and India. At the same time, the invention of the Internet, online banking and online brokerage created the instrument that enabled the transmission and dissemination of information about the new investment territories and brought these countries into a relationship of simultaneity and virtual proximity with the financial metropolises, i.e. these new territories were brought within "their" space.

Hand in hand with globalization which, in the domain of financial investments and financial markets, is more than just a spatial expansion, three major expansions of financial investments took place. Spatial expansion in a geographical sense was closely associated with informational expansion and the social expansion of financial investments. And the expansion of financial investments into wider sections of the population which had no previous engagement in the capital market introduces a third element, the phenomenon of debordering, to the historical dynamic towards spatial and informational expansion.

Globalization of the Capital Market as the Driver of Globalization of the World

The following processes, according to Klaus Müller, are commonly understood to be the defining features of globalization:

- Liberalization of financial markets,
- Transboundary ecological hazards,
- Transnational fusions,
- Mass media dissemination of western (consumer) models,
- Growing migration flows,
- Declining effectiveness of national policy.[1]

Müller puts the liberalization of financial markets at the head of his list, and indeed, the liberalization, internationalization and expansion of financial markets has to be described as the most powerful driving force of the process of globalization. Another common factor to all the features of the process of globalization mentioned is the increasing, non-place-dependent, ubiquitous access to knowledge. People's decision-making space and decision-making time became global because knowledge about the entire world is available more rapidly than in past eras and can be documented on digital media.[2] Conversely, we can only perceive globalization because our information systems provide us with momentary knowledge of the global reality, or at least parts of it. With the Internet and the globalization of information, the earlier disparity – indeed, the hiatus – between the center and the periphery of knowledge is increasingly being leveled off or even negated. The catalogues of the world's great libraries have become accessible even from the remotest village in the world, as long as it has a telephone line.

What is meant by the social debordering of financial institutions? In 1976, Peter Drucker published his book on "pension fund socialism".[3] As far back as the 1970s the pension funds were already bringing about a socialization of investment. They forged ahead with a tendency, already identified by Marx in the joint-stock company, to sever the relationship between capital ownership and managing a firm. Whether or not pension fund capitalism is actually equivalent to real socialism can be put aside for now. The fact is, however, that the pension and investment funds led to a previously unseen widening of the class of capital owners – 56% of households in the USA own corporate shares – and that they comprise an element of socialization of the ownership of means of production and drive forward the debordering of the capital market.

Another "driver" of the expansion of the capital market is a further trend observed since the 1980s: many employees in the USA engage in stock market speculation in the attempt to top up their income and generate a second income.[4] All four tendencies mentioned caused a debordering of the capital market with the effect of a

---

[1] KLAUS MÜLLER: *Globalisierung*, Frankfurt, New York (Campus) 2002.

[2] ROBERT J. SHILLER: *Irrational Exuberance*, Princeton and Oxford (Princeton University Press) 6th edn. 2001, points out that the laying of the first transatlantic telephone cable had a similar effect to the Internet. Crucially, however, unlike the telephone, the Internet enables instantaneous, documentable information transfer.

[3] PETER DRUCKER: *The Unseen Revolution: How Pension Fund Socialism Came to America*, New York (Harper and Row) 1976.

[4] The significance of this desire to augment one's income with a second income from capital market investment and speculation has been pointed out primarily by SHILLER (2001).

volume of amounts invested and a volume of trade hitherto unprecedented in economic history. The expansion is magnified by the new hybrid and synthetic financing instruments like asset-backed securities and structured financial instruments as well as expansion of the derivatives and options markets.

The debordering and worldwide internationalization of financial investments and of the capital market is perhaps the most important characteristic of globalization. Globalization is more than internationalization, even in the domain of finance. It comprises not just operating internationally and maintaining a presence in another country, but creating an integrated trading space of the stock exchange, which becomes technically feasible thanks to the Internet.

Values and Valuations in the Capital Market

The duties of participants in organizations or other institutions are determined by the purpose of the institution of which they are part. The question to be addressed is therefore what the purpose of the capital market is, and what duties arise from its stated purpose? If one analyses the purpose of the capital market in developed society, one arrives at three main functions: first, the capital market is expected to supply companies with the financial resources and capital that they require for investment in long-term investment projects; second, it should give the saver various means of putting his savings to productive use and becoming an investor, thus fulfilling the deposit function; finally, and this function of the capital market has risen to increasing prominence of late, it is the market for corporate control, in which investors, through the vehicle of their investments, control and put pressure on the management of large firms to deliver acceptable performance. If a large corporation's management team begins to underperform, it is replaced in a takeover by other companies or investors.

The relative weightings of the purposes of the capital market can shift. In this shift, the law specifies the rules of the capital market, codifies them and makes them justiciable. Values, by contrast, are only conditionally justiciable. They cannot be enforced through the courts; nevertheless, they fulfill a function as a background orientation of action, as the "spirit of conduct" so to speak.

Participants in the capital market can be held to rules and duties but not forced to accept particular values. In spite of this, values of virtue can be adopted additionally as a voluntary self-commitment. This problem of the relationship between legal duties and virtues was thematized long ago in Kant's writings on legal philosophy and ethics. Kant talks about duties of right and duties of virtue, which prompted Schleiermacher's critique that Kant first says that duties are only those which are unconditionally binding, and can therefore only be duties of right, yet he then talks about duties of virtue as imperfect duties to make some virtue or attitude into an obligation.[5]

---

[5]Cf. PETER KOSLOWSKI: *Principles of Ethical Economy*, Dordrecht, Boston, London (Kluwer, now Springer) 2001 (Issues in Business Ethics, Vol. 17).

If we ask which reality influences the capital market and which values it brings forth, we will have to break through the veil of greed and enrichment found in the capital market as in all domains of human exchange. It is one of the objections to the capital market that it unduly encourages greed and enrichment, and that speculation gives rise to greed and a loss of sense of reality.

The sole value of the capital market, it might be said, is cash value. Initially it is undeniable that the stock exchange revolves around the cash value of equities and corporate shareholdings. This means, however, that it is concerned with the cash value of investments which will generate yields at some future date in anticipation of future economic products and activity.

American pragmatism posed the question as to the value of truth – as Pontius Pilate famously asked, "What is truth?" – satirically. What is the value of truth, and since value is shown ultimately in cash value, pragmatism asked the question: "What is the cash value of truth?" If truth has to be revealed in pragmatic utility, the truth of the capital market and the stock exchange must be revealed particularly in its utility, namely in cash value. Truth in the economic sense is to pursue the right strategy which matches the needs of the consumer. "Truth" or rightness in the market is the correct anticipation of consumer demand and hence the correct anticipation of investment yields and investment strategies resulting from the successful meeting of needs. These always have a speculative element since we cannot know what people might want to have in future. We can only anticipate it. The right strategy is revealed in the cash value that it generates. The right prediction gives a better payback on the stock exchange and in the capital market than anywhere else, which is why everyone tries to make the right prediction by means of shares. The stock exchange cash value of truth is especially high, and so is the risk of loss.

Values are attitudes and preferential choices, which it is an imperfect duty to espouse. They become a perfect duty only when one is a member of an organization and placed under such an obligation by the organizational agent under the terms of a contract of employment, and only to the extent that the organizational agent is entitled to do so within the scope of general legislation.

The term "value" derives from the language of the merchant, who knows the market value, the cash value, the repurchase value, and so on. These different values reflect differing valuations of one and the same object. The translation of the value concept into ethics creates difficulties because value is supposed to express something that transcends this very subjectivity, namely objective values, but can only do so in the language of subjective evaluations, i.e. values. Therefore the concept of value always carries somewhat arbitrary, subjective connotations.

For that reason, it cannot stand alone at the center of law and ethics but has to be flanked in ethics by rules, duties and virtues. Rules are the ordering of an institutional context. An ordering in this sense is nothing other than a collection – a set – of rules. Duties are the binding obligations that follow from rules and role expectations. Virtues or values determine the attitudes and the spirit of conduct. In this sense, the capital market, like every market, sets out rules, justifies duties, welcomes virtues and is borne up by values, but it is not rooted in moral values.

Only organizations can make it a duty for their members to have certain values. Markets cannot do this, because they are primarily institutions for the coordination of subjective valuations and values.[6] For instance, the Frankfurt stock exchange can impose the duty on its accredited traders, as organizational members of the Frankfurt stock exchange, to abide by certain values in the conduct of all their business activity, but it cannot bind participants in the stock exchange itself, sellers or buyers, to abide by particular values. The capital market is defined by rules and duties – legal and ethical rules and duties – and, only insofar as they derive from those, by values.

Another question is whether the financial advisers and financial intermediaries, whose role is becoming more and more important in the capital market, need to adopt certain values in the capital market over and above compliance with the rules and duties of law.

Values are attitudes, preference rules and preferential choices that go above and beyond the economic concept of value. They define the identity of an organization and the spirit of conduct within organizations, particularly in areas not subject to formal regulation and grey zones which cannot be described in terms of well-defined rules and duties. Identification and orientation are thus attributes of values.[7]

Values are expressions of general attitudes in organizations but not in markets and states. An organization can make values binding because it is voluntary to join the organization, and the member of the organization could just as easily join another organization which does not make these values binding. The same cannot be said of states. Therefore it is problematic to talk about the "value system of the constitution". The citizens of a state can only be obliged to obey its laws. They cannot be obliged to internalize the value system of these laws. Nevertheless, it is not meaningless to talk about a value system that underpins the laws and perhaps also influences the intention of the law. But these values, as identification with the intention of the law, cannot be made obligatory.

Fulfillment of duty can be made easier, in human organizations, by adopting values. The rendering of services within the organization is encouraged by means of "organizational commitment", i.e. commitment to and identification with the organization. Nevertheless, ultimately the law can only make the fulfillment of duty, but not the adoption of the underlying values behind laws, into a "legal duty". The capital market is a market and not an organization. It is a point of confluence for many different values. While some investors will pursue "socially responsible investing", others will pursue moral goals that are not nearly so lofty. Thus there are ethical funds which impose stricter moral "values" on the firms in which they invest, but

---

[6]Cf. PETER KOSLOWSKI: *Gesellschaftliche Koordination. Eine ontologische und kulturwissenschaftliche Theorie der Marktwirtschaft* [Social coordination. An ontological and cultural theory of the market], Tübingen (Mohr Siebeck) 1991.

[7]Cf. JOSEF WIELAND: *WerteManagementSystem^{ZfW}. Prinzipien und Bausteine für Nachhaltigkeit in der Unternehmensführung* [ZfW Values Management System. Principles and components for sustainability in corporate governance] (manuscript).

there are also funds like the "Morgan Funshares" in the USA which assure their investors that their money is invested mostly in alcohol, tobacco and casinos.

Legal duties also incorporate duties of diligence, however, which possibly pre-suppose certain attitudes and values. Particularly in the ethical codes of professions like doctors and lawyers, the degree of care that members of these professions are expected to exercise presupposes certain attitudes and values. These heightened legal duties of care and "due diligence", as well as the duty to espouse the values of the profession which are conducive to fulfilling those professional duties, only apply to certain well-defined professional groups, not all citizens. Citizens living in a democratic state have to espouse their legal duties, but not the entire "value system of the constitution".[8] To demand that every citizen should internalize an entire state-defined value system is either totalitarian or romantic.[9]

Which Values Should Determine the Actions of Financial Intermediaries in the Capital Market?

Considerable ethical problems arise out of the position of trust of financial interme-diaries who operate as trustees and brokers for investors. To the extent that people's retirement provision will be transferred from state social insurance schemes into fully-funded private insurance schemes, the role of financial intermediaries will become increasingly important. Financial intermediaries must advise people seek-ing retirement provision fairly and appropriately to the matter at issue. The financial intermediary is in a fiduciary relationship with the client, which gives rise to height-ened duties: the service provider assumes the role of a guarantor and trustee who is trusted by his or her client. The trustee initially has the negative duty to refrain from gaining any personal or private advantage from the fiduciary relationship beyond the fee agreed in the contract as payment for his or her services. The service provider has the further duty to observe good faith and due diligence. The question that arises, therefore, is whether it is necessary and useful to bind the financial services provider in the capital market more specifically to certain values.

The necessity of heightening the professionalization of financial intermediaries arises from the fact that they administer the wealth of others, and their decisions are of the utmost importance for securing the future existence of their clients. The role of the financial intermediary is comparable to that of the doctor, for whom an elevated duty of diligence and a guarantor role is legally stipulated because of the higher risk of his conduct to the life and the health of the patients. Although the domain of financial services is not a matter of life and death, it

---

[8]The state can demand this of its organization-members, the civil servants, but not from all citizens. Nevertheless, it can encourage citizens to identify with the value system of their state.

[9]The state has no organizational purpose in this sense and no organizational values, because it is not a special-purpose organization. It provides the conditions for others, individuals and organizations, to pursue their own purposes within it.

has far-reaching consequences for people's life planning. On the one hand, this would necessitate professionalization of these occupations and stronger commitment to particular values as conditions of compliant practice. On the other hand, what should be avoided is bringing all financial services providers into the same guarantor role for all clients by force of law, since this would undoubtedly make financial services more expensive, and some clients are prepared to accept some tempering of the financial intermediary's guarantor role and bear any resulting risk themselves.

What are the arguments in favor of professionalization and stronger commitment of financial intermediaries to particular values? First, it is known from the history of ethics that the development of a professional ethic is often the first step that helps occupational groups seeking greater recognition for their work as a profession to achieve this aim. With a professional ethic, a profession shows that it is in the public interest. This kind of "ethicalization" and professionalization process is, in fact, currently taking place in the domain of financial services in Germany. Certain groups are coming together, endeavoring to have their activities certified, and organizing into associations that award quality seals and so on. All codes of professional ethics emphasize the obligation of a professional class to the common good, and make the commitment – which is also justiciable – that they will be guided by ideals such as integrity, objectivity, competence, diligence, confidentiality and the avoidance of conflicts of interest.[10]

Here it has to be emphasized that professional, academic, and quality-label associations are types of organization which make more extensive demands upon their members, and hence expect more extensive value-orientations from them than are demanded by state law or the rules of the market. The members of these associations, as members of organizations, commit themselves to a stronger value-orientation than applies outside the organization. They also submit to the sanctions that these organizations impose for breaching the self-commitment to their organizational values. The fact that such associations are armed with sanctions is of great importance because it enables the customer or demander of services to rely on compliance with the rules with some degree of certainty. It is likely that a trend in the direction of a more professionalized ethics of financial services, overseen by professional associations, will take root in the German capital market, a process that is already well advanced in the United Kingdom and the USA. The transfer of pension services out of the social insurance system into private pension planning in the capital market will drive this process forward in the other countries of continental Europe, too. The professions that will profit the most from the privatization of pension planning and from the introduction of pension funds backed by government subsidies and/or tax advantages – like the German "Riester pension" – will be the financial consultants, brokers and financial intermediaries.

---

[10]Cf. BOATRIGHT (1999), p. 44, and RENA A. GORLIN (ed.): *Codes of Professional Responsibility*, Washington, DC (Bureau of National Affairs) 3rd edn. 1994.

On the Ethics of Financial Consulting

Any inquiry into the economic-ethical duties of the financial advisor is bound to address the question of good conduct in the institutional context of the capital market. Advisors are obliged by their fiduciary role to act in the best interests of the customer and not in their own best interests. They are subject to fiduciary duties and duties of care, the latter being further differentiated in American law and business ethics into the duties of prudence and due diligence. Any other form of imprudent or non-diligent conduct by a financial advisor or any failure to protect the client's interests contravenes these duties and constitutes a breach of the fiduciary relationship.

In the capital market, this risk is most virulent in the temptation of the financial services provider to engage in "churning", "twisting" or "flipping" of customer investments. "Churning" is excessive stock-trading which generates commission for the bank or broker but produces no benefit for the client. Stock and trading tips which lead to churning breach the broker's fiduciary obligation only to recommend suitable investments and to disclose the risks associated with them. The financial advisor in this scenario faces a host of expectations and these often lead to conflicts of interest which are morally problematic. As the employee of a bank, for instance, the employee must act in the customer's interests whilst also giving due regard to the bank's interest in generating commission and fee income.

Non-professional day-traders are a special case because instead of having advisors who practice churning, they do it for themselves. According to the observations of Germany's Federal Securities Supervisory Authority (the predecessor of today's Federal Financial Supervisory Authority, the BAFin) from the year 2001, most day-traders lose their capital as a result of their constant buying and selling of the same shares, because they pay ever-rising commission fees to the online banks for their trading, which frequently more than consume the share-price gains notionally observed by the day-trader.

"Twisting" is replacing an existing insurance policy with a new one which is no real improvement for the insured but generates commission for the insurance broker and hence also costs for the insured; "flipping" is replacing a credit agreement with one or more new ones, which similarly promise to offer the borrower an improvement of his debt situation but generally fail to deliver because only the credit broker makes a profit from the commission.

All three phenomena, churning, twisting and flipping, are a breach of the fiduciary relationship and a dereliction of duty, not just an infringement of values, by the financial services provider. Not only can this dereliction of duty be combated through the ethical value-orientation of the financial services provider, but it must also be made justiciable and armed with the sanction of law – in other words, punished by imposing damages payments or fines, as the case may be, on the financial services provider. This only applies, however, where an explicit fiduciary relationship has been established. If customers waive this and want to act on the principle of *caveat emptor* (Let the buyer beware!), they cannot retrospectively foist an enhanced fiduciary duty on the financial services provider.

Another problem arises when analysts, as financial services providers, are not independent. Analysts are frequently paid by those whom they are evaluating and ranking, so that the objectivity of their analysis is impaired by their interest in the continuation of the business relationship with the corporation under scrutiny. They are also notoriously over-optimistic in evaluating the share price trend.[11]

The Tasks of the Capital Market and the Duties of the Participants in the Capital Market

How can we approach the ethical analysis of the capital market and the conduct of its actors? An economic-ethical analysis of the capital market looks at the ethical presuppositions of the functional conditions and rationality of the capital market and of the conduct of its actors. A crucial test of these functional conditions is the question of whether conduct in this market brings forth unintended side-effects which contradict or disrupt the task or "functional dedication" of the capital market. If the side-effects reach a certain scale, institutional changes need to be set in train. If traders are flourishing, for example, but they are doing so by churning investors to create high trade volumes that generate high commissions and fees, then investors will end up paying more in fees than they earn in profits, and institutional precautions need to be taken against churning.

If we apply the three principles of legal justification introduced by Radbruch to the institutional context of the capital market, the first question we need to address is the capital market's purpose. A structure as complex as the market for capital and corporate control generally fulfills multiple purposes. Moreover, there may be a certain amount of tension between them.

The purposes or functions of the capital market can be broken down into four sub-purposes:

1. The savings function: the capital market acts as a savings repository;
2. The wealth function: the capital market safeguards purchasing power over longer periods of time;
3. The liquidity function: the capital market gives investors the facility to convert their financial investments back into cash, ensuring that liquid funds can be at their disposal at all times;

---

[11]Cf. MALCOLM BAKER: "Review of John C. Bogle: The Battle for the Soul of Capitalism, New Haven and London: Yale University Press, 2005," *Journal of Economic Literature*, 22 (September 2008), p. 732: "Analysts move markets with recommendations, but annual earnings estimates and long-term growth forecasts are systematically too optimistic. Analysts often act as if they are paid by the firms they are covering – and it turns out they were, [...] taking a slice of investment banking revenue. This has reemerged with S&P and Moody's, who are explicitly paid by issuers of debt instruments."

4. The economic policy function of the capital and money market: the government
   can make use of capital market policy and monetary policy to steer economic
   activity and macroeconomic demand.[12]

By increasing or decreasing the money supply, the government can stimulate or
dampen demand for shares and thus exert an influence on share prices. A rise or
fall in share prices, in turn, raises or lowers consumer spending, because individual
consumer spending depends on the individual's net wealth. If share prices are high,
investors have greater wealth at their disposal and, *ceteris paribus*, they will indulge
in greater consumer spending. If the government reduces the money supply and
induces a rise in the interest rate, the effect is that share prices fall. When share
prices are falling, individuals tend to consume less because they feel worse off.

This mechanism implies that the government can use the money supply and the
interest rate as levers to influence the value of share assets and the individuals'
rate of consumption, which is influenced by asset value, and thus dampen or stimulate the economy. The American government's policy of easy money in the years
2002/2003 deliberately supported share prices so as to raise the value of consumers'
private wealth, as a means of propping up consumption during the recession that
followed the IT crisis of 2001. Since consumption is also a function of consumer
wealth, this increased private consumption.

In the capital market, the purpose of efficient allocation of capital is central. The
question of where capital should be invested is of the utmost importance to every
society. It encompasses the question of which projects, technologies and regions
society should invest in and which investments for the future are given consideration. Since investors decide *ex ante* which development they believe to be right and
desirable, their decisions are always laden with great uncertainty. Consumers in the
market, by contrast, decide *ex post* what they like about companies' products and
services, which result from decisions made some time previously, and hence they
can be more certain about which of the companies' decisions were right than the
firms could be when they made the decisions.

A society fundamentally has three mechanisms at its disposal for arriving at decisions on capital allocation. It can either leave the allocation decision to the banks,
or to the state's investment decision in a centralized planned economy, or to a dedicated market in which investors and companies coordinate their plans and their
expectations. It is obvious that a capital market as a coordination mechanism for the
allocation of capital is more in keeping with a democratic society than coordination
by major banks or by central steering of the economy.[13] Like other markets, the

---

[12]On the functions of the capital and money market cf. PETER S. ROSE: *Money and Capital
Markets. Financial Institutions and Instruments in a Global Marketplace*, Boston etc. (McGraw-
Hill) 7th edn. 2000, pp. 6ff.

[13]The analogy between democracy and the stock market as a democratic way of securing capi-
tal allocation is emphasized by OSWALD VON NELL-BREUNING: *Grundzüge der Börsenmoral*,
Freiburg im Breisgau (Herder) 1928, p. 9, and NELL-BREUNING: "Volkswirtschaftlicher Wert und
Unwert der Börsenspekulation" [Economic value and non-value of stock exchange speculation],

capital market proves to be a means of diffusing and controlling economic power since it creates competition between suppliers and demanders of capital. It is also open to new concepts and gives an opportunity for the new, the unknown and even the outlandish.[14]

If the capital market is to assume this function, however, it requires speculation on a grand scale. In the capital market, speculation is unavoidable and indeed desirable, for two reasons. For one thing, it is only possible to speculate on the future potential returns up to a point, since the future demand for products and goods is not something we can know right now. This is a phenomenon that is familiar from philosophical and theological speculation, namely that speculative knowledge begins where complete information and complete empiricism become impossible, but where it is impossible to dispense with empiricism altogether. Rather, inferences are drawn from fragmentary experience and imperfect empiricism onto a broader context. Stock market speculation is not therefore a game or a gamble, but the anticipation of future development based on incomplete information and empiricism, which incorporates the anticipation of what the other speculators are anticipating plus an element of gaming.

The unavoidability of speculation follows logically from the problem of uncertainty about the future. The two key uncertainties that arise in the capital market are uncertainty about the future profits of companies and uncertainty about the future development of capital gains from changes in the capital value of a firm or in the value of shares. Accordingly, speculation is targeted both towards correct anticipation of corporate earnings or – in the case of the joint-stock corporation – dividends, and towards the correct anticipation of movements in the value of its shares, i.e. the share price trend.

The second reason that speculation is necessary is in order to create the trade volumes of equity shares that are necessary in order to fulfill the liquidity function of the capital market. The strength of the stock market is that long-term investments in companies can be liquidated at any time by shareholders, if not always at a profit,

---

Stimmen der Zeit, 114 (1928), pp. 46–56, here p. 52. NELL-BREUNING's ground-breaking book *Grundzüge der Börsenmoral* [Principles of the ethics of the stock exchange] was published at a time when the stock exchange and speculation were heavily criticized in Germany after the breakdown of the German currency in the year 1923 and the period with occasional famines following it and leading to the rise of the Nazis.

[14]Cf. also BAKER (2008), p. 734: "Winston Churchill's line that 'democracy is the worst form of government except all the others that have been tried' is instructive. The same can be said about capital markets. Widespread participation, for example, has costs and benefits. In an earlier era and in other parts of the world, there are fewer, but more activist owners – a good thing – but also a higher cost and lower access to capital for firms, and the spoils of capitalism delivered to a smaller number of owners. Similarly, the world of lending before securitization involved less distance between lenders and borrowers and higher standards – a good thing – but also banks that were more constrained by their own balance sheets, making loans costlier and more difficult to obtain. The financial system is supposed to allocate capital actively and intelligently and to share risks and rewards broadly. Sometimes, these two goals are at odds. We can and should hope for a financial system that can deliver the best of both, but the global credit crisis is the latest reminder that this is a battle that will be hard to win."

and converted into cash. But liquidation of long-term investments and conversion into cash is only possible if there is professional speculation and professional stock trading, because otherwise investors would run the risk that no supply of buyers would be on hand in the event that they wanted to sell.

For both reasons, owing to the inevitable uncertainty about future corporate earnings and owing to the need to create liquidity in the market for corporate shares, speculation in the stock market is unavoidable, and without speculation an efficient capital market is unthinkable. Therefore resentments against stock exchange speculation have to be qualified. It is no coincidence that in Germany under the National Socialist regime, the Nazis directed polemic at speculation and prohibited parts of the capital market, the options market for instance.

Speculation is useful and fits the purpose of the capital market. It should not therefore be prevented. Comments made in autumn 2001 by the then German Minister of Finance, Hans Eichel, that speculation ought to be prohibited, find no justification in the functional conditions of the capital markets. Similarly the German government's proposal in connection with the privatization of Deutsche Telekom and Deutsche Post to offer the public "people's shares" (*Volksaktien*) is open to criticism, given the insight that speculation is unavoidable. Since the equities market is necessarily speculative, there can be no "people's share" that is not subject to speculation and uncertainties about the future. Any shares, even shares in former state monopoly firms like Telekom or Deutsche Post, are subject to price risk and stock-exchange volatility. It is one of the weaknesses of small investors that they usually underestimate the risks of share price development. Risk is also a moral problem, and realism or a sense of reality is a moral imperative.

Instead of advocating and issuing "people's shares", a more useful aspiration to strive for than a "people's share" would have been the goal of developing a "people's capitalism". In a democratic society it is desirable that as many people as possible take part in decisions about investments and companies, and hence about future economic strategies, and that ideally the entire economic knowledge of a nation and the individual assessments of all economic subjects flow into the capital market. In this regard, the goal of a "people's capitalism" which is serviced by the capital market is certainly worth striving for. In order to achieve the function of the efficient management of capital allocation, however, it is desirable not to concentrate on a few "people's shares" but on a broad range of investment activity in the equities of many innovative companies, not forgetting smaller firms.

If one sums up the purposes or functions of the capital market, it is clear that the efficient channeling of capital into investible purposes under the condition of information efficiency and liquidity, the convertibility of the investment into liquid funds, are the central functions of the capital market.[15]

This makes it possible to answer the question of what ethical and economic values must be given consideration in the globalized capital market. In order to meet

---

[15]Cf. also GERHARD PICOT: "M&A aus Sicht der Kapitalmärkte", in: G. PICOT: *Handbuch Mergers & Acquisitions*, Stuttgart (Schäffer-Poeschel) 2000, pp. 33–52.

the demands of information efficiency and fulfill the liquidity function, as many suppliers and demanders as possible must be active in a market in order to generate large enough volumes of supply and demand so that genuine markets for companies and corporate strategies emerge. Globalization, by enlarging the market, tends to be conducive to information efficiency and stock market liquidity. An efficient capital market calls for adequate liquidity so that investors are not "locked in" to their investments.[16] Conversely the preservation of wealth and the safekeeping of means of purchasing in the capital market is a purpose which requires that fluctuations in the value of assets in the capital market do not become excessive. In the capital market, then, important considerations will be that decisions in the capital market direct capital quickly and flexibly to whatever is the best use, but without giving rise to unnecessary fluctuations in value which cause uncertainty to savers and investors and drive them out of the capital market.

The mobility of capital and its efficient allocation on the one hand, and the conditions of stability and liquidity of the capital market on the other hand, are mutually antagonistic aims to some extent, partly because of speculation. Stock exchange speculation must on the one hand seek out the minutest changes in the potential returns on investments and bring them to evidence in the market. On the other hand, however, it must avoid creating artificial fluctuations in value which have no "substance" in the net asset values of shares and firms. Consequently, speculation is meant to be highly speculative on the one hand, and must find the tiniest differentials in value, but should not produce any artificial volatility on the other hand. In the orientation of the values of capital market actors, a tension arises here between speculative dynamism and the stabilization of volatility through speculation.

It must not be overlooked, however, that stock market speculation rewards the kinds of speculative anticipations which have correctly anticipated improbable increases in value. By doing this, the capital market rewards the highly speculative speculation which dampens price fluctuations and removes greater volatility from the market. The popular view that speculation always amplifies price fluctuation is wide of the mark.

---

[16]BOATRIGHT (1999), p. 116, points out that the lack of liquidity options for sizeable packages of shares can be a problem for large pension funds because these are often not in a position to voice their protest against weak management teams by selling the shares in their companies. They must therefore resort to influencing management by remaining invested in the company and exerting direct influence over the leadership of the company. A pension fund like CalPERS (California Public Employees' Retirement System) which is invested in shares with a market value of 198.9 billion US dollars (as of 15 September 2009, cf. http://www.calpers.ca.gov/) has difficulty in selling a package of Microsoft shares to the value of 1 billion dollars on the stock exchange without taking a price hit. – The change in the form of capitalism from private ownership capitalism to "pension fund capitalism" can be traced from the following figures: "In 1970, individuals held more than 72 percent of shares, while institutional investors (pensions, mutual funds, insurance companies, and private trusts and endowments) accounted for about 16%. By 1990, the holdings of institutions had risen to more than 53%, with private and public pension funds owning approx. 28% of the equities of US firms." (quoted after BOATRIGHT (1999), p. 114).

Speculation and Finance Ethics

The capital market assumes two tasks in which it resembles the credit market. Like the latter, the capital market serves as a transfer process in which savings are channeled into investments, and as a transformation process in which investments of different time horizons are transformed into investments of long-term ownership titles or shares. In the capital market for shares, the conversion of savings and the transformation of time periods are achieved not through the banks as financial intermediaries but by conversion of the savings into risk-bearing securities, by their subsequent securitization and marketability on the stock exchange, and by the institutionalization of speculative trading in securities. The control function that the banks fulfill in the credit market is fulfilled on the stock exchange by other institutions: by control over the issue of new shares, which is exercised by the stock exchange supervisory authority or the government,[17] by the marketability of the shares and securities, and by professional and public speculation about the future prices of shares.

In comparison with bank balances or mortgage bonds, investing in shares in the capital market is a higher-risk investment. The stock market serves as a means of allocation for directing investible funds to firms. The prices of corporate shares reflect the expected profit and the expected risk attached to such results for those firms that participate in the capital market. Stock prices show how the firms listed on the capital market are assessed by market participants. The prices of equities reflect estimations of their profit and risk, arrived at by means of the capital market.

Shareholders are investors who, as owners, bear the full risk of their invested capital. On condition that there is complete transparency regarding the past and present performance and the future strategy of the firm, the share price in the market reflects the estimation of past and present performance and of expected future returns and risks by market participants, and, in the ideal scenario, fully reflects the risks and returns at stake.

In an ideal market, every share would have a certain market price. Stock trading would barely take place since the price of the corporate share would be the same for everyone at every point in time. In reality, however, huge trade volumes exist in modern-day capital markets. According to Friedman, the annual volume of trade on the New York stock exchange normally amounts to almost half the total value of all currently listed shares.[18] Friedman explains this massive trade in corporate

---

[17] In Germany and Switzerland, the so-called "anchoring principle" has applied. It is stipulated in law that bonds or equities in one of the currencies of these two countries can only be issued by banks that are established in the country in question. This regulation was given up in the euro zone with the introduction of the euro in 2002, in Switzerland in the year 2004. On the impact of this principle in the German capital market, cf. R.E. BREUER.: "Die Deutsche Terminbörse als Vorreiter einer Börsenlandschaft der 90er Jahre?" [The German options and futures exchange (DTB) as the precursor of a stock-exchange landscape of the 90s], *Zeitschrift für Bankrecht und Bankwirtschaft*, 2 (1990), No. 3, p. 101.

[18] FRIEDMAN (1987), p. 323.

shares in terms of different estimations of risk by investors, but he does not mention the differences that pertain to the intended duration of the investment and to the chance timing of selling decisions. Corporate shares are short-term or longer-term risk-bearing investments. The title to ownership that they define remains constant, but their actual owners change over time. The time periods in which corporate shares are held can be transformed at low transaction costs; low in comparison with other kinds of titles to property.

This transformation is made possible by the fact that corporate shares are marketable and tradable on the stock exchange. The marketability of corporate shares presupposes, in turn, that the supply of a certain share will always be met with demand for the same share at any given point in time, even if the buyer's and seller's original intentions regarding the duration of the investment in the corporate share do not coincide. The transformation of different holding periods is guaranteed by stock trading. The supply, demand and marketability of corporate shares are massively amplified by an occupational group whose specialized niche within the economy is stock trading: the group of professional speculators.

The Functions of Speculation in the Capital Market: Bearing Uncertainty and Risk as Well as Enabling the Division of Labor Between Calculation and Speculation

Professional speculation creates a large trade volume by generating additional supply and additional demand for corporate shares on the stock exchange, which far exceed the volume that would exist if there were no speculation, i.e. if investments in corporate shares were only ever made for the returns on very long-term if not permanent investments. Speculation is the kind of economic activity which seeks to turn a profit from the differences between current and future stock prices. The speculator who goes "long" assumes that the future price of the share will be higher than the current price. Speculating by going "short" assumes that the price will be lower. The long speculator attempts to turn a profit from buying shares now and selling them in the future. The investment decision does not concentrate on the expected return from dividends, but primarily on the differences between the future and current price of the stock.

The division of labor in the capital market between those who concentrate on the profit yields and the capital value of the corporate share, investors in the real sense, and those who concentrate on the differences and fluctuations in the share price over time, the speculators, ensures that an investment in shares can be liquidated at any point in time.[19] Speculation in shares increases the marketability of corporate shares and thereby the transformability of time periods for the capital invested in the capital market. Professional stock market speculation reduces the risk that one may not be

---

[19]Cf. WILHELM RÖPKE: article on "Spekulation", in: *Handwörterbuch der Staatswissenschaften*, 4th edn., Jena (Gustav Fischer) 1926, Vol. 7, pp. 706–710, here p. 708.

in a position to transform the periods of stock investment and disinvestment. It thus performs an important service for the economy.

Speculation assumes a portion of the uncertainty about future random change in holding periods and increases the investor's independence from other investors' time horizons, i.e. from their schedule for investment or disinvestment in corporate shares. The gains from speculation are the price that non-speculative investors have to pay for the additional trade volume in corporate shares that is available to them. Professional speculation, although it has other problematic aspects, is an intelligent game of chance and gain which produces the side-effect of boosting trade in corporate shares and easing the transformation of holding periods. Speculation in the spot market for corporate shares is equivalent to speculation in options and in futures and forwards insofar as they both bring about an increase in the trade volume for the spot and futures markets.

Speculation in the futures markets for commodities, currency or shares creates the possibility of hedging the prices of those commodities and shares whose producers or investors/owners do not want to speculate but want to have predictable commodity prices with which to calculate for the future. Speculation in futures acts as an insurance policy, giving non-speculators certainty about future prices or protecting them against future price fluctuations. In the same way, the increased trade in corporate shares through speculation in spot markets is an insurance policy for those who want to be free in their decisions about the time period and duration of their investment in corporate shares. Speculation in the spot market for corporate shares assures non-speculative investors that they will be in a position to find demand for their shares whenever they want to sell them and disinvest. In all of these cases, it is the non-speculators who must buy the insurance policy against price fluctuations and pay the price for it to the speculators.

In the market for futures, the division of labor between the speculators and the market participants who practice hedging to limit their risk comes about because some people have to speculate so that others can calculate with assured, or even certain, future prices.[20] In the spot market for corporate shares, the effect of speculation is not complete hedging of future prices but the reassurance that stock-investment holding periods in the future will be transformable by virtue of the ability to sell or buy on the stock exchange.

Assurance of the transformability of share holding periods by speculation on the stock exchange is only economically advantageous if the speculation has no vested interest in amplifying the price fluctuations of shares, and if it does not in fact amplify these fluctuations over the course of time. If professional speculation increases price fluctuations in order to turn a profit from them, it is very probable

---

[20]This relationship has already been pointed out by NELL-BREUNING (1928), p. 129. Professional speculation meets "the need to lighten the load of those sections of the economy who 'do not want to speculate but would just like to calculate' (Terhalle)" (own trans. from the German). Nell-Breuning draws on the thoughts of the public finance scholar Fritz Terhalle.

that the negative impact of the more pronounced price fluctuations caused by speculation will cancel out the welfare effects deriving from the increased marketability of shares.

Economic theory makes a distinction between speculation in shares with a negative and a positive expected elasticity of demand for shares, as measured against the stock exchange's expectations. Speculation with a negative expected elasticity describes speculative investment in shares which operates counter to the market's expectations, and thus buys shares when the market expects prices to be lower in the future. This kind of speculation reduces stock price fluctuations by means of a countercyclical investment strategy. Speculation with a positive expected elasticity of demand for shares, in contrast, buys and sells shares in agreement with the prevailing expectations of the market, trading cyclically along with the majority of market participants. This kind of speculation further increases price fluctuations and generates a negative welfare effect.

Stock market speculation is, however, most successful under two conditions: firstly, if its anticipations regarding the future prices of shares are accurate, and secondly, if it invests and disinvests countercyclically to the general market expectations with negative expected elasticity of demand for shares. Speculation is not very profitable if it follows the market expectations with positive elasticity and it is absolutely unprofitable if its predictions of future prices are wrong. There is nevertheless a tendency inherent to speculation, induced by the profit motive, to anticipate future stock price changes correctly, and there is an incentive to speculate in such a way that, because of the higher profit-rate of speculation under negative expected elasticity, the higher profits likely to be yielded by countercyclical speculation tend to lessen the fluctuations of the stock exchange.

The insight that speculation in the spot market for corporate shares decreases uncertainty about the future transformability of holding periods justifies the conclusion that the function of speculation in the market for corporate shares is to reduce the uncertainty of market participants, and that this function cannot be performed with other instruments. The risk attaching to a firm's earnings or its insolvency can be reckoned approximately by the market. However, no probability calculus can help it to reckon the uncertainty concerning the duration of future holding periods, i.e. the time-spans for which investors will want to hold their investments.[21] This uncertainty is a matter for "speculation" alone.

The two components of speculation should therefore be differentiated. Speculation can be divided into one part of pure speculation about the trajectory of securities prices, a trend line that takes shape under conditions of chance and uncertainty and is independent of earnings, and its counterpart which is genuine, long-term investment in corporate shares and bears risk as an owner and partner. Although these two components of speculation should be clearly differentiated

---

[21]On the distinction between risk and uncertainty cf. FRANK KNIGHT: *Risk, Uncertainty, and Profit*, New York (Houghton Mifflin) 1921.

analytically, in real capital market practice it is the case that speculators can only speculate if they also invest in corporate shares, i.e. if they are investors.

Capital market speculation is ethically permissible since it fulfills an objective function in the economy: it reduces uncertainty about the marketability of corporate shares on the stock exchange. Profits from speculation are thus payments for the service that speculation makes available to the public on the stock exchange, and it is justified by the economic added value that speculation creates.

Since professional speculation can claim an economic and ethical justification by virtue of its contribution to the common good by reducing uncertainty, the converse implication is that speculation is not economically or ethically justifiable if it does not actually reduce some uncertainty which cannot be reduced by any other means than speculation. Speculation is justified by its task of absorbing uncertainty in situations in which there is no other means of doing so. Where uncertainty can be reduced by less costly means than speculation, those are the means that should be used. Where speculation does not really reduce uncertainty, it is not justified.

Chapter 4
Insider Knowledge and Insider Trading as Central Problems of Finance Ethics

The stock exchange is the central institution charged with mediating supply and demand in the market for capital. The question of what conduct is appropriate to the matter of the capital market is a matter of intense debate, particularly with reference to insider trading. Indeed, insider trading is a central problem in the economic ethics of the capital market and the stock exchange. In Germany it has been prohibited since 1 August 1994, when the Second Financial Market Promotion Act was adopted.[1] Yet within the various schools of economics and jurisprudence, the debate has not arrived at any consensus on the question of whether or not insider trading is harmful, and hence, whether or not it should actually be illegal.

Insider trading is not the only problem of economic ethics in the capital market. There are other issues that raise questions of what conduct is materially appropriate to this particular domain: the ethics of investment and of the selection of shares are aspects of the economic ethics of the investor, while the conduct of exchange-listed firms towards their shareholders and the stock exchange is part of corporate ethics. Important questions of economic ethics can also be explored by inquiring into the ethics of the intermediaries and brokers in the capital market, the investment advisors and bankers. These questions go beyond the insider-trading problem.

However, as the problem of insider trading touches on the ethics of all three groups of capital market actors – the investors as suppliers of capital, the finance departments of corporations as demanders of capital, and the financial intermediaries as brokers between supply and demand – we can zero in on the ethics of the capital market or a theory of ethical economy by analyzing the arguments for and against insider trading. The German and the international debate on insider trading is riven with controversy. The "front lines" of the discussion by and large mirror the frontiers that divide economists and jurists. Whereas many economists advocate insider trading based on the argument that insider trading raises the allocative

---

[1] *Zweites Finanzmarktförderungsgesetz (Gesetz über den Wertpapierhandel und zur Änderung börsenrechtlicher und wertpapierrechtlicher Vorschriften*: German Act Governing Securities Trading and for the Modification of Regulations Governing the Stock Exchanges and Securities) of 26 July 1994. Its main parts took force on 1 August 1994, the Act in its entirety on 1 January 1995.

efficiency of the stock exchange,[2] most jurists reject that argument and favor the prohibition of insider trading, drawing on arguments from justice, particularly the principle of parity of rights for all shareholders and that of legal certainty and legal stability at the stock exchange.[3]

This conflict between the standpoints from which economists and jurists assess insider trading reveals a deeper-seated difference between the normative criteria of the two disciplines. While the economists have a tendency to concentrate on the efficiency aspect of allocation and the allocative function of the capital market, the jurists generally argue from a standpoint that takes account of several normative criteria. In its attempt to synthesize the criteria of efficiency and justice, here the ethical economy approach is closer to the juristic approach than to the purely economic approach, since the former is more open to the integration of several normative criteria.

Compared with a purely economic view, the judgment we arrive at from the perspective of ethical economy or economic ethics is of a higher order, because it aims to incorporate both aspects of the good – the aspects of efficiency and justice – into its criteriology. If we apply this to the capital market and the issue of insider trading, the question to be addressed from the perspective of economic ethics is not whether insider trading is *either* efficient *or* fair, but whether it is *both* efficient *and* fair. If the dimension of law is added to that of economic ethics, the further criteria of legal certainty, the calculability of rules, and the justiciability of rule-violations in the capital market enter our field of vision. The law is defined both by its ability to guarantee certainty of expectation, and hence legal certainty, and by its capacity to render potential conflicts justiciable, i.e. adjudicable and enforceable before a court.

The question of the ethical economy of the capital market and the permissibility of insider trading is twofold in nature. In the first place, we have to ask questions about the institutional ethics and economics of the capital market, considered as an institution. These are part of the ethics and economics of the broader cultural domain or subsystem of society that we call the economy. By those lights, it is also an inquiry that touches on business law. Secondly, though, if we ask questions about the economic ethics of insider trading, we are looking into the personal ethics of those who make a living by operating within the rules of the stock exchange.

A duty is derived from the purpose or the teleology of the institution, from the idea of justice, and from the requirements of legal certainty. The duties applicable in stock-exchange ethics and the law are determined partly by the purpose of the

---

[2]Cf. ENGEL (1991) and DIETER SCHNEIDER: "Wider Insiderhandelsverbot und die Informationseffizienz des Kapitalmarkts" [Against prohibiting insider trading and the information-efficiency of the capital market], *Der Betrieb*, 46 (1993), Heft/Issue 29, pp. 1429–1435.

[3]Cf. B GRUNEWALD.: "Neue Regeln zum Insiderhandel" [New regulations on insider trading], *Zeitschrift für Bankrecht und Bankwirtschaft*, 2 (1990), No. 3, pp. 128–133, and K. J. HOPT: "Europäisches und deutsches Insiderrecht", *Zeitschrift für Unternehmens- und Gesellschaftsrecht*, 20 (1991), pp. 17–73.

cultural domain and the legal domain under discussion, namely by the purpose of the capital market, which is to intermediate between the demand and supply of capital, but also by the idea of justice – particularly as formal justice in the sense of equality under the law – and by the demands for consistency of expectations in legislation and legal adjudication.

Insider Trading as Pseudo-Speculation and Agiotage

The problem of insider trading on the stock exchange is that insider traders make a profit from a situation in which no real uncertainty exists, since the facts of the insider information are already known. This being the case, the legitimation for speculation – i.e. exposure to uncertainty and risk – is patently not in evidence.

If Geko, a shareholder or owner, gives Miller, his broker or employee, a tip to buy shares in firm ABC because firm BCD wishes to take over firm ABC and will soon be keen to buy up his newly acquired shares at a higher price, this knowledge about the future is already on hand; it is not something that Miller the broker has just produced.

In this situation, there is a less costly means of overcoming uncertainty, namely to publish the insider information to the trading public. The insider is not producing an actual good or rendering any service to participants in the capital market that the corporation concerned could not accomplish just as well simply by publishing the insider facts. Speculation by insiders is a kind of pseudo-speculation because an insider-speculator has no exposure to uncertainty, but is only reducing some pseudo-uncertainty about the facts of the insider information – facts that are already known.

Of course, the insider still bears a certain degree of risk because the takeover might not take place after all, whatever the insider has been told. Or a recommendation by a business journalist to buy a particular share may have a far less spectacular effect than the insider perhaps anticipated, and consequently the gains from the insider's speculation may amount to nothing. Nevertheless, the insider's risk is always very much lower than that of other speculators operating in the same market.

Profits from professional speculation are the reward for the value-adding activity of the absorption of uncertainty. Where the efforts of speculators add no value because they are only exposed to pseudo-uncertainty, speculation can claim no legitimation to "earn" a profit. The insider-speculator absorbs only pseudo-uncertainty, and is not therefore entitled to retain the profit arising from his insider dealing. By analogy with games of chance, the insider-speculator can be compared to a player who uses marked cards which reduce the element of chance and uncertainty. In that same way, the insider-speculator reduces the element of uncertainty and chance for himself alone, but not for the other players. The insider-speculator plays the game with less exposure to uncertainty than his fellow players, and the profit that

he makes from playing with marked cards does not equate to any economic effort
or value creation on his part.

Arbitrage, Speculation, Agiotage

The pseudo-productive effect of speculation via insider trading is neither arbitrage
nor true speculation but agiotage (the mere pocketing of a premium). Arbitrage is
the value-adding activity of making a profit by equalizing geographical variations
in pricing. The arbitrageur generates a profit by minimizing the price differentials
between different places at the same point in time. If the interest rate for loans is
low in Tokyo and high in Rome at the same point in time, it is profitable arbitrage
to borrow money at low interest rates in Tokyo and lend it at high interest rates in
Rome. The arbitrageur reduces the differences between prices in different locations
and equalizes the price level between two locations by eliminating an oversupply in
one trading venue and alleviating a scarcity of supply – in our case, a scarce supply
of loans – in another location. Arbitrage creates welfare effects by equalizing prices
across different markets at the same point in time. Speculation brings about the
equalization of prices between different points in time in the same marketplace.
Speculation is therefore arbitrage between different points in the dimension of time,
not space. Both arbitrage and speculation perform a useful service for the economy
in equalizing price differentials.

Agiotage must be differentiated from arbitrage and speculation. Agiotage refers
to the practice of turning a profit purely by adding a surcharge, a premium, to the
price of a given good or service without adding any kind of value. The price difference between the share-buying and the share-selling price in this case is just a
surcharge or a premium charged by the stockjobber. The insider is a stockjobber
who, although he purchases at one point in time, t, and sells at another, t + 1, adds
no value to the traded goods, in our case the shares, since the information on which
he bases his profit was already available at the first point in time, t. The distinction
between the value-adding economic activities of arbitrage in space and speculation
as a form of arbitrage between points in time, on the one hand, and agiotage or
the pure levying of a surcharge without adding value, on the other, permits insider
dealing to be classified as mere agiotage and differentiated from other activities on
the stock exchange, like arbitrage in the dimension of space and speculation in the
dimension of time, which do add value.

This distinction was familiar even to Scholastic theoreticians of economic ethics
and economic theology, such as John Duns Scotus, and to the Spanish natural
law thinkers of the Early Modern period. Duns Scotus asserted that profit is only
ethically permissible if the trader or speculator has performed some kind of value-
adding activity and thereby rendered a service to the community. "They who neither
transport nor store nor improve, and also if the commodity is not improved by their
effort, nor is someone who is uninformed assured of the value of the commodity to
be bought, ergo: if someone merely buys in order to resell at once without fulfilling
even one of these conditions, this one should be cast out of the republic and exiled

from it."[4] Lugo[5] and Molina[6] further argued, that profits from arbitrage and speculation are perfectly legitimate if they produce real added value for the economy, but
that agiotage, which is nothing but levying a surcharge, demands too high a price
from the other party and therefore violates the principle of justice, i.e. of giving
every man his due.[7]

Insider Trading and the Fiduciary Relationship

Insider speculation as mere agiotage, i.e. reselling the same good without refin-
ing it and without making any productive contribution to the community through
its resale, is not in keeping with the nature of speculative trading. This analysis
stands up, even in those situations when insider trading is beneficial to a third party.
Consider the case of a corporation that is planning a takeover. The management or
one of the shareholders can now tip off an inside trader to buy shares in this firm
that is about to be taken over in the near future. This tip is likely to earn the insider
some additional profit. The corporation that passed on the information can spread
the purchasing of the other firm's shares over a longer period of time. By spreading its demand for the shares of the takeover candidate over time, it can probably
acquire the shares later – from the inside trader and from others – at a lower price.
In this way, the inside trader is supplied with information in the interests of the
informant's firm, which is the firm planning the takeover, and is urged to buy shares
in the takeover-target firm and sell them later at an insider profit. In this example,
the insider trader also renders a certain service to the economy by facilitating the
takeover-bidder's acquisition of the takeover candidate firm.

This service could equally well be achieved, however, if the corporation planning
the acquisition bought the shares itself, or if the fiduciary bought the shares himself
under the contract that he is acting on behalf of the corporation. The corporation that
is planning a takeover is not forced to resort to informing an insider trader, thereby
using an ethically dubious means to an end which can be achieved just as well by
ethical and legal means.

The existence of cases where insider trading is in the interests of the third party,
the manager or shareholder who passes on the information, a "victimless crime" in
other words, does not disprove the thesis that insider trading is mere agiotage and

---

[4]JOHN DUNS SCOTUS: *Quaestiones in Lib. IV. Sententiarum*, Vol. 9, Lyon (Laurentius Durand)
1639, reprint Hildesheim (Olms) 1968, dist. 15, q. 2, n. 23: "*Qui nec transferunt nec conservant
nec eorum industria melioratur res venalis nec certificatur aliquis alius simplex de valore rei emen-
dae, sed modo emit, ut statim sine omnibus istis condicionibus vendat, iste esset exterminandus a
republica et exulandus.*" John Duns Scotus was born around 1265/66 in Maxton (Scotland) and
died in Cologne (Germany) in 1308.

[5]JUAN DE LUGO: *De iustitia et iure*, Lyon 1670, disp. 28, Section 10, n. 132. Juan de Lugo was
born in Madrid in 1583 and died in Rome in 1660.

[6]LUIS DE MOLINA: *De iustitia et iure*, Madrid 1602, tr. 2, disp. 410, n. 11.

[7]Cf. NELL-BREUNING (1928), p. 107f.

not productive speculation. The corporation supplying the information already has the knowledge at its disposal on which the insider trading is based. It has the option to disseminate this knowledge or, if dissemination would harm its own business, to withhold it and act on the information itself by purchasing the shares itself over time.[8]

The example of the insider deal in which an insider acquires shares on his private account on behalf of a third party shows that insider trading cannot be described as unethical solely because it violates a fiduciary relationship.[9] In many instances, this is indeed the case, and insider trading is then unethical based on the fact that it constitutes a breach of fiduciary duties. In a few cases, however, what happens is that the person who established the fiduciary relationship passes on the insider information to another person who is asked to act in the first person's private interest. Some arguments in favor of insider trading claim that insider trading improves the allocative function of the market by virtue of the fact that trading in the shares does disseminate information about the insider facts. Such arguments rest on the assumption that insider trading is not only in the interests of the insider trader or broker, but can also be in the interests of the client or principal.[10]

To recapitulate this point: neither the advantage of the inside trader, nor the advantage of the client, nor the minor allocative effect of insider trading upon price formation in the securities market can offer any justification for insider trading, if its unethical character is due to the fact that the insider dealing violates the nature of the matter at issue, i.e. the nature of speculation in the stock market; in other words, if the insider speculation serves some other purpose than reducing real uncertainty. Insider trading does not really reduce uncertainty because the insider information is already in existence. Since all shareholders have the same right to information about the corporation, the management is not allowed to pass on information about a pending takeover just to enrich a select few third parties.[11] Even individual shareholders may not pass on insider knowledge to selected other individuals because, if they did, they would be violating the right of other shareholders to this knowledge. The principle of parity of rights for all shareholders demands that either all shareholders should know the insider information and be able to pass it on, or none of

---

[8]The Second Financial Market Promotion Act of 26 July 1994, Section 21, obliges all corporations listed on the German stock exchange to report acquisitions or sales of shares in other corporations which exceed 5, 10, 25, 50 or 75% of the other corporation's total equity. The Federal Supervisory Authority can, however, exempt a corporation from this duty if compliance with the duty could cause the corporation substantial damage (Section 25, no. 4).

[9]J. MOORE: "What is Really Unethical About Insider Trading", *Journal of Business Ethics*, 9 (1990), pp. 171–182, claims that insider trading is unethical because it breaches the fiduciary relationship. Certainly this is often true, but not in every case of insider trading.

[10]The main proponent of this thesis is H. G. MANNE: *Insider Trading and the Stock Market*, New York (The Free Press) 1966.

[11]The aspect of the parity of rights of all shareholders is particularly emphasized by HOPT (1991).

them should. If all shareholders pass it on, the information naturally ceases to be insider information.

German and American legislation on insider trading therefore prohibits shareholders from passing on their insider information in the same way as it prohibits the management of the corporation from doing so.[12] The legislation does not invoke the fiduciary relationship but the principle of parity of rights, i.e. the equal rights of all shareholders to information, as well as the conditions for value-adding speculation on the stock exchange in order to justify the legal ban on insider trading.

Insider Trading as Perverse Incentive

The conditions whereby speculation on the stock exchange is productive and serves the common good by absorbing uncertainty are not merely violated by the detrimental effects of insider trading when it occurs. In point of fact, these detrimental effects are also intensified by the perverse or counterproductive incentives that arise from insider trading, which would be further exaggerated by its legalization. Brokers and intermediaries in financial markets have strong incentives to invest in seeking opportunities for insider trading, if insider trading is allowed. Instead of seeking to anticipate future events correctly in their speculation, they will seek insider information about a future that is not actually the future at all, but the here and now. They will become neglectful of their proper, speculative task, and turn their attention to opportunities for insider investments.

Since the opportunities for insider investments are increased through random price fluctuations and, above all, by the high amplitudes of such fluctuations, the incentives for insider trading seduce the financial brokers still further to encourage price fluctuations instead of minimizing them. Any legalization of insider trading therefore creates additional perverse incentives, which heighten rather than lessen uncertainty for other market participants.[13] Permitting insider trading within the law diverts the efforts of financial brokers and stock market speculators away from investing in the reduction of uncertainty and towards investing in the search for insider information, i.e. in investing in the production of knowledge that already exists, and in strategies for heightening external uncertainty by increasing price fluctuations in the stock market. The perverse incentives that arise from insider trading divert resources into the search for unproductive rather than productive knowledge.

---

[12]German law prohibits all shareholders, not just shareholders with large packages of shares, from passing on insider information, cf. Financial Market Promotion Act, Section 13, nos. 1, 2. For the comparative legislation cf. R. J. WOJTEK.: *Insider Trading im deutschen und amerikanischen Recht* [Insider trading in German and American law], Berlin (Duncker & Humblot) 1978, pp. 56ff.

[13]Thus MOORE (1990), p. 179, HOPT (1991).

Knowledge that already exists but is withheld by the market, for the purposes of private exploitation by agiotage, is unproductive knowledge.[14]

Insider Trading and Short-Termism

Insider trading in the stock market is unproductive, because it is used neither for arbitrage (the equalization of price differentials between different points in space) nor for speculation (the equalization of price differentials between different points in time). Insider trading is carried out within the same market, and aims to make short-term capital gains without bridging longer periods of time. Above all else, the short-termism of insider trading indicates that it serves neither the purpose of absorbing uncertainty nor that of true capital investment. Both the absorption of uncertainty and the investment of capital require investments to be held for longer periods.

But insider trading cannot be prohibited by law purely because it is short-termist. If the speculator, abiding by correct and responsible practices, reaches the conclusion that it is the right economic decision to close out an investment after an ultra-short holding period because changes in the economic fundamentals require it, this can be perfectly moral and is also the economically efficient solution. Therefore, the short-term nature of an investment is not, per se, an indicator of insider trading, nor is it a sufficient reason to prohibit and preclude it by law.[15] At this point, the decisive factor is the intention, i.e. whether the investor was intent upon insider trading from the outset, or had in mind a serious, long-term investment and/or the useful, uncertainty-absorbing form of speculation.

Insider Trading and the Duty of Ad Hoc Publicity

Insider information is unproductive information, because the general availability of this information is only impeded by the fact that it is deliberately withheld from the market. The use of insider information has no beneficial effect on the economy, because it is not an act of arbitrage between venues or of speculation between points in time. McGee bases his argument in favor of the legalization of insider trading on the fact that in transactions of the arbitrage type, the arbitrageur is not obliged to inform the potential buyer that the good offered by the arbitrageur is on sale at a

---

[14]For the distinction between productive and unproductive knowledge, cf. H.-B. SCHÄFER, C. OTT: *Lehrbuch der ökonomischen Analyse des Zivilrechts* [Economic analysis of civil law], Berlin, New York, Tokyo (Springer) 1986, pp. 300ff.

[15]RICHARD T. DeGEORGE.: "Ethics and the Financial Community: An Overview", in: O. F. WILLIAMS, F. K. REILLY, J. W. HOUCK (eds.): *Ethics and the Investment Industry*, Savage (Rowman & Littlefield) 1989, p. 213, bases his critique of insider trading on its short-termism and calls for tax legislation to levy a 100% tax rate on short-term capital gains.

lower price in some other venue, or, in the case of speculative trading, that the price will probably decrease in the future.

McGee quotes Thomas Aquinas,[16] who disputed that the seller had any duty to inform the purchaser about such price differentials between geographical venues or points in time. McGee, however, overlooks the premises underlying Thomas Aquinas's argument, namely that arbitrage is economically and socially beneficial because it equalizes price differentials between different markets.[17] Arbitrage will only take place if there are incentives for it, namely the chance of making profits by bridging price differentials between different markets. Where these incentives do not exist, arbitrage will not take place. If a buyer had the duty to inform a seller of grain in place A that grain actually commanded a higher price in place B, the seller would not sell him the commodity but would ship it to market B himself and sell it there. By doing so, the seller would take possession of the earnings from the efforts invested by the arbitrageur, whose work would then go uncompensated. In order to encourage useful trading it is therefore necessary to permit arbitrage in trading. This is why Thomas Aquinas and the theory of natural law permit arbitrage trading.

Where trade consists solely of agiotage or pocketing a mark-up, rather than arbitrage or speculation, the buyer or seller is not entitled to withhold the information on which the transaction is based or to derive a profit from his knowledge about future price changes. Since the insider has not invested in productive but unproductive knowledge, he is not entitled to derive a profit from a knowledge advantage that he has gained over his competitors illegally, or that is not value-adding in character.

Detrimental Effects of Insider Trading on Allocation, Distribution, and Stability

Insider trading leads to a reallocation of resources from speculation towards pseudo-speculation, and from the dissemination of knowledge towards the withholding of knowledge. There is reason to concede that share purchases by insider traders can give rise to a minor knowledge-dissemination effect in the stock market, and also that a minor effect from the spreading of share purchases over time, which can be helpful in cases involving corporate takeovers, is brought about or supported by insider traders. Nevertheless, these beneficial allocative effects are far outweighed by the misallocation of resources into the search for unproductive insider information, by the perverse incentives of insider trading to increase price fluctuations and destabilize the stock market, and by the problematic distributive effect of profits from insider trading.

---

[16]MCGEE (1988), p. 37, discussing THOMAS AQUINAS, *Summa theologiae* II-II, p. 77, art. 3(4).

[17]THOMAS AQUINAS, *Summa theologiae* II-II, qu. 77, art. 3(4), discusses this question and explicitly accords arbitrage an important, morally justified economic function.

The perverse incentives of insider trading lead to questionable insider investments and profits. The problematic capital gains from insider trading, its short-termism and other flaws also lead to a socially destabilizing and economically and ethically dubious distribution of incomes. The public criticism of the income distribution that results from insider profits[18] cannot simply be brushed aside as an envy complex.[19] It is not so much the resulting distribution as the repercussions of this distribution on the incentive structure, and on the allocation of value-adding efforts in the financial markets, which must give cause for concern. Since allocation and distribution cannot be separated, if vast profits can be made from insider trading then resources will be diverted for use in insider trading.

All three economic criteria – allocation, distribution and stability – call out for the suppression of insider trading. The arguments from allocative efficiency, distributive justice, and the economic stability of the capital market all concur with the judgment that derives from the nature of the matter at issue, namely from the nature of the capital market. The economic and ethical arguments lead to the conclusion that the actors in the capital market have the duty to engage in investments that add value, and in the service of absorbing uncertainty, but not in the pseudo-speculation of insider trading.[20]

The fact that prohibiting insider trading has the effect of favoring professional speculation at the expense of amateur speculation should not be criticized, as in Schneider,[21] but welcomed. If prohibiting insider trading reduces the gambling element that is very much present in stock market speculation, and replaces it with professional speculation, it reins in the part of the capital market that deals only with uncertainty, and shrinks it to its unavoidable minimum. The prohibition of insider trading eliminates factors on the stock exchange which create unnecessary and avoidable uncertainty. The stock exchange should not be the venue for gambling-style speculation but an institution that serves the economy and society, an institution that provides the service of intermediating capital and absorbing uncertainty.[22]

More than 80 years ago, Nell-Breuning posed the question of whether the stock exchange needs speculation in shares or whether it could work without it.[23] The analysis of insider trading shows that the stock market can function without pseudo-speculation, whereas professional speculation plays an indispensable role in the assimilation and absorption of irreducible uncertainty.

---

[18]Concern about the effects of financial speculation on income distribution and distributive justice has been a topic since Aristotle. Cf. SEN (1993), p. 211.

[19]Thus R. W. McGEE: "Insider Trading: An Economic and Philosophical Analysis", *Mid-Atlantic Journal of Business*, 25 (1988), p. 42.

[20]GRUNEWALD (1990), p. 133, comes to the similar conclusion that insider trading must be prohibited in the interest of the functional capacity of the capital market.

[21]SCHNEIDER (1993).

[22]Cf. NELL-BREUNING's emphasis (1928), p. 23, on the "service mentality of the stock exchange", i.e. the conscious awareness that the stock exchange produces a service for the real economy.

[23]NELL-BREUNING (1928a), p. 54.

The assessment of insider trading can be summed up in the following conclusions: the nature and function of speculation on the stock exchange demands the strict suppression of pseudo-speculation in the form of insider trading, the absorption of pseudo-uncertainty. The principle of parity of rights in the justification of economic norms demands that all shareholders and speculators have an equal right of access to information. Therefore, the shareholders' parity of rights precludes any passing of insider tips to third parties by management or an individual shareholder. Ultimately the principles of economic and legal security and stability demand that insider trading be forbidden on the basis of its perverse incentive effects. Forms of speculation which cannot be justified on the basis of the capital market's function of absorbing, and transforming, risk and uncertainty must not be allowed to amplify price fluctuations in the stock market.

Experiences After the Entry into Force of the Laws Against Insider Trading in Germany

Economic commentators were tenacious in their insistence that the implementation and enforcement of a law against insider trading would be extremely difficult. The difficulties have turned out, however, to be less onerous than expected. But of course, even difficulties of the anticipated degree of severity do not stand up as a legal argument against an insider trading ban. By way of evidence that the law is enforceable, in the first quarter of 1995, the first quarter after statutory provisions against insider trading took force in Germany, around 200 notifications pursuant to Section 15 of the Federal Securities Trading Act (*Wertpapierhandelsgesetz*, WpHG) were submitted to the Frankfurt stock exchange. According to the Federal Supervisory Authority, the figure reached 100 notices a month on average, whereas earlier in the year, according to Hans-Joachim Schwarze, the average was around two to three notifications.[24]

Compliance with the law is higher than we might be led to expect by the ostensibly great incentives to circumvent the insider ban. One explanation for this, we will have to assume, is that the deterrent effect of the law is directed primarily against the source of the tip. The threat of prison sentences for passing on insider information and tips from which others can benefit has the effect of making individuals in possession of insider knowledge think very carefully about whether to take the risk of passing on some piece of insider information, when the main beneficiary of any profit from exploitation of this knowledge will be the recipient of the tip. It is plausible that, for this reason, the main effect of the legal prohibition is to discourage insider tips at source.

---

[24]Thus H.-J. SCHWARZE: "Ad-hoc-Publizität und die Problematik der Notierungsaussetzung" [Ad hoc publicity and problems of suspended trading], in: J. BAETGE: *Insiderrecht und Ad-hoc-Publizität*, Düsseldorf (IDW-Verlag) 1995, p. 100.

For large joint-stock corporations, the duty to publicly disclose facts relevant to
the share price under the statutory provisions against insider trading is part of their
general public relations policy. Since maintaining a consistent share price is one
of the objectives pursued by the public relations work and the investor relations
departments of most major corporations, the interests of the joint-stock corporation
go hand in hand with the intentions of the statutory provisions against insider trading. Compliance with the duty of public disclosure is becoming an element in the
general information policy of the corporation.[25]

Corporations can also substantially allay any compliance fears stemming from
the comparative imprecision of the legal concept of the "price-sensitive fact", which
they have a duty to disclose, by following the maxim, "*In dubio*, opt for disclosure!"[26] The law also follows this maxim by extending the requirement for ad hoc
public disclosure of price-sensitive facts in that corporations must now inform the
public about such facts prior to the annual general meeting; merely informing those
present at the joint-stock corporation's annual general meeting is no longer sufficient
to meet public disclosure requirements.[27]

It had been feared that the new statutory provisions on insider trading would
impair the functional capacity of the stock exchange because trading in the
corporation's shares frequently had to be suspended following notification of a
price-sensitive fact. Since the suspension of trading often leads to rumors about the
corporation concerned, this was assumed to have a destabilizing effect on the capital market. However, the suspension of trading is evidently a problem that the stock
exchange is capable of addressing. Nowadays, trading is suspended only briefly after
publication of a price-sensitive fact, not for an entire day.[28]

We can assume the deterrent effect of the laws against insider trading to be
especially significant. For instance, a Swiss banker told the author in 1995 that
Switzerland's laws against insider trading had been in force for three years, but in
all that time, nobody had yet been convicted of any insider trading offense. It seems
reasonable to attribute this not only to a high level of undetected offenses but also,
as already mentioned, to the strong deterrent effect on individuals who contemplate
passing on a tip.

Insider knowledge is a universal phenomenon that goes far beyond the utilization
of insider knowledge on the stock exchange. It is clear from the overall phenomenon

---

[25]Thus H.-G. BRUNS: "Finanzpublizität nach Inkrafttreten des 2. Finanzmarktförderungsgesetzes
– Zur praktischen Umsetzung bei Daimler-Benz" [Publicity duties under Germany's Second
Financial Market Promotion Act – practice at Daimler-Benz], in: J. BAETGE: *Insiderrecht und
Ad-hoc-Publizität*, Düsseldorf (IDW-Verlag) 1995, pp. 110ff.

[26]Thus Caspari in J. BAETGE: *Insiderrecht und Ad-hoc-Publizität* [Law on insiders and ad hoc
publicity], Düsseldorf (IDW-Verlag) 1995, p. 81.

[27]Cf. K. J. HOPT: "Das neue Insiderrecht nach §§ 12 ff WpHG – Funktion, Dogmatik,
Reichweite" [Germany's new insider trading law – function, dogmatics, scope], in: *Das Zweite
Finanzmarktförderungsgesetz in der praktischen Umsetzung. Bankrechtstag 1995*, Berlin, New
York (Walter de Gruyter) 1996, p. 19.

[28]Cf. SCHWARZE (1995), p. 105.

of insider trading and knowledge, therefore, that the utilization of economically relevant knowledge is tied to statutory regulations, and the law distinguishes between the type of knowledge that may be utilized for profit and the type – examples being all knowledge divulged to a doctor, a tax consultant or a father-confessor, which is covered by a duty of secrecy – that may not be utilized for gain.

The problems of insider trading also touch on the question of which economic activities may rightfully yield a profit, i.e. the problem of the generation and justification of profit. This becomes clear from the fact that even in the utilization of insider knowledge on the stock exchange, distinctions are made once again between the target groups of the statutory provisions. Thus, on the one hand, much more stringent provisions are applicable to banks than to state or government agencies, which are permitted to make use of insider knowledge.

Refraining from acquiring or selling insider securities on the basis of insider information is not a purchase or sale transaction and is not therefore covered by the prohibition on insider deals. For banks, however, stricter requirements are applicable in some circumstances.[29]

When the utilization of insider knowledge benefits the community and is not for private gain, it is permissible. Thus, state bodies may make use of insider knowledge or transactions made "in pursuit of monetary, exchange-rate or public-debt management policies enacted by the Federation, one of its special funds, a state of the union (*Land*), the German Central Bank (Deutsche Bundesbank), a foreign state or its central bank or another body commissioned to conduct such transactions or with any person acting for their account."[30]

The statutory provisions on insider trading simultaneously define rights to make profits and draw a line between those activities from which profit can legally be made and those from which profit-making is not permitted.

The Abuse of Insider Knowledge as a Form of Corruption

Insider trading on the stock exchange can be seen as a form of corruption of those who work at the stock exchange and in financial institutions and markets. As in the case of the universal phenomenon of corruption, they violate their position of trust and abuse information that has been entrusted to them in confidence for the purpose of personal enrichment. Even where the stockbroker or financial intermediary has been authorized by the shareholder to make use of the insider knowledge, corruption is still evident, since the broker is violating his position of trust in relation

---

[29]Thus HOPT (1996), p. 17.

[30]Transactions using insider knowledge are permitted if they are enacted "*aus geld- oder währungspolitischen Gründen oder im Rahmen der öffentlichen Schuldenverwaltung vom Bund, einem seiner Sondervermögen, einem Land, der Deutschen Bundesbank, einem ausländischen Staat oder dessen Zentralbank oder einer anderen mit diesen Geschäften beauftragten Organisation oder mit für deren Rechnung handelnden Personen getätigt werden.*" Quoted after HOPT (1996), p. 27f., who discusses Section 20 WpHG. (Own trans. from the German).

to the other shareholders of the firm that supplies the tip and in relation to stock-exchange rules. The phenomenon of exploiting the knowledge of confidential facts can be deemed a more or less universal characteristic of corruption, and taken as the foundation of a general theory of corruption.

Supposing that a doctor's patient receives a terminal diagnosis, which is divulged to the doctor under his duty of professional confidentiality, and the doctor, in return for commission, informs an estate agent that the patient's house will soon be up for sale since the diagnosis does not give him long to live, that doctor is corrupt, is abusing his professional position and is violating the duties of that profession.

The employees of a firm cannot enter a prize competition that their own firm has organized; nor may they use any insider knowledge about this prize competition that they possess by virtue of their employment, in order to gain an advantage for themselves over other competition entrants or to divulge details to others to give them an advantage.

The official responsible for highway and bridge construction in a city may not use his insider knowledge about that city's construction policy in order to pre-emptively purchase the land necessary for the bridges at a low price in order to sell it on to the city at a higher price.

The architect who is building a house for a customer should not simultaneously act as an agent who procures construction contracts for building firms and receives agent's commissions from them in addition to his architect's fees. If he does, he is abusing his professional position as a neutral advisor of his client, his insider knowledge as the client's architect, and his architect-client contract in order to engage in insider dealing with the construction firm. He is abusing the fiduciary relationship between his client and himself in order to enter into transactions on a commission basis with firms that he should be dealing with as an impartial advisor and advisor to the client. It is obvious that in such a case he is being paid twice for the same service, which would only be acceptable if he reduced his architect's fee by the amount that the construction firm paid him in commission.

The abuse of insider knowledge or of facts divulged in confidentiality is at the root of the most subtle forms of corruption in the private and public sector. Corruption is the misuse of official power or a position of trust in order to make decisions which go against the intention and the rules of the office or the client in order to make profits on one's own account or to procure illegal advantages for a third party. Procurement of advantage by the official himself or by a third party, be it in private-sector corporations or in the public sector, is always based on some special insider knowledge, which only the person concerned possesses and which is used inappropriately in order to make insider profits.

The more blatant forms of corruption are becoming more and more impracticable for officials in democratic states under the rule of law, because legal controls and a democratic public generally put a stop to them quickly. A judge cannot blatantly favor the rich and powerful and rule to the detriment of widows and orphans, as the biblical prophets used to lament. Nevertheless, judges can utilize insider knowledge to pass information to one party so that they gain an advantage in the proceedings. Nowadays, the Prime Minister can no longer make his wife a Cabinet minister as used to be possible under communist regimes. But he can make use of his insider knowledge by tipping off his friends. The use of insider knowledge by members of the council of a country's central bank, for instance, can be worth billions of dollars. If the central bank of the United States lowers the interest rate by one percentage point, it causes the Dow Jones index to rise by several points. And someone who has this knowledge 24 hours earlier than everybody else could certainly make profits to the tune of millions of dollars from stock-trading. Profits made from corruption and the abuse of information known only to the individual concerned by virtue of his official function violate economic law and economic ethics for three reasons: corruption and the abuse of insider knowledge violate the principle of parity of rights, the principle of economic efficiency, and the principle under the democratic rule of law that all citizens have the democratic right of equal access to political and administrative power and official institutions, and the right to hold private and public holders of office accountable for their actions in office.

By means of corruption, those who practice bribery gain an unjust advantage over others. If this were not the case, they would not "invest" in corruption. This procurement of advantage is supposed to be prevented through the rules of public tendering for state building projects and through the public advertisement of positions by state or private sector employers. What all forms of corruption and insider knowledge have in common is not just that they violate the position of trust and the principal-agent relationship, the relationship between beneficiary and fiduciary, but also that they set perverse incentives, which divert the individual's attention and effort to precisely those activities which are not in the interests of the common good nor the good of the individual's employer.

The theory of perverse incentives, which has documented this effect for insider trading on the stock exchange, does not apply to the capital market alone. The corruption-induced striving for insider knowledge creates perverse incentives among workers who, instead of concentrating on their actual tasks, look out for ways of procuring advantages by exercising their official role or their professional position corruptly.

For the entrepreneur and manager, this prompts the necessity to combat all forms of corruption, at home or abroad, because they are not in the long-term interests of the firm. Even where a firm can attract contracts by paying bribes to a foreign middleman, the repercussions of this practice of bribery on the internal economic ethics and business practices of employees are so negative that it is better dispensed with. The acceptance of offshore corruption, of corrupt practices in countries beyond the scope of domestic law, compromises the moral integrity not only in one's own country but also in one's own firm.[31]

---

[31] The borderline between legal commission payments and bribes is not always clear-cut. Consider the following scenario, for instance: you are taking your firm into a new market in which you have never operated before, and in which your firm has no business contacts of any kind. Your firm sends you as manager to a Latin American country, where your remit is to organize the distribution of its products. Mr X from a supplier firm gives you the name of a Mr Y in Nuevo Berlin, who (he assures

Corruption and the exploitation of insider knowledge often occur where one contracting party is still unfamiliar with the market or where it is difficult to determine a commonly accepted market price. This begins with a phenomenon that everyone will recognize, namely that there is almost no country on Earth where the taxi drivers at the airport are not corrupt in the sense that the naive newcomer who steps off the plane without a clue about the market rate for taxi fares will be comprehensively gouged, and will be able to do little about it because he or she does not know the market price. Corrupt practices can also be easier in this case if the right for taxis to stop and pick up passengers can be controlled by a monopolist or a Mafia at the airport, and all the taxis not approved by their cartel can be forced to drive away empty. On the other hand, it would be difficult and inordinately expensive for such an organization to control all the journeys conveying people *to* the airport.[32]

An expert in the problem of offshore corruption, George Moody Stuart, has pointed out that weapons exports can easily fall victim to corruption for the same reasons. The difficulties reside in the nature of the arms trade: firstly, it is difficult to determine a market price for a fighter plane, demand for which is limited to only three customers, i.e. the defense ministries of three countries, and the production of which requires feats of technical virtuosity which are likewise difficult to value at market prices. Secondly, weapons exports are also very popular as exports to third countries, especially Third World countries, because where such exports are concerned, the payments of facilitation money can be concealed in the purchase price. This simplification of corruption by the nature of the arms export trade applies both to the buyer and the seller side.

The dictator of a country will not find it as easy to conceal payments of facilitation money to himself or family members in connection with deliveries of

---

you) can open the necessary doors for you. Mr Y presents himself as extremely cooperative and is prepared to put you in contact with the important people at the Ministry of Economic Affairs and with the representatives of firms who might be potential customers. He also makes himself available to act as your interpreter. In the course of negotiations prior to signing your first contract, it now emerges that for his contact-brokering and interpretation services he expects a fee of 20% of the contract sum, for a contract that runs to several millions of US dollars. His services have been of great benefit to you and your firm, which has saved substantial amounts of money as a result. But still, you cannot help but think that the amount seems too high. Transparency International, an organization that has taken on the mission to combat corruption in the world, recommends that the question to be asked in such cases is whether the commission payments and special fees are publishable. The demarcation line between commissions and gifts, on the one side, and bribes, on the other, can generally be drawn where it is unproblematic – in the case of a commission or a gift – to make it public or at least to inform affected third parties, whereas bribes cannot be made public. A further distinction must be observed between facilitation money and bribes. In terms of economic ethics, a very different view is taken of "facilitation money" to speed up legal acts, and a bribe to procure an illegal act that benefits the person committing bribery.

[32]This control of market-access for taxis at the airport led to a situation in an Eastern European capital city, for example, where the journey from the capital's airport used to cost three times as much as the same journey in the opposite direction. It also meant that the taxi driver to the airport always asked to be paid a few kilometers before reaching the airport so as to look like a private driver when dropping off passengers at the airport itself.

automobiles, which have the same market price everywhere, as with the delivery of high-tech armaments, the market price of which nobody in his country can possibly know. This example is not intended to mean that all arms exports involve corruption, but merely to show that the opportunity for corruption arises more frequently in connection with goods that are not substitutable for other goods and therefore have no comparison price.

Another problematic result of this fact is the diversion of demand from corrupt governments. Given the greater opportunity to conceal bribes within the price of non-marketable armaments, the demand of government "insiders" for imports will be distorted and diverted towards those kinds of goods. Since they expect it to be easier to obtain, and conceal, commissions or even bribes in the context of armaments, they will disproportionately demand armaments as opposed to other, more urgently needed goods. This kind of arms/bribes spiral leads, eventually, to an over-consumption of weapons, and this in turn contributes to a further deterioration in economic development.[33]

Ethical Duties of the Investor and of the Firm Quoted on the Capital Market

Does the investor have ethical duties in the capital market, beyond the duty of refraining from insider trading?[34] The now defining concept of maximizing share-holder value seems to contain no other imperative to guide the investor's actions than that of maximizing the value of one's own shares, and thereby maximizing the allocative efficiency of the economy. In terms of the ethical economy model, this restriction of the investor's criteria to mere wealth maximization is inadequate, and must be enriched with the ethical criterion of acting in a way that is comprehensively good and in keeping with the nature of the domain of investment. The investor has the ethical duty to examine, in doubtful cases, where and for what purpose he is investing.

Finance ethics must also provide help with deciding how to act in grey zones. At the same time, by analyzing economic action in the grey zones, insights can be gleaned which are useful for determining the applicable norms in the clear zones. The scholar of economic ethics is not a specialist in grey zones, and nor is it the task of economic ethics to provide the all-too-shrewd entrepreneur or economist with the necessary know-how in these areas to get away with actions which, in themselves, verge on the indefensible.

---

[33]On the problem of the dependency of Third World countries resulting from arms deals, cf. also CHRISTIAN CATRINA: *Arms Transfers and Dependence*, New York (Taylor & Francis) 1988 (=United Nations Institute for Disarmament Research. UNIDIR and Dissertation, University of Zurich).

[34]For the economic ethics of shareholders, cf. also G. CORBETTA: "Shareholders", in: B. Harvey (ed.): *Business Ethics. A European Approach,* Hemel Hempstead (Prentice Hall) 1994, pp. 88–102.

Instead, it is interesting to apply economic ethics to contentious issues because grey zones, in which it is not clear from the outset what correct behavior is, can arise even for people who set out with *intentio recta*, or good intentions. An entrepreneur confronted with the problem of competing for a foreign contract against competitor firms, all of which are resorting to bribery, faces a dilemma: not because he welcomes corruption and wants to support it, but because for the sake of securing the continuity of his business and the employment it provides, he may have no choice but to adapt to some "sordid" practice in his sector, perhaps in relation to foreign clients.

According to Messner, investment in shares or corporations which pursue morally questionable production objectives are unethical. He cites the example of investments by colonial corporations in firms which exploit the manpower of the local people.[35]

Another ethical issue in the field of investment is whether the investor should be free to invest wherever in the world he likes. It should be mentioned in advance that the global capital market should be as free as possible. From the ethical standpoint, however, the investor is nevertheless obliged to ask himself whether the investment should be made in his home country or abroad. Situations involving severe draining of capital from one country to another, e.g. by elites in developing countries to the centers in the industrialized world, raise the question of whether investors are obliged to invest part of their capital in their own country on the grounds of justice.[36] This obligation cannot and should not be a legal one that is enforced by the state. A law like that would have too many detrimental effects on economic efficiency. It should, however, be an ethical obligation.

Although the holder of a few shares in a corporation has a very limited direct influence on the policy of that corporation, shareholders have an obligation to find out which projects, regions and countries the corporation in which they hold shares is investing in. Messner also acknowledges a duty to invest; the duty to invest one's capital at rational risk rather than hoarding it. The hoarding of money and mere amassing of wealth is not in keeping with the obligation to invest.[37]

The ethical obligation of property is part of the German constitution, the Basic Law (*Grundgesetz*). Art. 14 § 2 of the Basic Law states: "Property entails obligations. Its use shall also serve the public good." The "social obligations conferred by property", i.e. the duties of property owners towards society defined in this article,

---

[35]MESSNER (1955), p. 426, and J. MESSNER: *Das Naturrecht. Handbuch der Gesellschaftsethik, Staatsethik und Wirtschaftsethik* [Social Ethics: Natural Law], Berlin (Duncker & Humblot) 7th edn. 1984, p. 1073ff.

[36]From this it is possible to derive an obligation on the part of rich countries to invest in the developing countries, in order to combat this capital drain and to minimize the great differentials in capital stock within the global economy. Rohatyn emphasizes the necessity of a functional capital market in developing countries as a precondition for attracting foreign investment. Cf. F. ROHATYN: "World Capital: The Need and the Risks", *The New York Review of Books*, Vol. 41, no. 13, 14 July 1994, pp. 48–53.

[37]MESSNER (1955), p. 424.

are normally applied to questions concerning the permissibility of expropriation and to the possibility for the government and local authorities to place constraints on the use of private property when this is in the public interest.[38] However, the obligation of the investor – especially the investor of large capital sums – to take account of criteria of ethical appropriateness and the public good in his investment decisions is formulated in the article as a "shall obligation" and not as a "must law".

These same ethical obligations on investment apply equally to the management boards of firms preparing for stock market flotation, when making their decisions on business strategy and business policy. In addition to these ethical obligations concerning the strategy and business activity of a corporate management that is issuing the shares, corporations preparing to go public are obliged, most of all, to keep their shareholders and the market appropriately informed. Publicly listed firms must provide investors with all relevant information about themselves, since it is in the nature of the capital market that corporate managers have better access to information about their corporation's status and economic position than the public and shareholders, especially minority shareholders who only hold negligible interests in the corporation.

Since the payment of dividends is one of the main signals that the corporation gives the public about its business position and status, the firm is obliged to operate a rational dividend policy which neither retains excessive dividends for equity financing nor pays dividends at a level that is not matched by the corporation's performance. The firm must not mislead the public by paying unduly high dividends in order to portray corporate performance in a better light than is borne out by the reality of the situation.[39]

---

[38]Cf. D. HESSELBERGER: *Das Grundgesetz. Kommentar für die politische Bildung* [Germany's Basic Law. Commentary for political education], Neuwied (Luchterhand) 8th edn. 1991, pp. 136ff.

[39]On the problem of dividend policy cf. DAVID E. R. GAY: Article on "Dividend Policy", in: *The New Palgrave. A Dictionary of Economics*, London (Macmillan), New York (Stockton), Tokyo (Maruzen) 1987, Vol. 1, pp. 896–899.

Chapter 5
The Ethical Economy of the Market for Corporate Control and for Corporate Know-How

Buying up qualified percentages or majority holdings of the total shares of a firm is a somewhat peculiar kind of transaction, which makes it justifiable to differentiate between trading in shares to gain control over a corporation and normal trading in company shares. Although trading that has the purpose of gaining corporate control is conducted in the same market as normal trading, namely on the stock exchange, it is obvious that this type of trading conforms to a different pattern.

The percentages of the total company shares that are necessary to gain control over the appointment of board members can only be acquired at a price that is somewhat higher than the cost of acquiring "non-critical" percentages of shares. It will cost disproportionately more to acquire 51% of the total shares than to acquire just 49%, for example. Paradoxically, it is possible for the whole firm to cost more than the total sum of its shares. A price-premium is paid for the entrepreneurial function of disposition and management. Nell-Breuning observed that there was a difference between "normal" shares and the holding that confers control over the corporation. To explain this fact, he concluded that there is no market for corporations as such.[1] There is just a market for corporate control, which is part of the general capital market.

Hostile and Friendly Takeovers: The Finance Ethics of Corporate Control and Corporate Takeovers

The market for corporate domination and corporate control is especially relevant for a theory of ethics of the capital market. The trading that takes place in this market is not for the capital shares and the capital-owner relation alone. Rather, capital ownership confers the right to exercise control over firms through majority stakes and holdings. What is traded is not capital for its own sake, but the capital that brings with it factual control over the corporation. The capital that confers corporate control is subject to demand and supply.

---

[1] NELL-BREUNING (1928), p. 82.

P. Koslowski, *The Ethics of Banking*, Issues in Business Ethics 30, DOI 10.1007/978-94-007-0656-9_5, © Springer Science+Business Media B.V. 2011

Control of the corporation by a majority shareholder implies more power than mere ownership of shares by minority shareholders, and consequently it also entails more responsibility. It compels an awareness of the ethical dimension of one's own economic conduct. If the right intention – the *intentio recta* – is important in the market for company shares, it is even more so in the market for corporate control, a market in which the degree of freedom to take decisions and power to exert control over the corporation are far greater than for stock-trading in the normal capital market.

It is the intention behind the conduct of participants in the market for corporate control that actually defines what they do. Their intentions define whether they are just asset-stripping – or cannibalizing – firms, or whether they are attempting to improve the management of a firm that was previously loss-making by taking it over.

The *intentio recta*, or the ethically justifiable motivation to engage in economic activity, determines which type of strategy is at work in mergers and takeovers. The intention behind a takeover differentiates the mode of operation into a "friendly" or a "hostile" takeover of one corporation by another. Mergers by means of a leveraged buyout are not unethical in themselves. They become unethical when their sole objective is the cannibalization of the firm. Cannibalization means buying a firm, splitting and breaking up its assets and selling them off with the sole intention of making a profit for the purchaser, and without any thought to the firm's purpose and its contribution to the overall economy.

Takeover bids and mergers, if their only purpose is to make profit by means of asset-stripping and selling off the enterprise or its parts, or to gratify a power-hungry board, violate the overall objectives of the economy. They utterly divorce the purchaser's profit motive from the interests of the acquired firm as such. A takeover for cannibalization alone denies the firm a purpose and a teleology of its own as a social unit of production.

The example of the leveraged buyout is especially interesting for the theory of ethical economy because it is not always clear from the outset whether or not a merger financed by a leveraged buyout is in keeping with the purpose of the economy and the nature of the domain of the capital market. The threat of a takeover can wake up a firm, put its management under pressure to improve performance, and hence serve the interests of both staff and shareholders. Such a takeover can result in a more efficient reallocation of resources. For this reason, leveraged buyouts cannot be condemned on ethical grounds.[2]

Nevertheless, the leveraged buyout may equally well be seen as a game (of chance) or a venture that flatters the narcissism of raiders who want to make profits without making an entrepreneurial contribution to the firm itself. If the firm's asset base is broken up and sold off to the highest bidder without regard to its synergies,

---

[2]N.-J. Weickart points out the positive influence of company takeovers on corporate competition. Cf. N.-J. WEICKART: "Firmenübernahme: Festung Deutschland" [Corporate takeovers: fortress Germany], in: *Manager Magazin*, 19 April 1989, pp. 128–139.

which may be present but latent, underutilized or undervalued, the only addition of value that takes place is extractive. This is only justified if the takeover target has objectively proved itself incapable of utilizing its assets to carry on a profitable and economically purposeful business.

It is impossible, here, to ignore the intention of those planning a corporate takeover, because in cases of merger or asset-stripping, the intentional actions are crucial for an ethical, albeit perhaps not a legal, definition of the economic facts. A merger for the purpose of cannibalizing the acquired firm is not a merger at all, but an asset-stripping operation, whereas a takeover with the purpose of realizing synergies between two firms raises the productivity of both firms and increases allocative efficiency within the economy. Therefore, this alone merits the designation "merger" in the sense of a constructive amalgamation.

In terms of economic ethics, whether a takeover is friendly or hostile, i.e. done in consultation with the board of the takeover target or without its cooperation, is not a crucial question, either. A hostile takeover may very well be justified in terms of economic ethics if the management of the target acquisition has been idling. If the management has grown slack and can only be tightened up by pushing through a merger against its will, this being the only way to replace the management, then a hostile takeover is justified, both economically and in terms of economic ethics. If the sole purpose of the merger is cannibalization yet the management agrees to it, influenced by the prospect of receiving generous payoffs, a "friendly" merger can be reprehensible from the viewpoint of economic ethics, irrespective of the management's consent. The objective material appropriateness of the merger, and the *intentio recta* of the economic actors – in this case, whoever is embarking on the merger or takeover – who is objectively intent upon acting appropriately to the domain of the economy, determine the ethical or unethical character of an action.

The example of the merger and the leveraged buyout make it clear that the economy is not just a formal context for market exchange, in which subjective demand and subjectively-defined suppliers meet one another and are intermediated, but that the economy serves an objective purpose which has to be realized in a subjective way, i.e. according to the subjectivity of economic actors. The economy does not primarily serve the profit-making intention of individuals; rather, the profit-making intention of individuals is the means by which the objective purpose of the economy, the satisfaction of consumer demand, is realized in the subjective pursuit of individual objectives.

In light of the criterion of material appropriateness to business, the concept of profit maximization also draws criticism, since it involves a reversal of ends and means. Positive (not maximum) profit is a necessary condition of corporate activity but not the ultimate purpose of the firm. Profit, i.e. market success, is the criterion of the firm's objective success in pursuit of its economic purpose; however, profit cannot be the sole and only purpose of entrepreneurial activity, not even in the capital market.

The profit motive cannot be formulated in the language of maximization, because the maximization of residual profit is not the corporate objective; rather, profit as a surplus is the yardstick for measuring the firm's objective success and performs the function of disciplining the overall enterprise, including the board or the business owner. Or, as one managing director put it: "Profit is like health. You need it, and the more the better. But it's not why you exist."[3]

What is said here about profit applies all the more to the theory that shareholder value is the ultimate purpose of the firm. According to this theory, management must maximize not only profit but also its own company's share price.

Mergers and Acquisitions: The Capital Market as a Market for Corporate Knowledge and Know-How

In the most recent evolution of the global capital market, an increasingly prominent function of the capital market as a market for company shares is to ensure that not just capital but also management capabilities and knowledge are allocated to whatever is their best use. A first question to ask is why, at the present time, such an explosion of mergers and acquisitions (M&A) can be observed. The globalization of the world economy is a driver of M&A. By buying other firms, the firm making the takeover bid gains advantages for its network. The integration of entire new firms, which frequently remain intact as business units after the merger, generates network advantages of growing importance in comparison with conventional vertical integration or with efficiency gains through economies of scale.

Purchasing the development stages of products and processes by buying firms in possession of this know-how also results in a shortening of the temporal duration of research and development. For a firm launching a takeover bid, the takeover is a means of buying knowledge and know-how, and thereby short-cutting parts of the development cycle. It is possible to exploit time zones in a completely new way: in the domain of research and development, the same project can be worked on globally for 24 hours a day if the corporation acquires different firms with research and development activities in all time zones.[4] Through corporate acquisitions or disposals, a corporation can make adjustments to corporate structure, size and scope, which would require more time if divisions had to be set up within the old organization. At the same time, the boundaries of the corporation become more fluid and flexible. The complexity of products is another factor that increasingly necessitates acquisitions instead of in-house development, once again in order to save time by acquiring a new production process rather than taking the laborious and time-consuming route of developing it oneself.

---

[3]Cf. Th. J. PETERS and R. H. WATERMAN JR. (1982): *In Search of Excellence. Lessons from America's Best-Run Companies*, New York (Harper & Row) 1982.

[4]Cf. STEPHAN A. JANSEN: *Mergers and Acquisitions. Unternehmensakquisitionen und -kooperationen Eine strategische, organisatorische und kapitalmarkttheoretische Einführung*, Wiesbaden (Gabler) 3rd edn. 2000, p. 5 f.

On the other hand, an objection leveled at the rising numbers of hostile and friendly takeovers is that very few corporate takeovers succeed. Studies by the consultancy firms Price Waterhouse and A. E. Kearny show, for the period 1996–2001, that 40,000 mergers took place worldwide with a total value of 5 trillion dollars. 80% of these merged corporations did not generate the capital costs of the transaction. 30% were either broken up or sold. A. E. Kearny estimates the failure rate at 60–75%.[5] These statistics are not necessarily an argument against hostile takeovers, because they do not include the effect of takeover threats on firms which were not taken over. The effect of a takeover threat on the management of all firms in the market is to impel all management teams to raise, or at least maintain, their performance. This effect acts as a kind of general deterrent against creeping complacency and slack.

The general deterrent effect of the takeover threat is not reflected in statistics on the success of the takeovers that actually took place. The possibility and threat of being taken over amounts to the market's general deterrence against complacency in management teams, where the decisive impact is not the actual number of completed and subsequently successful or unsuccessful mergers and takeovers, but the general prevention of "shirking", of management complacency.

In terms of economic ethics, then, how shall we assess hostile takeovers, i.e. those which take place against the express will of the acquisition target's management? Central to the economic and ethical value of mergers and acquisitions is the question as to the legitimacy of the hostile takeover. Does the hostile takeover deserve our disapproval as a "hostile" procedure, or does it serve the capital market's purpose of ensuring and improving capital allocation and the "control of corporate control"? The central legitimization for the hostile takeover resides in the right of company owners to sell their shares to whoever bids the highest price for them, or, if the owner is also the majority shareholder, in his right to replace the management if he comes to the substantiated opinion that management is harming the firm or failing to realize its maximum value-creating potential.

It follows from this logic of ownership rights that in the event of a takeover threat, in accordance with the owner or shareholder-value principle, the management of the target firm must not reject any offer that gives shareholders the opportunity to sell at a price higher than the given market share price. Defensive measures which prevent or prohibit owners from taking this opportunity to sell must therefore be evaluated from the viewpoint of value-destruction because they deprive owners of the opportunity to sell their property, namely the company shares, at a higher value. The justification of hostile takeovers when the target firm's management is underperforming is not, therefore, in doubt.

---

[5] Quoted after NIKOLAUS SCHWEIKART: "Der getriebene Chef. Shareholder value über alles – das US-Modell setzt sich durch" [The hounded boss. Shareholder value comes first – the US model is prevailing], *DIE ZEIT*, No. 20, 10 May 2001, p. 26.

Hostile and Friendly Takeovers and the Importance of the Global Competition Between Management Teams

In Germany, the ownership or takeover principle[6] is frequently countermanded by the principle of consensus between all those who work for the firm, i.e. all its stakeholders. Attention is also called to the codetermination principle in major German corporations, which gives labor representatives the right to be consulted on decisions concerning the management of the firm.

In contrast, the Anglo-American model relies on external control over the firm and its management by outside shareholders. This model is backed by fairly realistic assumptions about the risks to which corporations are exposed by their stakeholders. Situations are conceivable in which the management and the workforce make choices that enable them to have an easier life at the owners' expense, by consuming the value of the corporation and paying the owners or shareholders little or nothing in the way of dividends or earnings. On the presumption that all members of the organization will be tempted to take life easy in the firm, and that outside owners prevent this tendency, control of the corporation by its shareholders is evidently a necessity.

Among the explanatory hypotheses for hostile takeovers, Jensen's free cash flow hypothesis in particular is predicated on the danger of management complacency in mature corporations and sectors.[7] In mature sectors, free cash flow items can be amassed, i.e. surplus income from sales and amortization which, for the sake of efficient allocation of capital, should be distributed to the shareholders so that they can invest the proceeds in alternative projects by other firms. It is in the interests of the managers, however, to keep these income streams within the firm. By this means, they enhance their own freedom of action by several degrees because capital market control is weakened.

In globalized markets, the threat of the hostile takeover by international management teams reduces management's tendency to accumulate profits within the firm, as well as the concomitant tendency to inflate profitless turnover at the expense of profit, and hence to boost management earnings, which are linked to turnover performance, at the expense of dividends. The context that is analyzed by the free cash flow hypothesis can also be described in terms of the universal phenomenon that once people have built something up, they feel entitled to relax and stop working so hard. Naturally, this is not in the interests of the institutions for which they have done all the groundwork. On the other hand, in the case of a hostile takeover, it gives rise to the necessity to remunerate all the groundwork and the part played by management in the firm's added value – where this is not already remunerated by

---

[6]Cf. PETER KOSLOWSKI: "Shareholder Value und der Zweck des Unternehmens" [Shareholder value and the purpose of the firm], in: P. KOSLOWSKI (ed.): *Shareholder Value und die Kriterien des Unternehmenserfolgs*, Heidelberg (Physica) 1999, pp. 1–32.

[7]MICHAEL C. JENSEN: "Agency Cost of Free Cash Flow, Corporate Finance, and Takeover", *American Economic Review*, 76 (1986), pp. 323–329.

manager salaries – by means of compensation payments. For this reason, the criticism frequently voiced over high severance payouts to managers who are replaced in hostile takeovers needs to be tempered.

A further argument for permitting hostile takeovers as a necessity is that shareholders in general, and shareholders of large, anonymous joint-stock corporations in particular, cannot constantly be present in the company and assert their interests, and, therefore, can only avoid being taken advantage of via their right to appoint or dismiss the management team.

The argument that the threat of takeover raises the efficiency of management cannot be dismissed out of hand. It is, however, doubtful whether its application necessarily involves total acceptance of the theory of shareholder value. It could be that shareholder value is also a necessary principle of control, because of the disciplining effect of the threat of takeover, but this need not imply that shareholder-value maximization is the firm's purpose.[8]

Corporate Governance by Self-Control Through Stakeholder Consensus, and Corporate Governance by Competition from Outsiders: The German and the Anglo-American Model of Corporate Governance

In contrast, the German model of business management presumes that a consensus of all the stakeholder groups, for the very fact that it is a consensus, is best for the company and ensures the optimum decisions. Dissent between the company's workforce and stakeholder groups is viewed, in that culture, as a sign of crisis and inadequate management, whereas consensus – wholly in keeping with Habermas's consensus theory of truth – is seen as a guarantee of the rightness of decisions.

It is not hard to see that the discrepancy between the consensus principle and the shareholder-value principle is based on wide-ranging philosophical differences in the conception of governance, of management, leadership and government – indeed, of constitution, – which extend right into the political constitutional debate. Under the German or continental European understanding of republican government and constitution, the idea of self-government by consensus is the guiding model. In Anglo-American republicanism, the dominant idea is that of government by the representation of groups, and the replacement of adversarial political government teams and economic management teams by the mechanism of extrinsic, decisive competition for the approval of voters and shareholders. The globalization of the competition between management teams and the globalization of the capital markets foster the competition principle rather than the consensus principle, because globalization undermines if not destroys national and regional consensuses.

---

[8]On the shareholder value principle, cf. Chapter 9, below.

Consensus is no assurance of the truth of decisions taken in consensus. It is conceivable that a consensus of certain stakeholder groups might work to the detriment of other stakeholders. Alternatively, consider a situation in which all stakeholders in a firm are deluding themselves about the firm's actual condition and productivity, for which the only possible remedy is an extrinsic force, i.e. competition from alternative management teams, to shatter the "illusion" of consensus.

In the wake of the crisis in the financial markets, the European Union finds itself at a turning point in the debate on corporate governance and corporate constitution and about the role of the capital market. Decisions must be made on questions of principle concerning the model of corporate governance, given that the responsibility for the crisis in the financial markets can largely be attributed to the Anglo-American model. But this should be tackled with caution. The takeover principle, if it is understood restrictively in the sense described here, retains its justification.

In passing its Takeovers Directive, the EU Commission incorporated the takeover principle into the legislation and adjudication of the Member States. This Directive called for more effective corporate control by means of hostile takeovers and the abolition of laws reducing economic competition. Thus, for instance, rules such as the Volkswagen Law, conceding special rights to the German state of Lower Saxony as a state shareholder of Volkswagen AG, should be abolished.

It is interesting, philosophically, that the then Competition Commissioner of the European Union, Mario Monti, argued in 2001 that the European Union cannot discriminate between companies in private and in state ownership. State ownership of companies may no longer confer any competitive advantage, according to Monti, because this would distort competition between private and semi-state companies.[9]

We can consider this claim from two sides. One could object that the EU Commission is thus questioning the distinction between state and society, which is especially emphasized in Germany, by denying that the state has any privileged status among other groupings within society[10] and no longer conceding any special role to companies in which the state is a shareholder as opposed to private companies.

On the other hand, a response to this objection is that the privileging of a company in which the state has a holding overrides the very distinction between state and society by creating a third, hybrid form of political–economic management, which follows neither the market principles of competition, consumer sovereignty and the profit principle, nor political representation based exclusively on voter sovereignty. The semi-state companies are neither entirely exposed to competition and the profit objective, nor are they wholly for the public benefit because they do indeed make a profit, although the use to which this should be put is frequently a political

---

[9]Thus MARIO MONTI at the annual conference of the Verein für Socialpolitik (Society for German-speaking economists) on 27 September 2001 in Magdeburg, Germany.

[10]Cf. PETER KOSLOWSKI: *Gesellschaft und Staat. Ein unvermeidlicher Dualismus* [Society and state, an unavoidable dualism], with an introduction by Robert Spaemann, Stuttgart (Klett-Cotta) 1982.

decision.[11] They belong neither wholly to the sphere of the state, nor to that of society. They distort competition in the domain of the state-coordinated social economy in that they can reap the benefits of state privileges over their private-sector competitors.

In this respect, the dynamics of the single market of the European Union point in the same direction as the dynamics of the global market. Within the European Union, it is difficult to explain why the State of Lower Saxony's large shareholding in Volkswagen supposedly gives the firm competitive advantages over French competitors like Peugeot or Renault, which are also partly state-owned, or, vice versa, why this privileges French carmakers over Volkswagen. From the standpoint of making a clear distinction between state and society, it may help to safeguard state functions if the hybrid form of the semi-state, semi-societal joint-stock corporation makes way for fully privatized joint-stock corporations alongside fully state-run functional corporations which are also, in that case, wholly for the public benefit.[12]

If we inquire into which fundamental values and which identifications with basic principles underlie the controversy over the legality or illegality of hostile corporate takeovers, we arrive at the dichotomy between consensus and competition, self-control and extrinsic control. The German model of business management is based on the consensus principle and on the stakeholders controlling themselves. To the capital market, it ascribes only a subordinate role in the control of corporate management, and envisages the prime form of corporate control as the stakeholders themselves exercising control over themselves within the corporation. The Anglo-American model, on the other hand, assumes that consensus does not necessarily entail productivity because when an emphasis is placed on the value of consensus, it can lead participants in the discourse to be too easily satisfied with self-serving solutions.

Cultural traditions and religious persuasions also come into play here. The defining characteristic of the puritanical Calvinist Protestant tradition, as opposed to the Lutheran Protestant and the Catholic tradition, is a stronger mistrust of self-justification and self-control by groups and a greater reliance on the individual.

These confessional differences are matched by differences in the models of republicanism which emerged from the ideas that influenced the American Revolution, and from those that inspired the French Revolution. According to the Anglo-American, puritanical model, the people affected by decisions were not capable of assessing their own efforts due to the distortion of human knowledge caused by self-interest – or theologically, because their will is tainted by original sin. The

---

[11]This is probably also the reason why all Minister-Presidents of Lower Saxony, whatever their political hue, have staunchly retained the VW Law and the problematic role of the State of Lower Saxony as a privileged shareholder in Volkswagen.

[12]Assessing the special position of Germany's regional-state banks and savings banks presents a difficult problem. It may be useful that they make discounted credit available to small and medium-size enterprises thanks to the state deposit guarantee enjoyed by these banks. At the same time, the burdens of this discounting are paid for by the taxpayer, who is perhaps ambivalent as to the structure of the firms in a market and about subsidizing credit with taxes.

identity-democratic model of republicanism, of government and of corporate governance, by contrast, assumes that the truth-generating element of political and other governance processes lies precisely in consensus or in Rousseau's *volonté générale*.

The identity-philosophical interpretation of democracy as the unity of the governors and governed, which defines German and continental-European political philosophy and its understanding of government from Hegel to Habermas, is not as superior as it likes to suggest. In fact, it is founded on the questionable basic assumption that, in the same way that Hegel's absolute subject becomes conscious of itself as an object, the people or nation becomes objective and conscious of itself in the subject-object of the state.[13] Out of this putative identity of the subject and object of power, identity-philosophical thinking concludes that the conscious self-objectivization of the people in the state takes place in consensus, that it leads to the identity of people and state, author of the law and addressee of the law, and that through this identity, political power is neutralized and translated into self-government.

Discourse-theoretical theories of corporate governance also transfer this consensus- and identity-theoretical model of political government onto the firm and its management, and demand discourse and consensus of the corporation's stakeholders as the principle of corporate control.[14]

From the standpoint of the general anthropology of human self-interest and our lack of objectivity towards ourselves, discourse theory stops short of tackling the complexity that pervades the problems of controlling power. The tendency, observable in corporatism, to agreements and coalitions among influential interests or stakeholder groups requires an emphasis on the idea that political and economic power can be controlled through competition and through extrinsic scrutiny by individuals or institutions. Hostile takeovers are one of the possible control mechanisms against false forms of consensus and coalitions between management and stakeholder groups within the corporation. They should therefore be encouraged rather than prohibited by the German law on the legal structure of the firm. Greater control of the management of large German corporations by the threat of takeover

---

[13] Via the transition to people's sovereignty, it enables the national state of society according to Habermas to "influence itself" politically. Cf. JÜRGEN HABERMAS: "Die postnationale Konstellation und die Zukunft der Demokratie", in: J. HABERMAS: *Die postnationale Konstellation* [The Postnational Constellation], Frankfurt am Main (Suhrkamp) 1998, p. 100. According to K. A. SCHACHTSCHNEIDER: *Res publica res populi. Grundlegung einer allgemeinen Republiklehre. Ein Beitrag zur Freiheits-, Rechts-, und Staatslehre* [Groundwork for a general theory of the republic. A contribution to the theory of liberty, law and statehood], Berlin (Duncker & Humblot) 1994, p. 4, the republic is founded on a "constitution free of rule or dominion" (*Verfassung der Herrschaftslosigkeit*).

[14] As argued in papers on discourse-theoretical economic and corporate ethics in the circle of Horst Steinmann. Cf. ANDREAS GEORG SCHERER: *Die Rolle der Multinationalen Unternehmung im Prozeß der Globalisierung* [Role of the multinational corporation in the globalization process], Heidelberg (Physica-Verlag) 2003 (Ethische Ökonomie. Beiträge zur Wirtschaftsethik und Wirtschaftskultur, Vol. 7).

by competing management teams would have the effect of raising their business performance.

This does not rule out retaining the mechanism of codetermination as a form of workforce representation and involvement in corporate management. The rules of codetermination do not negate the principles of ownership and shareholder value, but explicitly confirm the owners' majority rights and therefore ultimate decision-making rights on the supervisory board of the joint-stock corporation. In conjunction with the control principle of the hostile takeover, the codetermination principle – as a principle of representation, not consensus – can raise the corporation's performance. Codetermination as labor representation increases the organization's capacity to learn and also performs a placatory function when conflict situations arise within the corporation.[15]

The synthesis between the Anglo-American principle of the capital market as a market for corporate control and the German principle of codetermination as work-force representation in the management of the corporation is also tenable – and performance-enhancing for the corporation – under the conditions of globalization. This is, in all probability, superior to both the pure capital market model without codetermination and to the pure codetermination model without hostile takeovers via the capital market. Globalization may well force company law in the EU and the USA in the direction of such a synthesis.

---

[15]On the precondition that the unions see themselves not as adversarial unions, i.e. industrial relations partners who are hostile to the owners, but as non-adversarial unions cooperating in corporate management, which can be said of the German trade unions. On the critique of the concept of the adversarial union, cf. RICHARD A. POSNER: *A Failure of Capitalism. The Crisis of '08 and the Descent into Depression*, Cambridge, MA (Harvard University Press) 2009, p. 224.

Chapter 6
The Ethical Economy of the Market for Derivatives: Trading with Values Derived from Other Values for Hedging, Speculation, and Arbitrage

It is useful to differentiate between the market for derivatives and the markets for credit and capital, despite the existence of some structured products which blend elements of credit-market and capital-market products – collateralized debt obligations, for instance. Share options are the classic example of capital-market derivatives, and interest-rate swaps the classic example of credit-market derivatives. Given the more complex nature of the market for derivative products, it seems appropriate to treat this market separately as a market in its own right, even if there are also credit-market derivatives, capital-market derivatives, and hybrid derivative products that can be seen as hybrids consisting of credit-market products and capital-market products, although they are not hybrid securities in the narrower sense, as convertible bonds are.[1]

Derivatives introduce a higher, more complex dimension to the financial system. Derivatives are financial contracts, the price of which is dependent on or "derived" from another value, namely that of the underlying asset. The basic function of the derivative is to provide protection against a decline in the value of the underlying asset. This is done either with a futures contract, which gives the buyer the right to buy or sell the underlying at a certain future point in time, or by means of an option. The option gives the option-buyer the right to buy or sell the underlying asset at a price determined in advance if a change in the value of the underlying asset occurs.

The economic function of derivatives is, in exchange for the payment of a fee, to enable the transfer of risk from those who are unwilling to bear risk to those who

---

[1] Similarly, ALEXANDER BATCHVAROV (ed.): *Hybrid Products. Instruments, Applications and Modelling*, London (Risk Books) 2005, cover text: "Traditionally, a hybrid product was any financial instrument that blended characteristics of debt and equity markets. An example would be convertible bonds. Today, that definition may be stretched to include instruments that blend aspects of other markets as well. Structured finance has produced a host of innovative hybrid products, some of which have sizeable markets. Examples include trust preferred securities (TruPS)." Cf. also CHRISTOPHER L. CULP: *Structured Finance and Insurance: The ART of Managing Capital and Risk*, New York (Wiley) 2006.

P. Koslowski, *The Ethics of Banking*, Issues in Business Ethics 30,
DOI 10.1007/978-94-007-0656-9_6, © Springer Science+Business Media B.V. 2011

are willing to do so.[2] Futures and options therefore serve the primary purpose of hedging, the protection of an asset or value against a future change in value and the transfer of the risk of such a movement in value from the party who would rather hedge than bear the risk to another party who is willing to bear the risk in exchange for a fee. However, for those in need of protection to be sure that their demand for futures and options will be matched by a supply, there must be suppliers of futures contracts who either hold the contrary expectation about the future, and have an equal demand for protection against the complementary movement in value that their complementary future expectation leads them to anticipate, or else a group of suppliers who are motivated by speculation and/or arbitrage to ensure a supply of futures or options. The demand for hedging and the meeting of that demand presupposes a supply of futures and options motivated by speculation, and hence a certain volume of speculation in futures and options. Both the hedging and the speculation motives determine the market for futures and options.

Structured finance products are investment vehicles like certificates (e.g. index or basket certificates) which comprise a least one derivative element.[3] Unlike shares or other capital-market products, but also unlike fixed-interest securities, they are structured by incorporating a derivative component. They can be seen as hybrids of credit-market and capital-market instruments, although the term "hybrid security" is used for products like convertible bonds which can actually be transformed in nature. A classic hybrid product is the convertible bond, a bond – i.e. a loan to the corporation – which is converted into a share in the corporation, a share of its common stock.

In fact, structured products themselves are hybrid securities, in that they are hybrid constructs consisting of a fixed-interest and a derivative component.[4] The invention of the collateralized debt obligation created a form of security and a financial instrument that combines loan elements with elements of equity financing. The distinction between the credit market and the capital market cannot be stringently maintained for these securities. They belong to both markets. The creation of structured products or certificates likewise results in financial instruments that are hybrid in character and cannot be ascribed to just one market or the other.

---

[2]Cf. also RENÉ M. STULZ: "Should We Fear Derivatives?", *Journal of Economic Perspectives*, 18 (2004), pp. 173–192, although he understates the risks of the massive expansion of derivatives.

[3]Cf. SARYAJIT DAS: *Structured Products and Hybrid Securities*, Hoboken, NJ (John Wiley) 2nd edn. 2001, p. 1: Structured products are "derivative-embedded securities, a security that combines the features of a fixed income instrument with the characteristics of a derivative transaction (in effect, the return profile of a forward or option on a selected class of asset.)"

[4]SARYAJIT DAS: *Structured Products 4: Equity, Commodity, Credit and New Markets*: 2, Hoboken, NJ (John Wiley) 2005 (Swaps & Financial Derivatives Library), gives a list of structured products including: equity derivatives (including equity swaps/options, convertible securities and equity linked notes), commodity derivatives (including energy, metal and agricultural derivatives), credit derivatives (including credit linked notes/collateralized debt obligations ("CDOs")), new derivative markets (including inflation linked derivatives and notes, insurance derivatives, weather derivatives, property, bandwidth/telephone minutes, macro-economic index and emission/environmental derivatives) and tax based applications of derivatives.

They are structured combinations of shares and options, or of loans and options, which link the credit and capital market with the market for futures and options. For this reason, in accordance with the scheme of classification into credit, capital and derivative markets, they will be dealt with separately here following the examination of the credit and capital market.

The derivative portion of structured products is an element of an investment strategy of intentional exposure to higher risk coupled with the use of higher leverage. Speculation is the pivotal motive for this derivative strategy. A structured product can also be used for hedging, however.

The hybrid makeup of structured products and derivative products is the root cause of the great complexity of these financial products, which is frequently sufficient to defeat the understanding of their sellers and buyers, not to mention the tax authorities.[5] *It is also the reason for the high costs of these products, which result from the less than entirely transparent or verifiable fees charged by the banks.* As one financial intermediary said, the banks have their own reasons for offering structured products: "The game is stealing money". Extra profits are also the reason for the banks' practice of buying each other's loans, or the risk of each other's loans, or both, in the form of CDOs.

Futures and Options: Non-Conditioned and Conditioned Forward Transactions

Derivatives encompass, firstly, the trade in financial instruments or other goods at a certain point in the future, known as forward transactions or futures, and secondly, the trade in financial instruments or other goods based on a condition to be realized at a certain future point in time, known as conditioned forward transactions or options.[6] Unlike the spot or cash market, in which direct deals are made for immediate payment and delivery of the object of the contract, the contracts concluded on the futures and options markets are for a deal that will take place in the future. Derivatives or derivative financial instruments are usually derived from assets such as shares, bonds and commodities, or from reference rates such as currencies, interest rates or indices. The underlying object is not fixed, and can be any kind of asset. Derivatives can also be seen as wagers on the price movement of an underlying asset.

The object of a non-conditioned or fixed forward contract[7] is the delivery of a good at a certain price at a certain point of time in the future. The forward

---

[5] On the complexity surrounding the taxation of hybrid financial instruments, cf. the Directive of the Australian government: http://www.treasury.gov.au/documents/196/PDF/round6.pdf

[6] For a clear presentation on options and futures in the markets of the German-speaking countries, including options and futures pricing, cf. ERNST MÜLLER-MÖHL: *Optionen und Futures. Grundlagen und Strategien für das Termingeschäft in Deutschland, Österreich und in der Schweiz,* Stuttgart (Schäffer-Poeschel) 5th edn. 2002.

[7] In the German-speaking discussion, the term "*nicht bedingtes Termingeschäft*" (non-conditioned future) seems more appropriate than the term "*unbedingtes Termingeschäft*" (unconditional future)

contract enables the quality and price of a good to be specified for delivery at a certain future point in time. Non-conditioned futures are differentiated into futures, which are standardized and exchange-tradable, and forwards, which are individually negotiated and non-exchange traded. The latter are known as "over-the-counter" (OTC) contracts.

Conditioned futures, known as options, heighten the complexity further. The option specifies the delivery of a good at a certain price at a certain point in time, contingent upon a specified condition concerning the value of the underlying; for instance, that the price of a specified index has reached a certain predefined price, which then determines the price of the (index) option.

Futures that are not conditioned, i.e. not dependent on the realization of a pre-defined condition, must be executed by the buyer, whereas options, as futures conditioned by another factor, may or may not be exercised by the option buyer. Both conditioned and non-conditioned futures incorporate future time into present time. The speculation on which the futures transaction is based is a heightened form of speculation. Unlike simple speculation, it is not merely arbitrage between points on the time axis from the present onwards, where the future point in time at which a good will be sold is left undecided; instead, it nominates a point in time (European options) or a time period (American options) in the future as well as a purchase or sale price. It anticipates the future in precisely specified conditions. Because it is designed to be dependent on the price movement of a good, not just in the future in general but at a fixed future point in time, it is characterized both by its higher contingency on a certain future point in time, but also by the certainty it provides for one of the contracting parties about the value of the option at a certain future point in time.

Derivatives are financial instruments, the prices of which are aligned with price changes or the price expectations of other investments. The party that accepts the risk, the derivative writer, undertakes to provide a financial service if a certain value of the underlying occurs. In order to create incentives for the derivative writer, derivatives must be constructed in such a way that they disproportionately reflect fluctuations in the prices of these investment assets. They can be used both to hedge against losses and, because they respond disproportionately to fluctuations in the price of the underlying asset, to speculate on price gains.

Variants of Derivatives: Futures, Options, Swaps, Structured Finance and Investment Products

The most important derivatives are futures, options, swaps and structured finance and investment products, which will be briefly presented here. Because of their

---

used by MÜLLER-MÖHL (2002), p. 22, since the latter has connotations of urgency or exigence that are out of place here.

significance, the structured finance products, especially collateralized debt obligations (CDOs), will be presented last and in more detail.

Non-Conditioned Futures and Forwards

Futures transactions are standardized transactions which enable the acquisition or sale at the present time of a commodity, a currency, a certain interest rate, or a share, at a certain price and at a certain point in time or period of time in the future. Futures are standardized by contract size and expiry term, and are transacted on the stock exchange via a bank or broker. Forwards are the same transactions without the standardization, transacted by individually negotiated contracts. The contract size and expiry terms for forwards are defined according to the wishes of the contract partners.

Conditioned Futures: Options

An option is the agreement whereby one contract partner is assured of the unilateral right to buy or sell a quantity of the good or an asset defined in advance at a fixed price within a defined period of time. For this agreement, a premium is paid. The value of the agreement is determined by the payment of the premium, known as the option premium. The option contract can be individual or standardized. Standardized options are traded on certain stock exchanges; in Germany, for instance, on the options and financial futures exchange EUREX.

The economic function of derivatives is, in exchange for the payment of a fee, to transfer the risk of a movement of value of an underlying asset from the party that does not want to bear it to another party that is willing to bear the risk. The buyer of a call option, to be able to buy a share at a certain value at a certain future point in time, transfers the risk of the share's movement in value to the seller of this option. The buyer expects the share price to rise, but does not want to bear the risk of the price movement; the seller is prepared to bear the risk of the price trend because he expects a fall in price. Both the buyer and the seller of the option are placing wagers in contrary, but complementary, directions on the price trend of the share. The buyer is prepared to pay the seller a fee for assuming the price risk; the seller is prepared to bear the price risk in exchange for this fee.

Swaps: A Sequence of Forwards or Options

Swaps are obligations to exchange payment flows. Their purpose is to stabilize payment flows, especially of interest payments. Interest-rate swaps together with credit-default swaps make up the most important class of swaps. Other categories that exist are currency swaps, equity swaps and commodity swaps. A swap contract is just a series of forward contracts that are tied together in a sequence. The contract obliges the two contracting parties to exchange payment streams.

Interest Rate Swaps

Imagine a firm that has agreed a variable interest rate for its borrowing. Nevertheless, it would like more certainty about its future interest payments and therefore wants to lock in a constant interest rate for a particular period of time. In a swap contract, it makes a deal with another firm or a bank which, in exchange for payment of a one-off fee and constant monthly interest at rate R, offers to pay the variable interest rate R^* on every due date. The variable interest rate payments R^* falling due on future dates $t + n$, expressed as Rt^* for $(t = 1...n)$, are replaced by the constant interest payments R, expressed as Rt for $t = 1...n$, and a forward-contract fee. The swap represents a sequence of forward contracts F, for $F = Fa^*$ and $a^* = 1...n$, which have been individually negotiated and tied together into a single swap contract.[8]

Credit-Default Swaps

In a credit-default swap, the swap seller or protection seller, usually a bank, enters into an obligation in exchange for a fee paid by the swap buyer or protection buyer, which is a finance company or an investor, that if the firm that issued the reference bond fails to make interest payments, the swap seller will make interest payments to the swap buyer, or if the bond issuer becomes insolvent, i.e. in the event of credit default, it will repay the loan in full. Again, the main motives for credit-default swaps are hedging by the lender and swap buyer in parallel with speculation by the swap buyer and/or the swap seller. The credit-default swap is equivalent to a credit insurance policy in that it insures the protection buyer against default by the reference debtor, whose debt is the underlying value of the credit-default swap.[9]

At the same time, however, there are important differences between the credit-default swap and credit insurance, which typify the problematic side of derivatives. The buyer of the credit-default swap, the protection buyer, needs not own the reference value, which can be identical with the underlying security but may differ from it; he need not even be exposed to loss by the reference value but can hold the credit-default swap for purely speculative reasons. The protection seller, the seller of the swap, need not be a legally regulated entity or hold any reserves in order to pay out to the protection buyer. Unlike insurance companies, which manage risks through

---

[8]Cf. also DONALD H. CHEW JR.: *The New Corporate Finance. Where Theory Meets Practice*, Boston (Irwin McGraw-Hill) 1999, pp. 468f.

[9]Cf. also GERALD BRAUNBERGER: "Credit Default Swaps. Das Produkt, das die Finanzkrise verschärfte" [The product that intensified the financial crisis], *Frankfurter Allgemeine Zeitung*, 3rd April 2009, No. 79, p. 24.

the law of large numbers, credit-default swap traders manage their risks by insuring them with other traders for compensation (hedging). Hans-Werner Sinn points out that the buyers of credit-default swaps are betting on the demise of a firm, and may develop an interest in using market power to engineer such a demise in order to benefit from the swap premium.[10]

Credit-default swaps emerged in the early 1990s. The first fully-fledged credit-default swaps were sold by JP Morgan Chase in 1997. Since then, the market volume for credit-default swaps has grown in leaps and bounds. At the end of 2007, the volume (notional value) of assets underlying credit-default swaps had reached 45 trillion US dollars. As a result of the financial market crisis, this fell to 38.6 trillion US dollars by the end of 2008.[11]

A finance swap is a derivative in which the contracting parties agree to swap one stream of cash flows for another, and in doing so, come to contrary but complementary conclusions about their assessment of the future development of these cash flows (in the examples: the interest payments and loan repayments). Both parties wager that the payment streams will move in contrary directions. In the above example of interest rate swaps, the swap seller, protection seller or "writer", who takes responsibility for the payments at the variable interest rate, wagers that the variable interest rates will fall, while the swap buyer or protection buyer expects the variable interest rates to rise, and seeks insurance against this eventuality. Interest rate swaps, too, can therefore be seen as a type of credit insurance. But they can also be used for mere speculation about changes in the direction of the prices underlying the swap, the interest rates. Most credit-default swaps are agreed between banks; in other words they are wagers placed by banks among themselves.

The Collateralized Debt Obligation as a Structured Finance Product and an Instrument of Credit Enhancement

Another type of derivative is the financial instrument known as the collateralized debt obligation (CDO), if it comprises a derivative element. This is principally the case for synthetic CDOs, which are largely identical with credit-default swaps.

CDOs are structured finance products that are used as instruments of credit enhancement.[12] In order to satisfy the increased demand for credit, financial

---

[10]Cf. SINN (2009), p. 315 (own trans.): "This market is the most obscure of all, because it is totally unregulated. [...] That the American International Group (AIG) invented CDSs to exploit a regulatory loophole and had to be nationalized in 2008 with an annual loss of US $100 billion, the highest loss made by any private firm in human history, speaks volumes."

[11]INTERNATIONAL SWAPS AND DERIVATIVES ASSOCIATION (ISDA): Market Survey, Year End 2008.

[12]Cf. RICHARD J. ROSEN: "The Role of Securitization in Mortgage Lending", *Chicago Fed Letter* (The Federal Reserve Bank of Chicago), n. 244 (November 2007), http://www.chicagofed.org/publications/fedletter/cflnovember2007_244.pdf. For a more critical view of CDOs, and a good presentation of securitization, see JAN PIETER KRAHNEN: "Der Handel von Kreditrisiken. Eine

institutions tried to find ways of increasing their means of supplying credit. Credit enhancement became a driving motive for the securitization of loans into structured finance products, i.e. products with derivative elements. At the same time, credit enhancement – the drive to extend lending beyond the constraints imposed by the regulatory capital requirement to maintain a certain ratio of equity to the bank's balance sheet total and by the obligatory minimum reserve the bank has to hold with the central bank, – became one of the causes of the IT crisis of 2000 and the financial market crisis of the years 2007–2008.

The main barrier that prevents banks from continuously expanding their lending is the obligatory ratio of equity to balance sheet total and the minimum reserve requirement in relation to risk-bearing loans. If the bank finds a way to lay off the risk for part of its loan book while keeping the collateral as equity, it can increase its lending and reduce its capital costs associated with the tied-up equity and reserve capital.

One of the main instruments for circumventing the equity to balance sheet total obligation became the securitization of loans as CDOs. Securitization is the process by which cash-producing assets, usually a pool of outstanding receivables, are turned into transferable securities which often also obtain a rating and can then be sold to investors. The securities are structured in such a way that they are paid primarily from the cash flow of the debt assets plus the revenues from the credit enhancement, but not by the seller – the originator – of the security. Bank loans are turned into tradable bonds, which are secured in turn by a share in the collateral for the loan. The security is asset-backed, i.e. backed by a claim. The collateral may be a general asset (asset-backed security), a mortgage (mortgage-backed securities) or a bond secured on a variety of loans, bonds or mortgages (collateralized debt, collateralized bond, collateralized mortgage obligation). CDOs are sold in tranches that create artificially differentiated classes of risk and define the seniority-rating of CDO buyers as creditors. In the event of debtor insolvency, the best-rated or most senior tranche is repaid first from the assets; the second-rated tranche is second in line, and so on. The tranches of the CDO with the derivative element are the structural features that make the CDO a structured finance product.

In collateralized debt obligations, loans are combined with other loans and securitized as bonds issued by a special purpose vehicle, which are secured by a share of the collateral and sold to investors outside the bank. In this type of CDO, also known as a "cash CDO", which has been created from the "true sale" of the claim or asset, the loan and the collateral and/or the asset disappear from the bank's balance sheet. The bank's equity is therefore reduced.

This is remedied by the synthetic CDO. With the synthetic CDO, only the risk and the coupon claim are sold, but the asset remains with the bank. The synthetic

---

neue Dimension des Kapitalmarkts" [The trade in credit risks. A new dimension of the capital market], *Perspektiven der Wirtschaftspolitik*, 6 (2005), pp. 499–519. Cf. also JOSHUA COVAL, JAKUB JUREK, ERIK STAFFORD: "The Economics of Structured Finance," *Journal of Economic Perspectives*, 23 (2009), pp. 3–25.

CDO synthetically – artificially – replicates a cash CDO. We talk about synthetic securitization when the claims of one or more banks are combined into a package (bundle, pool, special fund, portfolio) and a credit derivative is used to split off the credit risk, which is sold to a special purpose vehicle; however, the credit claim continues to figure on the bank's balance sheet (which differentiates it from a true-sale securitization).[13] The synthetic CDO, despite its synthetic, artificial nature, is easier and cheaper to create than the "true sale CDO" because it requires less legal expense. It hives off the loan but leaves the asset on which the loan is secured as a bank asset, and thus enhances the bank's equity and, therefore, its lending capacity.

Since only the credit risk is sold but not the asset, the synthetic CDO is the same thing as a credit-default swap. The different names for the same financial instrument can be explained by the different origins of each, and by the efforts of banks to remove lending risks from their balance sheets. The synthetic CDO is a credit-default swap issued by banks that want to reduce their equity requirement and maintain or even expand their capital base, whereas general credit-default swaps are agreed for the most diverse reasons by the protection buyer and seller.

Finally, there are also hybrid CDOs which are combinations of cash CDOs and synthetic CDOs. They are structured in such a way that in part they sell the loan collaterals to the CDO buyer and in part they sell the risk only.

The interest payments or bond coupons to the investors are settled out of the interest payments on the loan and the fees received by the bank that transfers the bond to a special purpose vehicle, and out of the enhanced credit made possible by the CDO. All three components of income must be higher than the costs of the CDO. The fees to be paid by the investor/buyer of the CDO to the issuer of the CDO, the originator, can be substantial. The expense of securitization is, as in many other areas of structured finance, high. This indicates a fundamental problem concerning the structuring of financial instruments: the fees for intermediation are high, whereas the actual value created by the intermediation, especially by multiple repetition of the same financial operation, is dubious.

Why do banks have an interest in transforming their loans into CDOs? The following reasons can be cited:

– Arbitrage gains from switching to another system of regulation (regulatory arbitrage)
– Individual adaptation of financing to customer needs (customization)
– Credit enhancement (enhanced credit creation)
– Adjustment of bond denominations to the customer's needs for retail denominations.

---

[13]Cf. *Monatsbericht der Deutschen Bundesbank* [Monthly Report of the German Bundesbank] of April 2004, p. 29, Monthly Report of the German Bundesbank of March 2006, p. 57 (clear example calculations), Monthly Bulletin of the European Central Bank of February 2008, pp. 92 ff. (schematic representation; explanations on particular forms of synthetic securitization; charts), page numbers refer to the German editions consulted. (Source: Gerhard Merk, University of Siegen).

The CDO creates the possibility, already described, of lowering the equity requirement and utilizing other regulatory arbitrage options by selling on the loans as bonds. That this arbitrage is in the private economic interest of the financial institution is obvious. Whether this arbitrage is also useful for the financial system and the wider economy is more than doubtful. Circumvention of the minimum equity requirement is not in the interest of the financial system.

Since major banks have better means of carrying out this arbitrage than smaller institutes, this possibility effectively induces greater concentration in the finance industry. The use of CDOs to adapt to the customer's financing wishes and to individualize the supply of financing is certainly in the customers' interests, as indeed is the facilitation of low denominations of bonds. The London Stock Exchange sets the "retail denomination" limit for bonds at €50,000. Anything above this sum is a "wholesale denomination".[14] Enhanced credit creation is also in the customer's interest if it is accompanied by a reduction in the price of credit.

However, since CDOs are associated with high fees to cover their structuring by the special purpose vehicle (SPV) and the management of the CDO, it is not clear whether the generation of fees by the originator is not a motive of at least equal importance. But even if the CDO benefits the customer, once again it is necessary to ask whether the circumvention of the minimum equity requirement is in the customer's long-term interest, because it jeopardizes the financial system, which will ultimately need to be rescued with taxpayers' money, i.e. customers' money, and supplied with new capital to rebuild the bank's equity.

The CDO creates incentives for its originator to pay more attention to the volume than to the quality of loans. The market for securitized loans suffers from the structural flaw that it prioritizes loan volumes over loan quality, and therefore neglects debtor monitoring.

The Functions of Speculation in the Derivatives Market: Enabling the Division of Labor Between Hedging and Speculation

Speculation in the markets for futures, options, and structured products based on commodities, currencies, loans, shares, or combinations of any of the latter, creates the possibility of hedging on the prices of these very commodities, currencies, loans and shares, whose producers or investors/owners do not want to speculate but prefer to calculate with predictable prices for future commodities or finance instruments. Hedging by means of the conditioned forward transaction, the option, in which the option buyer or protection buyer purchases from the writer the guarantee of a price, creates a further degree of freedom in that the option need not be exercised if it is not to the option buyer's advantage. Speculation in futures, options and structured products, the combination of a security with a derivative component, acts as

---

[14]LONDON STOCK EXCHANGE: "The Professional Securities Market," http://www.londonstockexchange.com/companies-and-advisors/psm/psmbgoverview.pdf

insurance which guarantees the future price or safeguards against future price fluctuations for non-speculators. Speculation in the spot market for corporate shares reassures the non-speculative investor that he can expect to encounter demand for his shares whenever he wants to sell them and thus disinvest. In the same way as the speculation-induced increase in spot-market trade in corporate shares provides insurance for those who want to be free to decide on the time-period and duration of their investment and disinvestment in corporate shares, because liquidity is always good in the stock market, the market for futures, options and structured products is a possibility of insuring oneself against price fluctuations through the purchase of futures, options or structured products on the basis of the liquidity in this market. This insurance can also be effectuated on an individual basis without an organized market, but is made more difficult, without an organized market, by the necessity of finding a contract partner and by the lesser liquidity of the supply.

In the market for futures, options and structured products, the division of labor between the speculating market participants and those who want to limit their risk, or practice hedging, comes about because some people must speculate so that others can calculate with assured, or even certain, future prices. In the spot market for corporate shares, the effect of speculation is not to protect future prices but to ensure that the time periods of investment in shares will be transformable in future, by virtue of the fact that they can be sold or bought at any time – if not at the same price – on the stock exchange.

From this consideration it becomes apparent that speculation supports liquidity in the market. The value creation effectuated by speculation is thus derivative. At the same time, it is clear that there can be an excess of speculation, namely when more speculation is taking place than is necessary to protect liquidity, and when speculation inflames rather than dampens the volatility of asset values.

Is there unnecessary speculation in the derivatives market? Speculation is essentially a wager on future price changes. Speculation in derivatives is a wager to the power of two. Not only is it a wager on the future, on future values of a given factor; it is also a wager about the effect that a nominated value of that factor will have on the future value of another factor at a nominated future point in time. It is evident that the winnings from the wager, if the wager is successful, are higher for the derivative wager than for the simple wager on the future value of shares or commodities. The prerequisite for a wager is to find someone who will place a counter-wager. Somebody who wants the protection of an interest-rate swap because he expects future interest-rate rises must find another party for the swap who will place the counter-wager that interest rates will fall. Since both parties have opposite but complementary future expectations, nothing stands in the way of their wager. In the case of derivatives, unlike other wagers, part of the stake is paid as a fee.

Anyone can use a wager to hedge against anything with anyone, if they both have opposing but complementary expectations about the future. The case is theoretically possible that half of the entire gross national income is staked by one half of the population on Ax, where $x = 1 \ldots n$, and by the other half of the population on not-Ax, $x = 1 \ldots n$. The macroeconomic value-added effect of this total wager is, however, zero because macroeconomically it is a zero sum game. Moreover, since wagering costs must also be reckoned – i.e. the commissions and fees charged in the financial markets – the total benefit gained, despite the income generated in wagering fees, is actually negative because productive activities are suppressed.

The example is naturally fictitious because no economy can be preoccupied with wagering to the exclusion of all else. The question that arises, however, is what scale of wagering an economy can really afford, even if wagering is useful for hedging against price fluctuations? In a free economy, nobody is in a position to stipulate what share of gross national income this should be. But it is the task of financial market actors to ask the question. Is the derivatives market a place of real value-creation for hedging purposes, or just a vast betting shop? What about the opportunity costs of derivatives speculation? Could time and intellectual effort have been deployed more productively than in speculation?

The market for derivatives has positively exploded in the last decade. The statistics on derivatives are evidence of the scale of these wagers:

According to a very liberal estimate, the volumes of derivatives contracts in the world amount to 1,600 trillion (= 1,600 million million or 1.6 million billion) US dollars.[15]

In 2004, the world's largest economy, the United States of America, recorded gross national income (GNI) of US\$12,969.56 billion; Germany's GNI for 2005 was US\$2,852.33 billion (source: World Bank, by the Atlas method). If we projected this volume of derivatives onto the USA alone, it would mean total wagers of US\$123.36 billion for every billion dollars of American GNI and a wager of US\$123 on every dollar of income. If we assume a notional average American income of US\$24,000 per year, then wagers amounting to US\$2,952,000 would be riding on the average annual income of every American. Luttermann estimates that derivatives to the value of 600 trillion dollars exist in the global market.[16] According to the considerably more conservative estimates of the International Swaps and Derivatives Association (ISDA), the total volume of issued derivatives contracts in 2007 rose from 327.4 to 454.5 trillion dollars.[17] Interest-rate derivatives such as interest-rate swaps accounted for the largest volume of contracts by far. According to the ISDA, the issued volume of interest-rate derivatives rose in 2007 from 285.7 to 382.3 trillion dollars.

If the ISDA-estimated volume is projected by the same procedure as the more liberal estimate, there are still wagers amounting to approx. US\$838,552 riding on the

---

[15]STEFFEN BOGS: "Warten auf Domino. Derivate sind der Renner im globalen Casino. Gehandelte Volumina werden auf 1600 Billionen US-Dollar geschätzt. Ein kräftiger Schubs könnte genügen" [Waiting for Domino. Everyone is piling into derivatives in the global casino. Volumes are estimated at 1600 trillion US dollars. One big push might be all that it takes], *Junge Welt*, 12 July 2007, p. 9. Online at: http://www.neo-liberalismus.de/forum/messages/5110.html

[16]According to CLAUS LUTTERMANN: "Der Wahrheitsstandard einer Weltfinanzordnung" [The standard of truth for a global financial system], *Frankfurter Allgemeine Zeitung*, 10 November 2008, No. 263, p. 20.

[17]"Finanzmärkte: Derivatemarkt wächst stark," *FAZNET*, 16 April 2008, http://www.faz.net/s/RubF3CE08B362D244869BE7984590CB6AC1/Doc~ E01C5CE6CC87149F8BE61DF204CD07505~ATpl~Ecommon~Scontent.html

average annual income of every American. Of course, these wagers are not placed in the USA alone. Projection onto the world population is difficult. Nevertheless, the volumes of derivatives wagers are staggering, and so are the volumes of wagering costs.

It is also evident that the wagering volume in derivatives far exceeds the volume of derivatives necessary to meet hedging needs, and serves the purpose of sheer speculation. There is a strong suspicion that banks are entering into too many wagers in the form of options or structured products. One wager may be rational, but hundreds of wagers are not. A thousand-fold wager on the same event is not an effective means of hedging. The only need it meets is the need of market players to place wagers. Wagering on this scale is comparable to tax-planning. When individuals in a fiscal state devote more time to tax-avoidance than to productive activities, there is a problem: what is rational for the individual's private economy is not rational for the economy as a whole. As in the case of the derivatives wagers, the amount of energy and effort used for tax-avoidance would be better deployed to productive uses.

Chapter 7
Interdependences Between the Financial Markets for Credit, Capital, and Derivatives, and the Challenges the Financial Markets Pose for Ethics

Universal banks intermediate between savings and investments within their own organizations, whereas in the capital market, investors find their own investment opportunities in the market for corporate shares.

A Capital Market Within Banks in Bank-Controlled Industries: The Corporatist Model

If the banks invest in industries on their own account, banks assume the investment risk and finance the investment fully or partly with their deposit customers' deposits. They decide on their customers' behalf where to invest their deposits and expose them to risk. Banks form an internal capital market, comparable to the internal labor market in any large industrial corporation.[1]

The advantage of the internalization of the capital market in banks might be that banks are highly professional investors and hence sometimes in a better position to manage investments than the amateur stock-exchange speculator. On the other hand, a shift of the external capital market into the bank's internal capital market turns banks into very powerful institutions. If sizeable parts of the capital market are brought inside the internal capital market of the banks, it increases the potential for concerted action between banks and industry. Comparisons between systems in which the internal capital market of the banks plays a greater role than the external capital market of the stock exchange show that in these economic systems, the banks wield greater control over industry and are more powerful than in economic systems with a strong stock-exchange-based capital market. But the process of consultation and concerted action between banks and industry can also produce high rates of growth in times of capital scarcity, as demonstrated by the historical examples of the

---

[1]For the theory of the internal market in firms, cf. O. E. WILLIAMSON: "Firms and Markets", in: S. WEINTRAUB (ed.): *Modern Economic Thought*, Philadelphia (University of Pennsylvania Press) 1977, and O. E. WILLIAMSON: "The Modern Corporation: Origins, Evolution, Attributes", *Journal of Economic Literature*, 19 (1981), pp. 1537–1570.

German and Japanese economies after the Second World War. These two economies were typically defined by close relationships between the banks and industry.[2]

Greater emphasis on the internal capital market of the banks, with concomitant state support for the financing of industrial development as part of the state's remit for industrial policy, describes the basic features of the corporatist model of banking and industrialization that was characteristic of the German and Japanese approach from 1870 until the Second World War. Emphasis on the external capital market of freely acting investors and of firms seeking stock-exchange listing is the hallmark not just of the American and British but also of the Swiss approach of a more conspicuously market-oriented society with a political system founded on democratic competition.

The stock exchange is an individualistic, democratic institution which intermediates between investors and capital-seeking companies without the intervention of banks or governments. The internal market of the banks, in contrast, corresponds to a corporatist model of society. The stock exchange can form a counterbalance to the power wielded by banks and the state.[3] In this regard, the appropriate division of labor between the credit market and the capital market is comparable to the appropriate dissemination of economic power, and hence, to the system of the constitutional separation of powers.

Corporatist economic systems in nations with strong banks and weak stock exchanges face the problem that banks in such systems can influence share prices by the power of their demand for shares and by supplying finance for the purchase of shares to individuals. But they can also influence the share price by manipulating the demand of third parties for shares by adjusting the interest rates applicable to leveraged share purchases.[4] Nevertheless, there is no ignoring the fact that amateur speculation on the stock exchange, however democratic, can cause serious stock market crises.[5]

In a universal banking system like Germany's, banks are not just intermediaries within their internal capital market. They also operate in the external capital market as investors, advisers, and supervisory board members. In their function as principal players in the credit and the capital market, banks must conduct their business with

---

[2]Cf. DAVID WILLIAMS: *Japan: Beyond the End of History*, London, New York (Routledge) 1994 (= The Nissan Institute/Routledge Japanese Studies Series), pp. 73ff.

[3]NELL-BREUNING (1928, p. 9) and (1928a, p. 52), writing in the 1920s during the Weimar Republic, emphasized the democratic character and the checking and balancing function of the stock exchange.

[4]Cf. NELL-BREUNING (1928a, p. 53), and MAX WEBER: *Die Börse, II. Der Börsenverkehr* [The stock exchange], Göttingen (Vandenhoeck & Ruprecht) 1896 (= Göttinger Arbeiterbibliothek Vol. 2, No. 2/3, S. 49–80), p. 78. Weber emphasizes above all – and this in 1896 – that banks have the means to manipulate futures prices by altering the interest rate for loans intended for the purchase of futures with leveraged financing.

[5]Both NELL-BREUNING (1928, p. 105) and WEBER (1896, Vol. 2, p. 72), point out that stock market crises have been induced not just by high finance but equally often by the activities of amateur speculators.

diligence, bearing in mind the many purposes they have to serve.[6] Their professional ethics should remind the banks of the advantages of the division of labor between banks and industrial firms, and keep them from the temptation to become industrialists or even super-industrialists themselves.[7] Meanwhile, the equivalent caveat applies to industrial firms. They, too, must resist the temptation to take up banking in place of, or as a complement to, their industrial activities. They must withstand the temptation to become "super-financiers", as the case of Porsche and other firms, which acted more and more like financial speculators in the years 2005–2009, showed.

A number of bankruptcies or heavy losses in German industry in recent years were induced by financial or speculative operations by industrial firms, which embarked on finance operations that lay outside their proper remit and competence as industrial producers. Heavy losses caused by finance operations occurred in the automobile, electrical, and metal industries.

The Information and Influence Asymmetry Between Banks and Manufacturing Firms: Banks as Monitors of Their Debtors' Firms

Banks have a tendency – naturally in their own interests – to warn industrial firms against encroaching on the role of banks and acting as banks or finance houses. They warn them not to open up internal financial markets within their own corporate structures. There is no ethical rule that prohibits overstepping the boundaries of the division of labor and one's own profession. There is, however, an ethical rule to be very cautious when overreaching the limits of one's own profession, and a recommendation implied by this rule that it is preferable not to do so.

Banks must monitor the conduct of industrial firms in order to prevent the destruction of capital in the credit market. This surveillance function confers on them a legitimate power of control, which is necessary because the avoidance of capital destruction resulting from distressed loans is the banks' central remit. In order to be able to exercise this power ethically, as for any form of conferred power,

---

[6]Major banks that are market leaders in the credit market, the capital market and the market for corporate control can become insiders from the mere fact of a position as a supervisory board member and as a firm's principal lender. J. DENNERT: "Insider Trading", Kyklos, 44 (1991), No. 2, p. 184 n. 3, recognizes the danger of another particular type of insider trading: "Due to the close links to the firms, the main creditor will in general obtain new firm-specific information earlier than the other creditors. Premature cancellation of credit has the same effects on the other creditors as insider trading on stock markets on the other shareholders." Equating the two forms of insider trading, as a creditor and as an investor in shares, is problematic but sets a challenge for future research. On this problem, cf. also GÜNTER FRANKE: "Inside Information in Bank Lending and the European Insider Directive," in: KLAUS HOPT, E. WYMEERSCH (eds.): European Insider Dealing, London (Butterworth) 1991, pp. 273–286.

[7]Cf. W. RÖLLER: "Zum Selbstverständnis der Banken in einer offenen Gesellschaft" [The self-conception of banks in an open society], in: A.-F. JACOB: Bankenmacht und Ethik, Stuttgart (Poeschel) 1990, p. 9.

it is necessary for those on whom power is conferred to have an intention to behave ethically, i.e. to possess the right intention, *intentio recta*, as well as the foresight to do justice to the material nature of their business and justice also to those who are affected by their decision-making power. Managing directors, especially of banks, must have regard to all aspects of their decision-making situation in its entirety. The requirements of ethics and foresight are even higher for banks than for other industrial firms, because one single bank must monitor several industrial firms at the same time, whereas an industrial firm does not have to monitor the actions of several banks, and nor can it inspect their business policy.

Owing to the bank's nature as the institution that gathers savings and intermediates between savings and investments, it engages with many industrial firms and has access to detailed information about their activity. However, its customer, the industrial firm, has no right to be kept informed about its bank's internal operations, let alone any right to be kept informed about the internal activities of *many* banks. One possible way of overcoming this asymmetry between banking firms and industrial firms might be for the industries to elect representatives so that each industry was represented with a seat on the supervisory boards of the major banks. Industry representatives on the supervisory boards of the banks would give industries a means of monitoring the conduct of the banks they work with. Their presence would convey to the industries concerned a sense that while the banks are monitoring them, they in turn can monitor how their banks do business.

The asymmetry between banks and industrial firms is unavoidable, yet at the same time it is the basis of the complaints commonly voiced by industrial firms about banks. In the end, banks can only deal appropriately with this very sensitive asymmetry by treating their industrial customers fairly and staying true to the material function of the credit market, by making financial resources available for rational investments in order to support capital creation and prevent capital destruction.

The Intangibility of the Merchandise Traded in Financial Markets as an Ethical Problem

The financial markets pose a substantial ethical challenge for market participants, particularly for financial intermediaries like bankers and stockbrokers. This challenge is caused by three characteristic features of these markets: (1) by the intangible, abstract, impersonal character, and the substitutability or fungibility of the traded objects, namely financial instruments and securities; (2) by the centrality of the fiduciary relationship to banking and brokerage; (3) by the inscrutable character of the finance sector, which makes the general public fearful of falling victim to conspiracies in the financial markets.

On the first point, personal control between the supplier and the consumer and a judgment about the quality of the delivered goods is much more difficult in financial markets than in markets with tangible and physically palpable material products, because what is traded is money: the most fungible, abstract and impersonal of goods. The financial institutions and markets are therefore beset with a dual challenge: as suppliers, they must fight the temptation to be beguiled by the inimitable character and the abstract and impalpable quality of their business, and they must resist the temptation to succumb to fictionalization and debordering of their own business. Banks and finance brokers are ethically bound to ensure that the services they offer are not merely fictive, or comprised of fictive elements. Whenever monetary values are determined, any degree of discretionary judgment harbors the risk that fictive values may come into play. Financial instruments and financial services can become fictive. Objectivity must therefore be the basic mindset of all those who work in the financial markets.

On the second point, banks and finance brokers act as trustees to their deposit and investment customers Trust is ethically relevant because, by its very nature, it cannot be replaced entirely by control. It contains an irreducible element of self-commitment on the part of the individual assigned as trustee. Self-commitment is the ethical relationship with oneself. Banks and finance brokers are therefore subject, in a special way, to the demands of an ethics of the fiduciary relationship.

On the third point, the goods traded in the capital and credit market are not palpable material goods but financial securities and financial rights deriving from them. The impalpable and "immaterial" nature of financial instruments and securities rules out simple empirical control of the quality of the traded goods. Hence, there is a constant risk that the public will feel at the mercy of the power of the banks and financial institutions because it is difficult to check their "products" even by taking a close look. This often sparks irrational fears about the secret power of the banks, or even "conspiracy theories" about the conduct of big banks and high finance. Transparency is one of the main remedies to combat these fears. The other remedy is to establish and then comply with a materially appropriate ethical code of conduct for financial services.

The financial markets call for huge resources of ethical motivation and ethics-driven coordination. On the other hand, the abstract and impersonal character of this industry hardly makes it easy to construct a personal and collective system of ethics, and does not therefore reinforce ethical conduct by means of face-to-face control between supplier and demander. Banks and professional financial intermediaries must therefore pay special attention to making the ethical rules of conduct known to their staff, and to ensuring that they comply.

Various applications of game theory to theories of social coordination[8] and ethical economy[9] have shown how ethics, as a means of coordinating human actions, falls foul of prisoner's-dilemma-type situations. These are defined as situations where it is in the shared interests of all members of the group if everyone complies with the ethical and legal rules, but where each group member has an incentive to break the rules for individual gain. Elaborations of this theory show that our willingness to comply with rules or to break them is dependent on our expectations

[8]Cf. AMARTYA SEN: "Isolation, Assurance, and the Social Rate of Discount", *Quarterly Journal of Economics,* 81 (1967), pp. 112–124.
[9]Cf. KOSLOWSKI (2001), pp. 17–37.

about what other people will do. If an individual can be certain that others will obey the rules, he or she will do the same. However, when there is no assurance that others will obey the rules, the individual will also be tempted to break them.

This positive theory of ethical economy can be applied to the problem of insider trading, and can analyze it as an empirical, non-normative problem of ethics-driven social coordination. Voluntary ethical obedience to the rule on refraining from insider trading will depend on expectations about the average conduct of other finance brokers and investors. If the individual stockbroker assumes that most other stockbrokers are practicing insider trading, he will have very few incentives to follow the ethical rule not to engage in the practice. Professional ethics, generally accepted and approved rules and customary codes of conduct in a profession will give the individual some assurance that others also obey the rules.

Nevertheless, even professional ethics and professional rules and standards cannot guarantee this absolutely. Professional ethics and professional associations are in a position to improve the standard of rule compliance, but cannot guarantee it. In situations where little control can be exercised in person and abstract contractual relationships predominate, coordination by means of ethical rules can break down and must then be supplemented with legal rules.

In the case of insider trading, this took place in the USA back in the 1930s. In Germany, by contrast, stock-exchange participants believed until well into the 1990s that the insider trading problem could be solved by the professional ethics of the stock exchange along with voluntary restraint on the part of its participants. Only after a series of insider trading cases in Germany, and only under duress from the European Community, the German Bundestag passed the Second Financial Market Promotion Act, which included a ban on insider trading.

The reason for this delay can partly be attributed to the lesser role that the capital market traditionally played in Germany. The American and the British stock exchanges fulfill the central task of the capital market for the pension funds, which operate on the stock exchange as probably the most important institutional investors. Pension provision in Germany is organized in a completely different way. The state organizes the social insurance system itself as a pay-as-you-go system and collects the funding for old-age pensions through social insurance contributions that are adjusted to the employee's income, i.e. by means of mandatory but individually adapted charges which are levied like a tax from members of the workforce and the firms that employ them. This means that in Germany, the vast sums of money earmarked for old-age pensions do not reach the capital market, in contrast to Great Britain and the United States, for instance, where the pension funds are the main investors on the stock exchange. The capital market is thus of the utmost importance, not just for the private investor but also for the institutional investor acting as a pension fund or on behalf of it.[10]

---

[10]RALF DAHRENDORF: "Europäisches Tagebuch (XII)" [European diary XII], *Merkur*, 48 No. 7 (1994), p. 639, rightly emphasizes the differences between Germany and Great Britain in the institutional organization of pension provision.

It is obvious that concern about insider trading must be greater in countries where the stock exchange plays a more important role in the coordination of investments, and where investments in shares are used to finance retirement pensions. Germany's delay in passing legislation against insider trading is explained, in part, by the fact that German retirement provision is not dependent upon share dividends. The case of the legislation against insider trading shows the complementary character of ethics and the law. Economic ethics cannot replace legislation on business law, but ethics and law complement one another.

Chapter 8
The "Banking Secret", the Right to Privacy, and the Banks' Duty to Confidentiality

Banks are obliged to maintain confidentiality about their business relationships with customers and about their customers' accounts. They must preserve banking secrecy or the "banking secret" (*Bankgeheimnis*) as it is called in German. First and foremost, the "banking secret" is just a subtype of the non-disclosure of facts communicated under confidentiality, and of the general class of professional and business secrets that are equally familiar from the medical profession, for instance, or from brokerage activities in the case of insider knowledge discussed earlier. Banking secrecy is the banking industry's own brand of professional confidentiality and trade secrecy. Any knowledge the bank comes by in the course of the business relationship must not be used for insider gain, a principle that follows from the fiduciary duty; nor must it be passed to others or publicly disclosed.

The Protection of Facts Communicated Under Confidentiality

Banking secrecy comprises the duty of confidentiality toward the customer and the bank's right to refuse information to third parties, including a country's tax authorities, about its customers.[1] It exists in most countries. It derives from civil contract law and is a product of contractual freedom. It does not derive directly from the constitutional principle of human dignity since it is not person-related but property-related,[2] although it belongs to the rights of personality that merit legal protection to prevent infringement of personal rights or invasion of the private sphere.[3] Since

---

[1] Cf. DIETER CAHL, JOACHIM KLOS: *Bankgeheimnis und Quellensteuer im Vergleich internationaler Finanzmärkte* [Banking secrecy and witholding tax, comparing international finance markets], Herne/Berlin (Neue Wirtschaftsbriefe) 1993, p. 5.

[2] On the other hand, it cannot be inferred from the association of banking secrecy with personal property and assets that it has no constitutional relevance to the protection of rights of personality, as CAHL and KLOS (1993), pp. 5ff. assume. The objects surrounding the person are relevant to personality.

[3] Cf. F. BEUTTER: "Geheimnischarakter des Geldes und ethische Grundlagen der Geheimhaltungspflicht", *Acta Monetaria*, 2 (1978), p. 15 (own trans.): "In the measure in which money, e.g. as remuneration for work done, has a close relation with the human person,

the protection of a person's rights of personality is a high constitutional priority, and banking secrecy plays a part in protecting those personality rights that reside in the things a person owns, it must also be accorded a value for contributing to the protection of such rights.

Banking secrecy has force in civil law, based on the agreement between the bank and the customer to preserve the customer's trust and confidentiality. However, it only has force in civil law as long as the bank in question is not obliged to disclose information by laws of higher precedence. This generally occurs when prosecuting authorities in a criminal trial demand information from the banks about the accused. In this case, penal law trumps civil law. Nowadays, in view of the growing importance attached to the taxation of financial assets, the banks' duty of disclosure in tax investigations and tax prosecutions is becoming the main problem in relation to the duty of secrecy and the limitations on banking secrecy.

Conflicts are flaring up, for instance, between the legal views of the German tax authorities and the civil-law provisions on banking secrecy in Germany's neighboring countries, including Switzerland, Austria, Luxembourg and Liechtenstein. It is impossible to ignore the fact that, in the main, banking secrecy is most extensive in these countries that share a border with Germany. Luxembourg's "tight-lipped" approach to banking secrecy surpasses even Switzerland's. According to the former German Minister of Finance, Peer Steinbrück, who attempted to put Switzerland under considerable pressure in early 2009, and German finance officials, the explanation for the stronger emphasis on banking secrecy in these countries can only be the aim of diverting international finance flows to their own countries.[4] Whether this view of things is accurate needs to be examined.

Banking Secrecy, the Investigation of Tax Avoidance, Tax Evasion, Money Laundering, and the Discussion Around the Swiss "Banking Secret"

It is well known that banking secrecy in Switzerland is protected more insistently and more extensively than in other industrialized countries. Therefore it is interesting to discuss the problem of the "banking secret" with reference to the example of Switzerland. The conditions under which Swiss banking secrecy can be breached are very restrictive. Banking secrecy cannot be penetrated by tax law. This is the critical difference from the USA and Germany: Switzerland adheres to the tenet that neither the interest of the revenue authorities in probing the affairs of Swiss citizens nor the interest of foreign fiscal authorities in information about their citizens' accounts in Swiss banks can override banking secrecy. In American law, banking secrecy enjoys

---

money participates in that personal sphere of legal protection. The norm governing the confidentiality of banking relationships is therefore: 'It is a fundamental ethical obligation to leave a person undisturbed in his private and intimate sphere [. . .] Secrets should be kept.' " (Ibid., p. 17).

[4]Cf. CAHL and KLOS (1993), p. 32.

no more than vestiges of protection. It is particularly alarming that the US Internal Revenue Service can penetrate banking secrecy in other countries to a degree that would once have been unacceptable between sovereign nations and, indeed, viewed as interference in the internal affairs of another country. German banks yield in obedience to the USA on this issue, with a notable haste that can only be explained by the ever-present threat of an American boycott of the banks' business.

The dissent between the Swiss law on banking secrecy, on the one hand, and German and American law, on the other, is rooted in the fact that Switzerland prioritizes the customer's interest in secrecy over the fiscal interest of the tax authorities, whereas in Germany the fiscal interest is prioritized over the customer's interest in secrecy. However, the discrepancy in legal views between Switzerland and other countries – it is important to emphasize – vanishes when it comes to the crucial matter of whether banking secrecy takes pre-eminence over the interest of penal prosecution in criminal trials. Even Swiss banking secrecy only applies up to the point that no prosecutable offense has been detected and no criminal prosecution is necessary.

It is best to start by mentioning the developments that make banking secrecy a problem deserving of analysis in terms of economic ethics and business law.[5] In the first place, the internationalization of the economy is a phenomenon that undoubtedly makes it necessary to internationalize the investigation of tax evasion. If profits are increasingly earned and hoarded abroad but losses from abroad are offset in the domestic economy, the domestic tax authorities must be guaranteed a certain right of access to the international operations of the domestic firms. This interest in internationalization and harmonization of tax laws and investigation of tax evasion is valid in all countries, because all countries – EU Member States as well as Switzerland – are affected by the internationalization of the economy. The European Union, the Council of Europe, the OECD and the United Nations have therefore called for international tax evasion to be combated.

The second development that makes banking secrecy a problem can be seen in the increase in dirty money in the world, and the consequent attempts to turn dirty money into clean money by means of money laundering. As far back as 1992, for instance, the annual turnover in the global drug trade had risen to DM 800 billion (approx. EUR 400 billion). The annual profits of crime in the heroin trade alone were estimated at DM 1.5 billion (approx. EUR 750 million).[6] The International Monetary Fund (IMF) estimates that the money laundered worldwide amounts to 2–5% of the global economy.

Money laundering is the exchange or transfer of assets, in the knowledge that these originate from criminal activity, for the purpose of masking their origin, and with the intention that the perpetrators will escape the legal consequences of their crime.[7]

---

[5] On Swiss banking secrecy, cf. also PETER, RUH, HÖHN (1981), Vols. I and II.
[6] CAHL and KLOS (1993), p. 72.
[7] Ibid., p. 76.

As long as money laundering was not a criminal offense, it could not be used to justify breaching banking secrecy. But all the time that banking secrecy was also applicable to huge sums of cash originating from the drug trade, which were laundered by transferring them through bank accounts, it was difficult to produce evidence of dirty money. In order to be able to override banking secrecy in the case of money laundering, it was necessary to criminalize money laundering, since banking secrecy could only be overridden in the case of criminal offenses. Legislation has now caught up with this requirement, which is unavoidable from the viewpoint of both business law and economic ethics, because it was incomprehensible that drug dealing should be criminalized but laundering of the financial proceeds should not. That said, questions are constantly raised as to which specific disclosure and verification duties the banks have to fulfill.

Switzerland was one of the first countries to introduce provisions against "money laundering".[8] Since 1990, the Swiss Penal Code has included a crime of money laundering (*Geldwäscherei*) according to Art. 305bis. In the case of cash transactions over CHF 25,000, the customer's identity must be established. In addition, screening systems have been refined and put in place to alert the banks to funds from unexplained sources, which enable them to detect dirty money. Because Switzerland has incorporated numerous penal provisions against money laundering into Swiss law, including the partial waiving of banking secrecy in the cases of criminal prosecution, some critics now claim that Swiss banking secrecy is as riddled with holes as a Swiss cheese. Detailed consideration of the situation lends no credence to this view.

For historically legitimate reasons, Switzerland stands resolutely by its banking secrecy. There is no ignoring the fact that Swiss banking secrecy prevented the Nazis from accessing Jewish accounts in Switzerland. Naturally, in perpetuating this tradition, Switzerland is also pursuing its own self-interest. With its closely co-located banking centers of Zurich, Geneva and Basel, ultimately it is the third-largest banking center in the world after New York and London, even ahead of Paris and Frankfurt. In foreign currencies alone, at the end of the 1990s over 500 billion Swiss francs were said to be deposited in Switzerland,[9] while according to another source, the Swiss banks were sitting on assets of around 3,000 billion Swiss francs.[10]

If we look more precisely at the conditions and situations in which Swiss banking secrecy can be overridden, it is apparent that these conditions are very restrictive. The first condition is that, in civil law, a mortality creates a legitimate duty of disclosure to the heirs. This duty of disclosure only extends to information about the testator's assets at the time of death, however, not to any prior account movements

---

[8]On the problem of money laundering, cf. also NIKLAUS SCHMID: "Insiderdelikte und Geldwäscherei – neuere und künftige Aspekte aus der Sicht der Banken", in: W. WIEGAND (ed.): *Aktuelle Probleme im Bankrecht, Berner Tage für die juristische Praxis* 1993, Bern (Stämpfli) 1994, pp. 189–215.

[9]Cf. CAHL and KLOS (1993), p. 89f.

[10]B. BRENNER: "Das Bankgeheimnis – abschaffen oder stärken?" [Banking secrecy – abolish or strengthen?], *Neue Zürcher Zeitung*, No. 242 (18/19 October 1997), p. 9.

and developments. Switzerland does not provide mutual judicial assistance in the field of debt enforcement and bankruptcy law.

It becomes apparent, secondly, that banking secrecy is not penetrated by tax law either. This is the critical difference from the USA and Germany; Switzerland adheres to the tenet that the revenue office's interest in probing the affairs of its citizens, and of course the interest of foreign fiscal authorities in obtaining information about their citizens' accounts in Swiss banks, do not override banking secrecy.

Thirdly, it is very much the case that criminal law overrides banking secrecy – if not to the same extent as in the USA and Germany. Straightforward tax evasion, either by Swiss citizens or by foreign account-holders, is not a legitimate ground for overriding banking secrecy. Only the persistent evasion of large amounts of tax gives Switzerland's special tax control organs (*Besondere Steuerkontrollorgane*, Besko) legitimate rights to pursue direct taxes of the Swiss Confederation.[11] Swiss banks are neither compelled nor allowed to pass information to foreign revenue offices except in cases of serious criminal proceedings. But even for Swiss citizens, the criminal law provides justification for overriding banking secrecy in cases of tax or customs fraud. This offense, defined by the falsification of documentation, is a criminal offense and overrides banking secrecy. To meet the criteria of tax or customs fraud, grave deception must have taken place, involving deliberate falsification of documents and such like.

From the viewpoint of economic ethics, the question posed is whether the Swiss regulations coincide with the principle of material appropriateness and the idea of justice. Critics of Swiss banking secrecy frequently claim that Switzerland's banking secrecy aids and abets tax evasion, and that the country is guilty of complicity in particularly serious cases of tax evasion and exploitative behavior, such as that of the former President Mobutu of Zaire. The question is whether it is defensible in terms of economic ethics for a country to accept that its own more extensive banking secrecy laws make it easier for the foreign investor to evade tax in their own country, since their revenue offices are denied access to information about the accounts they hold in Switzerland.

The question this raises is whether Switzerland is condoning the use of Swiss bank accounts by foreign citizens for tax evasion purposes, or whether it is merely declaring that tax investigations launched by other countries are beyond the scope of its powers. The first thing to say is that it would certainly look like condonement if Switzerland were to treat tax investigations launched against foreigners differently than those targeting Swiss residents. Analysis of Swiss law reveals, however, that the Swiss revenue authorities cannot access the Swiss bank accounts of Swiss citizens either, or at least, access is severely curtailed in comparison to Germany and the United States, so that banking secrecy and the increased difficulty of tax investigations apply even-handedly to Swiss residents and foreigners. We must therefore say that Swiss institutions do not encourage or promote tax evasion by foreigners living abroad, but uphold equal treatment for Swiss and foreign residents alike.

---

[11]CAHL and KLOS (1993), p. 94.

A further question is whether the Swiss authorities have any ethical duty to support tax investigations from abroad, when these are based on no more than suspicious facts or even dragnet investigations. In this case, restraint appears to be advisable. For one thing, Switzerland's right to use banking secrecy in order to attract international capital must be recognized. If capital is swayed by stricter banking secrecy to deposit money in Switzerland, Switzerland cannot be expected suddenly to minimize or even give up this comparative advantage by assisting tax investigations from abroad. The Swiss institutions can rightly argue that they are not responsible for the perhaps excessive tax rates of neighboring countries, and more-over, that a country has no ethical duty to enforce the collection of excessive taxes imposed by neighboring countries, or to support the recovery of such taxes.

Progressive income tax is not a natural right that every country has to respect and implement. Tax avoidance in the context of unduly high progressive tax rates does not contravene international private law, and need not be penalized by every country.

For Germany, the disparity between German tax rates and those of neighboring countries is beneficial at least to the extent that it prevents the "hungry" German revenue authority from turning the tax screw any tighter. Nevertheless, it has unfortunate consequences for distributive policy, since it enables only the wealthy classes in Germany to reduce their tax burden by moving their capital, a form of anti-tax protest that is not an option for the average person. This can undoubtedly be seen as the Achilles heel of Swiss banking secrecy, and concerns are raised repeatedly by critics based in Switzerland.

As a fundamental principle in a globalized economy, smaller countries can gain an advantage if they introduce lower domestic tax rates, thereby attracting foreign capital from heavily populated neighboring countries with high tax rates – especially countries whose citizens speak the same language. The loss of domestic tax revenue resulting from the lower tax rates can be more than balanced out by the capital inflows they attract, and the resulting additional tax payments or interest earnings from the accounts held in the banks. In the long term, this comparative advantage of small countries can undermine the tax basis of large countries to such an extent that they are forced to cut their tax rates substantially. This trend explains why advocates of the harmonization of tax rates among EU Member States are becoming increasingly vocal. The outcry is loudest in Germany, where high tax rates are coming under pressure from several smaller German-speaking neighboring countries simultaneously.

Tax harmonization within Europe is probably inevitable. But it is pointless to believe this will be an upward harmonization, toward higher average tax rates. Any harmonization will be downward, toward lower tax rates, and will probably herald the end of the fiscal state in Europe. The pressure exerted by Switzerland on the tax rates of EU Member States cannot be criticized, because even if Switzerland were to raise its tax rates and water down its banking secrecy, pressure would still come from countries like Austria, Liechtenstein and Luxembourg. Initiatives by the German government, toward the end of 2002, to grant an amnesty for the retrospective reporting of investment income parked abroad and not declared for tax purposes, point to a development in the direction of lower tax rates, which is, however, impeded by the immense increase in government borrowing due to the state sureties needed by banks as well as economic stimulus packages in the aftermath of the crisis in the financial markets.

The question of whether Swiss banking secrecy not only assists tax avoidance but also connives with tax evasion takes on an entirely different nature when the issue is not just a matter of different tax rates but the hoarding of illegally acquired, misappropriated or stolen property, or an instance of tax evasion that is already on official record as part of criminal proceedings in another country. If Switzerland allowed banking secrecy to conceal the movement of such assets into Switzerland, it would incriminate itself in receiving stolen property. Swiss law therefore waives banking secrecy if criminal proceedings are in hand and if the foreign revenue authority can prove that one of its citizens who holds an account in Switzerland has committed a serious customs or tax fraud. In such cases, Switzerland does not insist on banking secrecy to the detriment of the international prosecution interest. So it is only logical that in cases of tax fraud, Switzerland provides mutual administrative and judicial assistance to foreign states.[12]

Swiss banking secrecy succeeds in striking a balance between the interest of banking secrecy and that of allaying the suspicion of helping foreign account-holders to evade taxation.

This is evident from the fact that, firstly, the Swiss banks withhold the same data from their own fiscal authorities that they refuse to supply to foreign revenue authorities. The Swiss authorities will not pass any bank data to a foreign revenue authority that the banks are entitled to withhold from the Swiss revenue authority.

Secondly, because of its neutrality, Switzerland does not cooperate in judicial assistance in the investigation of offenses which it views as matters of political, military or foreign-exchange law. There appears to be no objection in economic ethics to this insistence on neutrality, even for offenses in tax law which arise from political, military, or foreign-exchange offenses.

Thirdly, Switzerland does not provide mutual judicial assistance if the object of the foreign proceedings is an act that breaches foreign tax, customs or currency regulations or contravenes foreign trade or economic-policy provisions. Here, it is less than clear whether the imperative of Swiss political neutrality really requires a neutral stance toward all tax-law provisions of foreign countries. On the other hand, nor is there any justification for waiving the imperative of neutrality on the grounds of foreign tax, customs or currency regulations, since neither human dignity nor overarching personality rights are affected.

The neutrality on questions of foreign tax, customs and currency law is counterbalanced by Switzerland's clear self-commitment to cooperate in mutual judicial assistance in cases where the foreigner's tax fraud represents an action that would fit the same description under Swiss law. Nevertheless, in cases of tax fraud,

---

[12] Ibid., p. 102.

Switzerland only provides "minor judicial assistance", i.e. it supplies documents from Switzerland to the foreign authorities, but does not enforce a foreign claim in Switzerland by, for instance, confiscating the foreigner's assets and accounts in Switzerland.[13]

In terms of economic ethics, the balance struck by Switzerland between neutrality toward the interests of foreign revenue authorities in recovering taxes and its clear support for foreign prosecution authorities in cases of unequivocal criminal offenses, appears to be defensible. There is little basis for imputing to a sovereign state any ethical duty to support another country's revenue authority.[14]

A valid question, however, is whether Switzerland's neutrality, and thus the strict validity of banking secrecy, can be upheld in the long term in the face of international tax, customs or currency regulations. If the Swiss economy also becomes more internationally integrated, and if the Swiss authorities themselves develop an interest in enforcing their legal claims on the assets of Swiss citizens abroad in the course of tax proceedings, they will not be able to avoid wider-ranging international cooperation on issues of tax investigation and recovery. Obviously the issue here is a weighing of conflicting interests, between Switzerland's interest in upholding banking secrecy and its interest in participating in international cooperation in the field of tax investigation.

How this weighing of interests will develop is not a question of economic ethics but one of Swiss *raison d'état*. As long as the benefits of neutrality on economic policy and tax law outweigh their costs, Switzerland – we may venture to predict – will adhere to them, and put up with any disadvantages to its exports and to international cooperation.

Should the disadvantages for Swiss industry and the Swiss revenue exceed the benefits to Swiss financial institutions and financial markets, however, restraints on banking secrecy will be introduced. Conflict can be anticipated on this issue between the Swiss banks and financial institutions, on one side, and the Swiss export industry, on the other. Which side will win is difficult to gauge, because how the relative weight of these industries will develop is difficult to predict, and the advantages and disadvantages that will arise on both sides are difficult to evaluate. Economic ethics does not yield any definitive answer to this question, which is not primarily an ethical one but a matter of economic and fiscal policy.

Swiss banking secrecy is one form of Switzerland's fiscal neutrality toward finance authorities abroad. Its reform or retention is, therefore, like all matters pertaining to reform or retention of Switzerland's traditional neutrality, a Swiss sovereign decision that the Swiss people must arrive at by reconciling the interests of the widely divergent Swiss stakeholders affected by this issue.

---

[13]Ibid., p. 103.

[14]In this regard, bear in mind that – contrary to the impression that may have been created by certain statements of the previously mentioned former German Minister of Finance, Peer Steinbrück, – it is over 750 years since the factual cessation and over 360 years since the legal cessation of Switzerland's membership of the Holy Roman Empire of the German Nation, and more than 200 years since even that, itself, ceased to exist.

Banking Secrecy, the Right to Privacy, and the State: Thoughts on Political Philosophy

Banking secrecy is an integral component of protection of the private sphere. It is a principle for the avoidance of envy and resentment, which should only be waived in very well justified cases such as genuine evidence of tax evasion. If the state conducts dragnet investigations and seeks to breach banking secrecy on the grounds of very slender suspicions, it is overstepping the limitations imposed on the state and jeopardizing the necessary distinction between the private and the public sphere. The tax law of the state, contrary to widespread views, is not pre-eminent over the right to privacy. There is, rather, a need to examine in each particular case whether or not the state is entitled to breach banking secrecy and the right to protection of the private sphere. This applies even in the present situation where sensitivities are heightened by international terrorism and its international finance operations.

The protection of the private sphere, including banking secrecy, is aligned with what is, in Western Europe, a deeply-rooted distinction between private and public, which is a constant in the European history of ideas. The protection of banking secrecy is a less momentous issue for the USA, a country not scarred to the same degree as Europe by a history of authoritarian state interference in the private sphere.

The Dualism of Private and Public, of Society and State

The right to privacy operates not by the state conceding us the right to privacy, but by the society of citizens granting the state rights of intervention, such as tax law, in well-defined legal situations. The right to property ranks above the tax law of the state, because tax is taken from the citizen's lawfully acquired income and property. Based on property law, banking secrecy is also protected from state intrusion. Only in the face of compelling suspicions can banking secrecy be waived.

To return to Aristotle's political philosophy, he makes the distinction between the sphere of the political and public, the *polis* or city, and the sphere of the economic and private, the *oikos* or household. He criticizes Plato's theory developed in his book *Politeia, The State,* which required the elimination of this distinction. As we know, Plato was a proponent of the thesis that in the ideal state, the *politeia,* there must be no distinction between private and public, *oikonomia* and *politeia.* For the community, according to Plato, what matters most is that everything affects everybody in the same way, without favor or distinction. If there is a private sphere, however, some people will be more affected by whatever befalls the state than others who can retreat into their private sphere.

This is one of the constantly recurring arguments against the right to privacy. The upshot of privacy is that not everything political has exactly the same repercussions for everyone. The right to privacy creates a private zone of protection and a differentiation from the public arena. This right, by its very nature, is not equal in its manifestation. Somebody who has a larger plot or apartment has a larger zone of privacy than somebody else whose private space is smaller. It is always the asso-ciation of privacy with inequality that provokes resentment against the principle of privacy, and the arguments against privacy are often similar to those against inequality.

The argument for privacy is the counterargument to the Platonic argument for the necessity of the equal bearing of adversity by all: the community has an inter-est in ensuring that, in times of political error or aberration, not everybody should be equally affected by adversity in the public sphere. The private sphere is a safe-guard against the totalism of wrongdoing perpetrated by politics. Naturally this also implies that the good public sphere is prevented by the same mechanism from exert-ing a good effect on the totality of the social world, because a private sphere can then assert itself beyond the confines of the public sphere.

Banking secrecy in Switzerland undoubtedly made it possible to prevent the Nazis from accessing Swiss bank accounts belonging to Jews. The Nazis' attack on private law in general, and the dereliction of any protection in private law for Jewish citizens, made way for totalitarian ideology and practices to pervade all spheres of German life during the Nazi period.

The protection of privacy is therefore akin to a technique for risk minimization, to counter the total intrusion of the state, and thus to mitigate its political, legal and cultural mistakes. Perhaps the right to privacy and the insistence on the distinction between the private sphere and the public sphere mean that the optimal state is never realized, because the citizens reserve the right to privacy, but at the same time, they prevent the worst outcome, namely the insinuation of the bad public sphere into all realms of society – totalism of the bad public sphere. The differentiation between private and public is necessary because the risk of the worst is always to be avoided, and because it is not always possible to realize the best. The imperative of halting totalism in the political sphere follows from the principle of law and from the ethic that we always have the duty to avoid wrongdoing but that we do not have the duty to induce the optimal by coercive means.

The imperative of upholding the distinction between private and public is a kind of negative utilitarianism. The prime concern is not to realize the monism and max-imal utility of the optimal public sphere, but to avoid the negative utility or harm done by totalism of the bad public sphere. This imperative follows from the frailty of human nature and the ever-present danger that this frailty will be potentiated and totalistically propagated by collective political action.

Aristotle himself states the crucial objections to be raised against the non-differentiation of private and public in his criticism of Plato's theory of communal property without any distinction between private and public, *oikos* and *polis*: his argument against Plato is that communal property is not really property, and that individuals will no longer care for things if there is no distinction between the public and the particular. He further criticizes that, by following Plato's political philoso-phy, the principle of the mixed constitution and of the separation of the power of several constitutional principles, as well as the principle of distinguishing between public and private, cannot be realized. In the state with communal property and elimination of the private sphere, there is no distinction between public and private and no safeguard against political power.[15]

It seems as though Plato accepted some of these points of criticism. In the retraction of his political philosophy in his *Laws,* he gives up the idea of communal property and of the elimination of the difference between *polis* and *oikos.*

Christianity in its infancy tended to heighten the distinction between private and public into the distinction between the public sphere and the sphere of religious inwardness. Latin Christianity's differentiation of state and church did its utmost to separate the sphere of politics from that of religion, and to distinguish the sphere of the private and of religious inwardness from the sphere of the public, including public religion.

Michael Oakshott has shown that civil society is a sphere in its own right, which is not constituted by the state. It is a sphere in which people pursue their own ends, whatever these may be, without being under any obligation – and free to reject any obligation – to pursue collective ends.

Protection of the Distinction Between Private and Public as a Consequence of Skepticism About Humans as Political Beings

The differentiation of public and private is a constant that is closely associated with Western skepticism about human nature, particularly toward man as a *zoon politikon,* a political animal. Associations with the theory of original sin spring to mind here. If even the individual is constantly tempted to do wrong, and often does wrong, how much more is that to be feared from people united in collective action? The demand for the differentiation of public and private arises from the insight that the collective potentiates badness, if the majority or a strong minority desires what is evil or bad. This badness can range from a trivial malaise like simple envy, through raging jealousy, to full-scale criminalization of the public sphere through forms of enslavement and genocide. The power of the unified forces of the state and the private sphere can tip over into evil, and magnify and potentiate it to far beyond the capacity of the individual act of evil. A tiny modification of the content of the word "good", if it is adopted publicly and universally, can tilt the public sphere into the realm of evil.

A key example is envy. Envy is the essential reason for protecting the private sphere. Envy is also the central argument for banking secrecy and the strictures of confidentiality in financial affairs. The impacts of envy and jealousy go far beyond those of individual envy if they are combined with political power and take on the shape of political resentment against individuals, groups or nations.

---

[15]Cf. PETER KOSLOWSKI: *Zum Verhältnis von Polis und Oikos bei Aristoteles. Politik und Ökonomie bei Aristoteles* 1976, 3rd edn. under the title *Politik und Ökonomie bei Aristoteles* [Politics and economics in Aristotle], Tübingen (Mohr Siebeck) 1993, and KOSLOWSKI (1982).

Barriers to information about the private sphere and barriers to undue transparency are often the best way to nip resentment in the bud. These are strategies for resentment-avoidance. Precisely when resentment and envy threaten to dominate entire groups and goad them into hostility toward minorities or members of other nationalities, defending the groups that come under attack from unjustified exposure to transparency and protecting their private sphere is the only way of containing and controlling resentment and envy. This control of envy is another of the functions of banking secrecy.

Part III
Financial Wagers, Hyper-Speculation, Financial Overstretch: The Financial Market Crisis of 2008

In the following, the causes that led to the financial market crisis will be analyzed. The financial market crisis is the consequence of an overextension of the finance sector, which bloated into a "financial overstretch" fuelled by financial wagers and hyper-speculation and which, for a time, disengaged from the real economy. The capital market, the market for corporate control, the market for credit, and the market for derivatives all fell prey to hyper-speculation. Speculation was not confined to the capital market and the derivatives market, where it performs a liquidity-boosting function; it also took hold in the credit market via structured products like CDOs, and in the market for corporate control under the influence of the shareholder primacy principle, which exhorts managers to exercise leadership in such a way as to drive the share price upward, even by speculative means, for the sake of capital gains.

In the domains of both lending and corporate management, speculation should be kept within limits since it increases the risks of these markets. In the markets for capital and for derivatives, speculation escalated to levels that were excessive. The trend was amplified not only by new options for "direct" access to the "trading floor" of the stock exchange via online banking and brokerage, but also – in Germany – by a tax regime which, until 31 December 2008, treated capital gains as tax free after shares had been held for the duration of one year.

As public speculation, facilitated by online banking and brokerage, spread to more shares and options, the risks were intensified, not least by the message conveyed to the public that the risks were lower than they really are, and because the amateur investor normally underestimates the risks of buying shares anyway. It is hard to believe that citizens would have invested the money they had saved for their children's university education in Lehman Brothers certificates on the scale that they did, had they been informed that certificates are actually financial wagers. Even the all-too-frequent appeals of the banks for customers to "trust" them with risk-laden and complex forms of investment, such as certificates, were ineffectual and heightened the hyper-speculation.

Chapter 9
Financial Wagers, Hyper-Speculation and Shareholder Primacy

During the period that culminated in the financial crisis, the financial wager had risen to a previously unknown prevalence. The wager's rise to dominance was evident in all financial markets. It was evident in the capital market, in which speculation on the capital gains of shares had risen dramatically. It was equally evident in the credit market, in which the policy of easy money had driven lending volumes to staggering heights, while the relaxation of requirements for loan collaterals had led to a higher tolerance of speculative uncertainty about debtors, and bad credit collaterals were purchased from the banks by speculative investors in the form of structured products. Finally, it was evident in the market for derivatives, in which something like an explosion of wagers on futures and options had taken place.[1]

Wager or Gambling: What Is Speculation?

Speculation, and even investment, has always comprised an element of the wager, because they both bet on movement in values, a movement which, by its very nature, is always uncertain because the future is uncertain. The investor and the speculator both make decisions about the future under conditions of uncertainty. Both attempt to reduce this uncertainty by adding to their knowledge, and both work on improving their forecasts although they know that these forecasts will never be free of an element of uncertainty. The fact that both investor and speculator attempt to marshal information about the object of their wager, in order to reduce uncertainty and increase the ratio of known information, is what differentiates investment and speculation from a mere gamble, a game of chance. The element of pure gambling is always higher in the speculator than in the investor; indeed, in the case of sheer speculation it can be absolutely pre-eminent. The speculator who trades in

---

[1] On the scale of trading in derivative instruments, cf. POSNER (2009), p. 144: "At its peak, the market in credit-default swaps was larger than the entire U.S. stock market (though that is misleading because swaps are largely offsetting)." – According to LUTTERMANN (2008), p. 20, more than 50 trillion dollars of credit-default swaps were used to wager on synthetic derivatives and short selling.

shares is aiming more for the capital gains than the dividend, whereas the ideal-typical investor pursues the opposite priority. Speculation is more uncertain than investment, because it is more focused on the time dependency of value-movements and more readily accepts that movements in value will be far more dependent on the speculations of other market participants. This dependency on speculative assessment by others makes speculation less effective than investment at reducing uncertainty about the future by marshalling knowledge about the object of speculation. General growth in the speculative element in financial markets tends to diminish the role of marshalling knowledge about the object of investment, while the dependency of value-movements on speculative assessments by other speculators rises in line with this trend. With this dependency on the speculation of others, value-movements are also more strongly influenced by speculative than by investment interests, and are susceptible to the crowd-following or "herding" behavior of speculative investors.

Since the 1990s, the speculative side of capital market investment has expanded without drawing attention to the expansion of the speculative element of uncertainty. On the contrary, buzzwords like "people's shares" and financial products such as certificates have suggested to the public that speculative capital market investments without uncertainty are perfectly possible. The use of the term "certificate" for a structured product is a euphemism, a neutralizing ploy, which rebrands the risky wager underlying these derivative-linked securities as something more certain. Furthermore, the public usually only got to hear about huge gains, never about huge losses on the stock market, creating a public perception that shares were a safe investment. The interest of the financial intermediaries in making the risks look harmless, rather than presenting them in a realistic way, exacerbated this trend.

Similarly euphemistic is the concept of "securitization", a term designed to create the impression that the securitized note has been made safe by means of the securitization process, although it has only undergone a rating process, which itself is not free of errors and uncertainties, and been converted into a legal form which in no way eliminates the economic risk.

The epoch before the financial market crisis must therefore be described as the period of hyper-speculation. The difficulty now is that the right level of speculation or financial wagering is difficult to determine, because even the impartial observer of financial market activity does not know the future and is unable to say *ex ante* when too much speculation and wagering behavior are rife in the financial markets. As the saying goes, you only feel a blister when it bursts. Or, you only find out who is swimming naked when the tide goes out, as Warren Buffett once remarked. The wager is part and parcel of capitalism, which rewards the right wager with a gain and punishes the wrong one with a loss. This principle applies a priori to every economic system. Every economic system rewards those within the system who successfully act in conformity with the system's rules, and punishes those within the system who do not. Capitalism, however, entertains a new affirmation of innovation, new products and new production methods, and rewards those who speculatively introduce successful innovations.

Innovation is always a wager on a new product and a new production method. Given the special rewards for innovation, it is pointless to bet on an old favorite; only a successful wager on new consumer benefits from new products and technologies is worthwhile. Every innovation originates as a wager on the success of a new product or a new technology. We talk about business-changing bets when a firm puts its faith in a new technology or a new product, and hence on the future trend.[2] The wager is lost if the competitor's counter-wager and counterstrategy proves more successful and more in tune with the trend. It is also possible for two strategies to emerge as viable paths, so that neither competitor is the sole victor. One strategy will nevertheless turn out to be the more successful wager, even if the other wager was not completely useless; it will still have contributed to the broadening of knowledge in technology and production.

There are three types of wager: the productive, knowledge-increasing and hence value-adding wager; the unproductive wager; and the wager for the sake of entertainment or the chance-driven wager. These should be clearly differentiated.

The Productive or Knowledge-Increasing Financial Wager

Every attempt to discover new knowledge is a wager on a particular research and technological approach. A researcher whose work has nothing staked on the possible outcome will never be immersed in the research. In the domains of technology and production, as opposed to scientific research, the wagering element is further intensified because the aim is not just to discover laws that exist independently of the researcher, but to assess how viable a new product and its technology will be in the marketplace, and with consumers, whose reactions have little in common with scientific laws. The success-backing and thus business-transforming element of the wager on product and technology is unavoidable and necessary. Firms that are not prepared to enter into such wagers cannot bring forth any deep-seated and market-changing innovations. The productive or knowledge-increasing financial wager enlarges knowledge. Even a wager with a less successful outcome still contributes to the enlargement of methodological and technical knowledge. It is also a

---

[2]Cf. MICHAEL V. COPELAND: "Intel's secret plan. This giant box contains a super-hush-hush project that promises to transform Intel's business. Can the company inside millions of PCs find a way to power billions of phones and other gadgets?", in: *Fortune*, 12 May 2009, http://money.cnn.com/2009/05/12/technology/copeland_intel.fortune/index.htm: "Intel has made company-changing bets before. Management seizes on a future trend, and the center of the company shifts. It happened in 1986, when then-CEO Andy Grove bet the future of Intel on the nascent PC and microprocessors. Several years later the company bet that speed would win the day, and in 1993 it unveiled another blockbuster, the Pentium chip, which helped desktop computers go mainstream. Otellini is entrusting his company's current bet on small gadgets to a team led by Elenora Yoeli [...]: Build a chip compatible with Intel's existing architecture, and make it consume one-tenth the power of the latest Centrino chip. She started with a $1 billion budget and a metaphorical blank sheet of paper."

necessary part of an experimental process, in which even the less successful attempt yields a knowledge-enlarging effect. In the developmental wager, both wagering approaches are integral to the necessary development process and its costs. Value is always added, not only by successful wagers but also by the less successful ones.

The Productive and the Unproductive Wager on Derivatives

In the case of unproductive wagers, it is less clear how much value is added. The underlying wager generates no new knowledge. Therefore the loss of the wager represents a cost only. The writer who sells an option for hedging creates more certainty for the option buyer, for which the latter pays an option fee. If the conditions specified in the option contract occur, the buyer's need for certainty is satisfied. The seller loses the wager, but keeps the option fee. Macro-economically, the risk is not reduced, just redistributed between option sellers and buyers. If the insured risk turns into an actual loss, the overall risk is not reduced by a gain in knowledge from the wager but only reapportioned between the option seller and the option buyer. The option seller bears the risk minus the option fee, which remains as the residual risk with the option buyer. It can be useful to redistribute risk in this way. The value that it adds is minimal, however. It becomes even more negligible if the risk is further divided up among other option buyers, without any reduction of risk on the macro-economic level through a modification of behavior or new knowledge. Further costs are the opportunity costs of time and attention to the option contracts. The added value of the option contracts is equally doubtful, because they represent costs that are not matched by any macro-economic risk-reduction resulting from this option trading. Furthermore, if the consequence of this trading is a reduction of risk-monitoring, because individuals are less concerned about risk, additional damage is occasioned in the allocative efficiency of the economy.

This process of de-monitoring risk by trading derivatives becomes particularly visible in the case of collateralized debt obligations. When the bank wants to pass on the credit risk to the investor, packaged as a CDO, in order to increase its capitalization or ratio of equity to balance sheet total, both the bank and the investor transfer the monitoring function to the rating agency that issues the rating for the CDO. The rating agency does not, however, bear the risk of a mistaken rating; that remains with the investor. The rating agency has a minimal incentive to carry out due diligence, to fulfill the duty of care, while it is virtually impossible for the investor to do so, since he has no knowledge of the original debtor and has to rely on the assessments of the originator and the rating agency. It was also common for the bank to sell a securitized bond, a synthetic CDO, to another bank, from which it would go on to buy a similar synthetic CDO. This, of all practices, is most obviously motivated by the interest in reducing the equity to balance sheet total requirement. The transaction takes on attributes of self-dealing between the two banks.[3]

---

[3]Cf. also POSNER (2009), p. 321.

The relationship between risk monitoring and liability is disturbed. By selling the credit risk, the bank is not reducing the macro-economic risk but increasing it. Macro-economically, risk is not reduced but increased by CDOs because the bank's duty of liability and obligatory minimum ratio of equity to balance sheet total are undermined. Moreover, there are the high costs of intermediation through the bank's special-purpose vehicle, which sells the CDOs to the investor for high fees but without adding value in the sense of reducing the overall risk of credit default. Even the principle of the financial wager is not clear in the case of the CDO. The investor who buys the CDO is not wagering that the creditworthiness of the debts underlying the CDO will be higher than the bank believes, because he knows nothing whatsoever about the debtor. The sole purpose of the CDO is that of reducing the bank's required minimum equity to balance sheet total ratio.

The wagers that underlie futures and options imply a zero-sum game: what the option buyer gains, the option seller loses, minus the amount retained in option fees. Such zero-sum games on a grand scale, resulting from the proliferation of wagers on the same underlying asset, make no sense in macro-economic terms. Given the fees incurred, only the banks get rich, while no macro-economic value is added. A zero-sum game after the deduction of fees becomes a negative-sum game from which everybody ends up losing. In contrast to the wager for entertainment, this type of betting is not even fun.

The Gambling Wager: Chance-Driven Betting for Fun or Good Fortune

Chance-driven bets are also part of the genre of wagers, but form a class of their own. The casino is similarly based on wagering on the outcome of the game. However, the element of knowledge recedes here almost entirely. The game of chance depends on luck, not on accurate knowledge of the future. In financial speculation, it is also possible to engage in mere gambling by placing financial wagers which are not wagers about the future values of assets made on the basis of (limited) knowledge and rational inferences, but a game of pure chance. Even playing the state lottery is a form of wager since it involves placing a bet on a certain set of numbers, but it is a wager on a chance outcome.

A notable judgment in this context was that of the German Imperial Court of Justice (*Deutsches Reichsgericht*) of 29 April 1882, according to which bookmaking at the horse races and betting via the totalizator are considered to be games of chance, although the participants consider themselves to be wagering and capable of influencing the outcome of the wager with their "factual knowledge".

Chance-driven betting is also a zero-sum game. However, gaming itself is perceived as a pleasure – but often also as its counterpart, an addiction. The enjoyment of the game can be seen as the value added. Also, it is difficult in a free society for gambling to be prohibited by the state. The state may take steps to channel and limit the demand for gambling, but cannot prohibit it. Addiction phenomena such as betting addiction and gambling addiction are the exceptions to this, since they harm the sufferers and, above all, their families.

The same is true for financial speculation, which cannot be completely prohibited, but can certainly be limited if practiced to excess. It can also be limited for the sake of social welfare and economic value-creation, if financial betting becomes rampant.

The Power of Gambling over Humankind in the Epic Mahabharata

Betting and gambling are "existentials" or *Existenziale,* basic situations and states-of-mind of human existence, in the terms of Heidegger's book *Time and Being* (*Sein und Zeit*). In the ancient Indian epic *Mahabharata*, the vast second book *Sabhaparva* is dedicated to a gripping account of the power of games of chance over humankind. The wise king Yudhisthira is challenged to play dice and is unable to resist, although he knows about the devastating power of gambling. He stakes first his kingdom and finally himself on the game – only to lose his kingdom, followed by his personal freedom. The messages of the *Mahabharata* are clear: gambling between kings who put their kingdoms at stake will lead to the destruction of their peoples.[4] The actual gambler who issues the challenge is King Sakuni. The challenger to the game sees the world as dominated by fate, to which the gambler must submit: "The whole universe moveth at the will of its Creator, under the controlling influence of Fate. It is not free."[5] But Vidura, his adviser, warns him not to gamble: "Vidura said: 'I know that gambling is the root of misery.' "[6] King Yudhishthira, who accepts the invitation to play, is aware that belief in fate robs people of their reason, just as a shining object robs the eyes of their sight. Nevertheless, he is unable to resist the invitation to play. The belief in fate has such a hold over humans that they bow to the power of destiny.[7]

His opponent, King Sakuni, persuades him to play with the subtle argument that wagers and games of chance are only about winning. Thus he draws attention to the narcissistic element of gaming. The player wants to feel like a winner. He adds the sophisticated argument that the motive for games of chance is neither truly dishonorable nor very honorable in order to deprive the opponent (who essentially wants to gamble) of the excuse that gambling is an unworthy pastime for a king. A game of chance is a contest like other contests and, as in all other contests, the main concern is winning.[8]

---

[4]*The Mahabharata* (written 400 BC to 400 AD but based on older sources), Book 2: *Sabha Parva of Krishna-Dwaipayana Vyasa*, translated by Kisari Mohan Ganguli [published between 1883 and 1896], Chapter 56, online edition: http://www.sacred-texts.com/hin/m02/m02080.htm

[5]*Mahabharata*, Ch. 56.

[6]*Mahabharata*, Ch. 57.

[7]*Mahabharata*, Ch. 57: "Like some brilliant body falling before the eyes, Fate depriveth us of reason, and man, tied as it were with a cord, submitteth to the sway of Providence."

[8]*Mahabharata*, Ch. 58: "Sakuni said, –'O Yudhishthira, it is from a desire of winning, which is not a very honest motive, that one high-born person approacheth another (in a contest of race superiority). So also it is from a desire of defeating, which is not a very honest motive, that one

Sakuni, who is a cheat, expands the narcissistic element of the game, i.e. that the player sees himself as superior in the skills necessary for the game, and emphasizes the neither dishonorable nor honorable character of the contest. The other actors in the epic, in contrast, recognize the desire to gamble as the desire to submit entirely to fate and the wish to experience the thrill of the loss of autonomy and ability to control one's own destiny.

The cheat represents the game as a fair contest and as a wager, which Sakuni, because he masters the game better and knows how to cheat, will win. Only the cheat can master the game. The genuine player in a game of chance entrusts the outcome to fate. He believes that fate and luck will smile on him. He passes up his autonomy, and derives excitement from the actively-chosen loss of control.

In the epic *Mahabharata*, fate and the willingness of the actors to submit to fate are so strong that the king himself, having lost his kingdom and regained it through mercy, sits down to play a second game. The outcome, as in the first game, is his own destruction.[9] Again he loses his kingdom, and he and his tribe must spend 13 years in the jungle before he is allowed to return to civilization. The punishment for abandoning reason and autonomy is regression to the pre-rational and pre-civilized condition: regression to the jungle.

Wagers and Gambling in Cultural Theory

Underlying the game of chance is a belief in fortune and fate, the belief that we are not free, and the desire to submit to fate's irresistible power, to indulge in the game as the antidote to reason. This desire also makes it almost impossible to be a rational player. Dostoevsky in his gambling period was convinced that he would always win if he could play with complete rationality and distance and remain unmoved by either good luck or bad. This position is self-contradictory and self-refuting. If the player plays with such complete distance, he does not experience the dependency on luck which is what the game is all about. If he feels like a gambler, somebody dependent on fate, he is no longer distanced from the game. In this period of his life, Dostoevsky conceded that he was not capable of distanced gambling for longer than 30 minutes.[10]

---

learned person approacheth another (in a contest of learning). Such motives, however, are scarcely regarded as really dishonest. So also, O Yudhishthira, a person skilled at dice approacheth one that is not so skilled from a desire of vanquishing him. One also who is conversant with the truths of science approacheth another that is not from desire of victory, which is scarcely an honest motive. But (as I have already said) such a motive is not really dishonest. And, O Yudhishthira, so also one that is skilled in weapons approacheth one that is not so skilled; the strong approacheth the weak. This is the practice in every contest.' "

[9]*Mahabharata*, Ch. 75: "And compelled by Fate they once more sat down at ease for gambling for the destruction of themselves."

[10]Quoted in E. J. CARTER: "Breaking the Bank: Gambling Casinos, Finance Capitalism, and German Unification", in: *Central European History*, 39 (2006), pp. 185–213, here p. 187. – CARTER, ibid., p. 188, n. 9, follows Joseph Frank's interpretation that ultimately, Dostoevsky

The fact that the gambler is enticed not by the rational but by the unfathomable element of chance and luck is also confirmed by the observations of Jackson Lears. Lears puts forward the view, in the American context, that the "culture of risk" and the "culture of control" must be separated.[11] For aristocrats, workers and marginalized ethnic groups, gambling served the purpose of setting the culture of risk apart from the culture of control. Gamblers reject the dominant ethic of self-denial for a future pay-off, of "deferred gratification", and of rational calculation, to throw in their lot with the more enigmatic power of luck and fate.[12] They reject the Puritan principle of "You must learn before you can earn." According to Kavanagh, the same is true of gambling for entertainment, as taken up by the European and American middle classes. Amateur gambling for entertainment appeals to the experience of luck as a force beyond rational control, and exhibits features of a subversion of the rational market economy into the "economy of gifts" and the effortlessness of "something for nothing".[13]

Unlike the game of chance and the chance-based wager, behind the rational wager stands the quite different type of belief in one's own capacity for knowledge, in one's own ability to be able to predict the future through superior knowledge. The wagerer is more narcissistically predisposed. He is overly convinced of his powers of knowledge, whereas the gambler is more prone to display traits of regression, of the abandonment of rationality in favor of surrender to fate. The gambler consciously wants to divest himself of his autonomy and surrender to blind fate. Yet the gambler lacks neither the narcissistic motive to force fate, nor the belief in his own ability to be able to do so. On the other hand, the wagerer is also familiar with the regressive element of surrendering to fate. Victory is important to both.

---

confirmed this inability on the basis of his anti-materialism: "Joseph Frank suggests that Dostoevsky's inability to restrain his emotions for more than thirty minutes confirmed his anti-materialist belief that humans are not motivated by rationality and interest alone, that spiritual demands trumped 'the icy self-domination of reason.' " Cf. JOSEPH FRANK: *Dostoevsky: The Stir of Liberation*, Princeton (Princeton University Press) 1986, p. 262. – The explanation that a purely rational game does not produce the satisfaction that the gambler is actively seeking, namely total dependency on luck, seems more plausible.

[11] JACKSON LEARS: *Something for Nothing: Luck in America*, New York (Viking) 2003, esp. Ch. 6. Cf. on working-class gambling, which is usually also seen as hostile to market rationality, MARK CLAPSON: *A Bit of a Flutter: Popular Gambling and English Society*, 1823–1961, Manchester (Manchester University Press) 1992; ROSS MCKIBBON: "Working-Class Gambling in Britain, 1880–1939," *Past & Present*, 82 (1979), pp. 147–178; and ROGER MUNTING: *An Economic and Social History of Gambling in Britain and the USA*, Manchester (Manchester University Press) 1996.

[12] Cf. also GERDA REITH: *The Age of Chance: Gambling in Western Culture*, New York (Routledge) 1999, p. XVII.

[13] Cf. THOMAS KAVANAGH: *Enlightenment and the Shadows of Chance: The Novel and the Culture of Gambling in Eighteenth-Century France*, Baltimore (Johns Hopkins University Press) 1993, p. 46. – In his more recent book, Kavanagh distinguishes the "nomological", regulated orientation of modern everyday life from the "ontological" orientation of the true gambler who is fixated on the "moment unregulated". THOMAS M. KAVANAGH: *Dice, Cards and Wheels: A Different History of French Culture*, Philadelphia (University of Pennsylvania Press) 2005, p. 21.

Wagers and Gambling in Civil Law and Economic History

The difference between the game of chance and the wager was introduced into German civil-law discourse by A. Krügelstein as long ago as 1869. The wager is the acceptable form of investment,[14] because it is based at least partly on skill or knowledge, whereas gambling and chance-driven bets are based purely on luck,

---

[14]Cf. A. KRÜGELSTEIN: *Über den begrifflichen Unterschied von Spiel und Wette. Eine civilistische Studie* [On the conceptual difference of gambling and wager. A study in civil law], Leipzig (Fues' Verlag) 1869, p. 65. – In a supreme court decision of 30 October 1998 on the enforceability of a betting debt, the Austrian Supreme Court of Justice (*Oberster Gerichtshof*, OGH) refers to the difference between a game of chance (*Glücksspiel*) and a bet or wager (*Wette*) and the possible legal consequence of such a distinction that the two are not equally enforceable. Online: www.ris.bka.gv.at/Dokumente/Justiz/JJT_19981030_OGH0002_0010OB00107_98M0000_000/JJT_19981030_OGH0002_0010OB00107_98M0000_000.rtf:

> "Insofar as the enforceability of a betting debt was brought to special prominence – for instance, in Freiburg and Frankfurt – towards the end of the 15th century, this was based on the influence of (classical) Roman law (Dreysel, ibid., 29). Accordingly, provided that its object was nothing illegal or immoral, a wager was a valid and enforceable legal transaction and was brought into legal effect either when – pursuant to one of the possible definitions in Section 1271 of the Austrian Civil Code (§ 1271 ABGB; cf. GlU 5967) – the parties to the wager deposited their stakes with a third party as adjudicator of the wager, in which case the winner could claim this deposit via the *actio praescriptis verbis*, or indeed if the parties to the wager merely promised each other by means of stipulations that the agreed stake would be paid (Arndts, GZ 1861, 401; Dreysel, ibid., 22; Krügelstein, *Über den begrifflichen Unterschied zwischen Spiel und Wette* [Leipzig 1869] 17 f.). In common law dogmatics, a controversy existed over whether games of chance and wagers should be judged according to the Roman or the (contrary) German legal tradition. The debt from a game was nevertheless held to be legally unenforceable by a considerable body of opinion. In contrast, there was fundamental insistence – mainly in keeping with the roots in Roman law – on the enforceability of the debt from a wager. (Dreysel, ibid., 30 ff; Moncke ibid., 14 ff). In the Prussian Law Code (*Allgemeines Landrecht für die Preussischen Staaten*) from which the provision of § 1271 ABGB followed, the opposing view prevailed that wagers were only enforceable when staked in cash and the stake deposited either with the court or with some other third party." (Own translation from the German.)

The Austrian Supreme Court of Justice rejects the distinction between gambling and wagering, holding that every gamble includes an element of the wager:

> "According to § 1272 ABGB, 'every game [is] [. . .] a kind of wager'. The legal nature of the game is thus at least similar in essence to that of the wager. The wager has the wider ambit, which also takes in the game. A distinction between game and wager is unnecessary with regard to their consequences in civil law, according to the prevailing view, because the same legal provisions – thus also § 1274 ABGB – are applicable to both legal transactions. [. . .] According to Amonn (*Spiel und spielartige Verträge*, in Schweizerisches Privatrecht VII/2, 463) the conceptual differentiation between game and wager, which is equally insignificant in Switzerland as to the consequences in civil law, is now only 'a meaningless relic of the Common Law', according to which, as has been explained, the debt from a wager but not from a game was enforceable. [...]"

The enlarged panel [of the Austrian Supreme Court] therefore formulates the following legal provision:

because their generating factor is not knowledge but chance. The sporting bet is the transitional form between the chance-driven wager and the knowledge-based wager, where it is not always clear whether a successful outcome is predominantly due to luck or factual knowledge. In the English discourse, when modern financial markets were first emerging in the nineteenth century, a distinction was made not between financial betting and gambling, but between financial speculation and gambling, i.e. legitimate speculation and mere chance-driven gambling.[15]

E. J. Carter shows how, after the differentiation of wagering and games of chance in nineteenth-century Germany before and after the founding of the German Empire in 1871, both advocates and critics of the new forms of financial speculation grappled to properly understand financial speculation and to differentiate between speculation and games of chance.[16] Unlike France, Germany in the second half of the nineteenth century wanted to realize a German mode of economy without excessive speculation. The futures market for commodities and stock futures came under particular criticism, and some parties called for regulation of the futures markets.

In his article "Börsenspiel" [Stock market gambling] in 1891, Emil Struck pointed out that between one-sixth and one-tenth of trade on the European stock exchanges at the time led to no change of ownership. He argued that this disparity between trading and exchange of ownership suggested a high volume of pure gambling on the stock exchange and cast the stock exchange in a questionable light, even if one granted stock exchanges a positive role as capital markets.[17]

In 1892, after a financial crisis in Argentina, a government commission led by Imperial Chancellor Count Leo von Caprivi (who had replaced Otto von

---

"Wagers on sporting events placed with bookmakers on the basis of a state-government license to carry on such a bookmaking business are 'state lotteries' within the meaning of § 1274 ABGB. Accordingly, such a bookmaker's betting debt is, in any case, enforceable provided that his contract partner has actually paid or deposited the stake. In contrast, if such a bookmaker has credited the amount of the stake and the contract partner has lost the wager, a claim for the stake is unenforceable." (Own trans. from the German.)

One might critically object that the enforceability of a gambling bet does not necessitate the elimination of the distinction between a game of chance and a wager. If the game, as the Austrian Supreme Court requires, conforms to certain formal conditions, it can still provide grounds for enforceable performance even if it does not form a common genre with the wager.

[15] DAVID C. ITZKOWITZ: "Fair Enterprise or Extravagant Speculation: Investment, Speculation, and Gambling in Victorian England," *Victorian Studies*, 45 (2002), pp. 121–147, here p. 143. Cf. also URS STÄHELI: *Spektakuläre Spekulation. Das Populäre der Ökonomie* [Spectacular speculation. The popular side of the economy and of economics], Frankfurt am Main (Suhrkamp) 2007, who makes reference to England and the USA, and NANCY HENRY, CANNON SCHMITT (eds.): *Victorian Investments: New Perspectives on Finance and Culture*, Bloomington, IN (Indiana University Press) 2008.

[16] The author derived important insights for the historical considerations on speculation and games of chance from Session 153: "Political Culture of Speculation: Stock Markets and Gambling Casinos in Nineteenth-Century Europe" at the 2003 Annual Meeting of the American Historical Association, Chicago, 5 January 2003, and particularly in the paper given by C. J. Carter at this session, which was incorporated into CARTER (2006).

[17] EMIL STRUCK, article on "Börsenspiel" [Stock market gambling], in: *Handwörterbuch der Staatswissenschaften*, Jena (Gustav Fischer) 1891, pp. 695–704, here p. 695.

Bismarck in 1890) recommended the appointment of an enquête commission on stock exchanges, the prohibition of commodity futures transactions, and a massive limitation on forward trading in raw materials and shares. The Reichstag codified this decision in the German Stock Exchange Act of 1896. The Act overturned a civil-law court decision of 1872, which had ruled that speculation in futures can only be equated with gambling if it can be shown that neither party had the intention of ful-filling the contract, which was difficult to prove. The new law made it mandatory for participants in the market for futures to have their transactions recorded in a register. The purpose of the measure was to discourage speculation in futures, and to transfer a major part of the capital for futures speculation abroad.

According to Borchardt[18] and Carter[19] the stock exchanges in many countries were reformed during the 1890s, including Belgium, France, Holland, Russia, and the USA. But only in Germany did it come to a restructuring of the financial markets so overwhelmingly dictated by the authority of the state.

The Continuum from the Wager on Corporate Strategy and the Wager on Technological Development to the Gambling Wager: The Difference Between the Value-Creating and the Non-Value-Creating Wager

Again, these historical observations show that financial speculation is always a wager, a fact that they have in common with the philosophical or metaphysical wager, such as Pascal's Wager on the existence of God. Financial speculation, however, like the metaphysical wager, is no mere chance-driven wager because its rationality and its yield are increased through knowledge. On the other hand, the chance-driven wager and the sporting wager are also not entirely uninfluenced by the wagerer's knowledge and ability; and likewise, luck and chance certainly play a role in the outcome of a financial wager.

The different degrees of amalgamation between knowledge and chance in the different kinds of wagers shows that the concept of the wager is an umbrella term encompassing the class of actions whereby predictions about the future are made with incomplete knowledge and, based on these predictions, strategies for the future are adopted which are risk-laden, partly or totally dependent on luck, and associated with varied possibilities of gain. This definition applies across the spectrum, from the wager on corporate strategy via the speculative financial wager to the sport-ing and chance-driven wager. If wagers are arranged in a continuum, from a firm's wager on a corporate strategy to the chance-based wager, this continuum exhibits a consistently rising element of chance and luck and a consistently declining element of rational analysis and knowledge.

---

[18]KNUT BORCHARDT: "Einleitung" [Introduction], in: MAX WEBER: *Börsenwesen. Schriften und Reden 1893–1898* (Matters of the stock exchange. Writings and speeches), ed. Knut Borchardt, Tübingen (Mohr Siebeck) 1999, p. 25.

[19]CARTER (2006), p. 209.

The similarity between types of wager must not, however, mask the fact that the character and effects of the said wagers are highly disparate. The knowledge-enlarging wager is value-adding and a positive sum game, whereas the chance-driven wager is non-value-adding and a zero-sum game. The differentiation between the wager and the game of chance allows a distinction to be made between the acceptable form of investment with a speculative element, and mere chance-based gambling. The foundation and justification of the differing definition and valuation of the types of wager mentioned are the different degrees to which the wagerer's skills and knowledge influence the outcome of the wager, and the different degrees to which the different types of wagers contribute to value-creation in the economy. Although the element of luck plays a role in every wager, and hence also in speculative investment, the knowledge and prosperity-enhancing corporate wager in market competition represents an unavoidable and value-creating element of capitalism, indeed of every form of economic system, whereas this cannot be upheld for the chance-based wager.

The speculative element is also legitimate in wagers on corporate strategies, because without speculative entrepreneurial thinking, no new products and forms of production can be invented and put into practice.[20] Intel's one billion-dollar wager on a new type of microchip is a good example of the speculative character of the strategies of modern technology firms. It is therefore useful to maintain the distinction and differing legitimacy of chance-based games and wagers, without denying that even in games of chance there is an element of the wager.

The Functional and the Dysfunctional Extent of Financial Wagers on Derivatives

Financial wagers differ from games of chance only when they demonstrably provide some economic functionality, or a contribution to value-creation such as hedging, market liquidity, or arbitrage. But even if such functionality is present, that in itself is not sufficient to determine what volume of financial wagers is useful and value-creating. Even if financial wagers are demonstrably useful for the financial markets, more wagers may be placed than are necessary for this purpose, and the excess of wagers may not only be non-functional and inappropriate to the purpose, but may even be detrimental. The escalation of financial wagers to a dysfunctional scale encourages financial wagers of the gambling type and shifts the financial markets for these wagers in the direction of an arena for games of chance. Excessive financial wagers create excessive liquidity in the markets, which only serves the gambling motive and increases price fluctuations.

The rule for options is therefore: if options are to fulfill their function for hedging and arbitrage, for the fulfillment of these functions a certain extent of

---

[20]On speculation, cf. also HANNS LEISKOW: *Spekulation und öffentliche Meinung in der ersten Hälfte der 19. Jahrhunderts* (Speculation and public opinion in the first half of the 19th century), Jena (Gustav Fischer) 1930.

speculation is necessary to ensure the liquidity of the market for options. If this speculation in options significantly exceeds the amount necessary for this purpose, the element of gambling in speculation in derivatives may gain the upper hand. This danger exists when there is no obligation to register options and no cash deposit requirement. The deregulation of options, and the eschewal of any obligatory registration or deposit requirement, supported the tendency, in the run-up to the financial market crisis, toward the expansion or even overexpansion of options wagers.

Essentially, in the market for derivatives, a wager or an option contract can be arranged about anything and guaranteed by the option writer. As with other wagers, the extent of wagering activity and the stability of the market for derivatives in relation to the economic function of derivatives plays the decisive role. If non-value-creating wagers suppress other value-creating economic activities, an economic problem exists even where wagering causes no direct harm. The problem caused by excessive wagering activity is the opportunity cost of such activity: other, value-adding activities could have taken its place. The non-value-adding activity of derivatives wagering suppresses other, value-adding economic activities.

Some have to speculate as a pre-requisite so that others can merely calculate and invest. Both professional speculation, as well as the amateur speculation that rose dramatically in the run-up to the financial market crisis, enable others, who prefer not to speculate, to limit their risks by "hedging". When speculation is taken to excess, there is a portion of speculation which no longer serves non-speculative purposes, such as hedging and the liquidity of financial markets, but consists of self-dealing. The principle that "everything worth doing is worth doing in excess" cannot and must not govern financial speculation.

Richard Posner remarks at the beginning of his book on the analysis of the financial market crisis that this crisis had been prefaced by a massive upsurge in speculation.[21] At the end of his book, however, he arrives at the not exactly clear judgment that it is unclear whether the increase in speculation generated any added value at all.[22] This judgment is unduly cautious. When wagers amounting to many times gross national income are placed in the form of derivatives, the constructive and functional element of derivatives speculation is forgotten and the line to chance-based gambling has been crossed. Although this does not turn derivatives into weapons of mass destruction, as Warren Buffett claimed,[23] because no intention of harm exists, they are nonetheless financial wagers which have, for the most part, crossed the line into chance-based wagers and which therefore cause macro-economic harm due to their opportunity costs.

How was it possible for so many derivatives wagers to be placed for such high amounts? For the investor, the highly leveraged nature of derivatives trading makes

---

[21]POSNER (2009), p. 13.

[22]POSNER (2009), p. 296.

[23]BERKSHIRE HATHAWAY INC.: *2002 Annual Report: Chairman's Letter*, http://www. berkshirehathaway.com/2002ar/2002ar.pdf, p. 13: "We view them (derivatives) as time bombs." Ibid., p. 15: "In our view, however, derivatives are financial weapons of mass destruction, carrying dangers that, while now latent, are potentially lethal."

it easy to invest in the derivatives market but difficult to disinvest from it when the high option-wagers do not work out. To quote Buffett, options are like Hell: "easy to enter and almost impossible to exit".[24] In a certain sense, that applies to all wagers.

The Principle of Shareholder Primacy and Hyper-Speculation

The financial market crisis also resulted, in part, from the misunderstanding that shareholder value is the firm's ultimate purpose, and from a disproportionate emphasis within the remit of management on concern about the firm's share price. Both these misapprehensions are inherent to a style and culture of business which has given ever-growing weight to speculation as a means of generating corporate share-price growth. The thesis that the maximization of shareholder value is the absolute criterion for the work of a firm and takes precedence over all other corporate purposes (the doctrine of "shareholder primacy")[25] played a highly significant role in the speculative interpretation of investment and corporate control that characterized the run-up to the financial market crisis. The radical version of the shareholder-value approach, as expounded by Jensen and Meckling[26] and others, actually inverts the relationship between the firm's purpose and the firm's control principle: the control principle, shareholder value, is taken up as the firm's ultimate purpose.

In the theory of the firm, it was claimed that the firm works best when it serves the sole purpose of maximizing shareholder value. According to the "financial theory of the firm", the firm is just a nexus of contracts entered into by profit-maximizing and utility-maximizing individuals, amongst which the contract between management and shareholders or owners, and thus the imperative to maximize shareholder value, commands primacy. The doctrine of shareholder value introduced the innovation that management was expected to maximize not only profit, i.e. the firm's operating profit, over which the firm's management is largely in control, but also capital gains, i.e. growth in the firm's share price, a gain in value that largely depends on the capital market, over which the management does not have complete control.

The question at issue here is the task and purpose of the firm. Is the purpose of the firm exhaustively defined by the task of realizing maximum shareholder value and financial profit for its shareholders? A simple but important objection to this thesis is that the joint-stock corporation with its many shareholders is only one type of firm, and by no means the dominant type in Germany and Austria where, in

---

[24]Ibid., p. 15.

[25]Cf. also ANTOINE REBÉRIOUX: "Does shareholder primacy lead to a decline in managerial accountability?", *Cambridge Journal of Economics*, Advance Access published online on May 15, 2007.

[26]M. C. JENSEN and W. H. MECKLING: "The Theory of the Firm: Managerial Behavior, Agency Costs, and Ownership Structure", in: K. BRUNNER (ed.): *Economics and Social Institutions*, Boston (Martinus Nijhoff) 1979, pp. 163–231.

contrast to America, most firms are not organized as joint-stock structures.[27] The small- to medium-sized firms, the *Mittelstand,* all have owners, but not shareholders in the sense implied by the shareholder-value principle. In firms under family or individual ownership, the owner or owners will prioritize different purposes than in the firm with multiple owners who just hold anonymous shares in the firm's capital stock.

A further objection to the dominance of the shareholder firm is the crisis in the joint-stock corporation, the "public corporation" as it is called in the USA, with its onerous duties of public disclosure. The limitations of the public corporation are evidenced by the rise of private equity firms, which are the very opposite of "public" in comparison with public corporations, and which do not act for numerous shareholders but amass concentrated holdings of capital and corporate control rights.[28]

The limitations of the joint-stock company or public corporation reside in its higher bureaucratic and regulatory overhead. This is a necessity because otherwise the shareholders' rights in the widely dispersed and anonymous share-ownership cannot be guaranteed. Private equity firms try to alleviate this shortcoming, and at the cost of much-reduced transparency they generate higher returns for investors than joint-stock corporations.

The shareholder-value criterion is nevertheless significant even for firms with different legal structures, because it leads by extension, as the business ethicist Elaine Sternberg argues, to the idea that the maximization of capital gains for the firm's owner is the purpose of business. Elaine Sternberg therefore makes the purpose of maximizing owner value the defining feature, the specific differentiator of businesses from other, non-business organizations. Only an organization that makes the long-term maximization of owner or shareholder value its primary purpose is a business.[29] Any organization that does not pursue this purpose is not a business. Sternberg therefore considers the majority of large German companies to be political organizations rather than proper businesses, since in her opinion they maximize turnover, influence and power rather than shareholder value.[30]

---

[27]Cf. E. GAUGLER: "Shareholder Value und Unternehmensführung" (Shareholder value and the management of the firm), in: P. KOSLOWSKI (ed.): *Shareholder Value und die Kriterien des Unternehmenserfolgs,* Heidelberg (Physica) 1999, pp. 175–186.

[28]Private equity firms and even hedge funds proved more resilient to the financial market crisis than corporations with a joint-stock structure. Cf. POSNER (2009), p. 46: "One reason that hedge funds have not encountered problems of solvency as acute as those of commercial banks may be that no part of their capital is federally insured, so they have to worry that if they have too much leverage in their spatial structure, or otherwise overdo risk, they will face a run (as some have)." – Another reason could be the better monitoring of investment and risk in private equity firms and hedge funds.

[29]ELAINE STERNBERG: *Just Business: Business Ethics in Action,* Oxford (Oxford University Press) 2nd edn. 2000, p. 32: "The defining purpose of business is maximising owner value over the long term by selling goods or services."

[30]Ibid., pp. 44f.: "Japanese keiretsu have traditionally been more concerned with achieving market share to save jobs, while the German industrial complexes have focused on consolidating power."

The maximization of shareholder value is the central purpose of the advice that financial advisory firms or financial intermediaries give to equity investors, and is therefore the ultimate task of the financial institutions that provide advice to investment clients. This finality effectively makes shareholder value one of the core products of the financial institutions. Clearly, it was only a small step from this finality of shareholder value in the investment advisory business to the finality of shareholder value as the ultimate purpose of every firm. Shareholder value became so central to corporate governance partly because it filtered through from the financial advice sector, of which it is properly the purpose, into industrial firms.

The producing divisions of the firm become the object of its own holding firm and of its financial investments, which view the firm's producing divisions primarily as a financial investment. One example of this tendency, until 2009, was the firm Porsche, the management of which showed ever-increasing signs of understanding its role as that of managing a financial holding company which had invested in a production firm.

Many industrial firms underwent this transformation into firms with a financial holding company, and in the process, the firm's normal logic of means and ends was turned on its head: the "end" of production became a "means" of maximizing the financial "end" pursued by the holding company.

Why Was the Shareholder-Value Criterion Elevated to Primacy as the Corporate Purpose?

Two developments explain the elevation of shareholder value to such prominence in the debate. The first reason was that market opening and economic globalization had increased the competition between firms and between economies to attract capital. Most of all, a new demand for capital was stimulated by the opening of former communist economies which had previously been behind the Iron Curtain and cut off from the global capital market. The build-up of competitive pressure on the demand for capital, and on those offering investment opportunities, is inevitably followed by the demand for higher capital productivity because more firms and economies are competing for the same capital stock. Just as the production factor of labor has to achieve higher productivity under pressure of competition, the factor of capital has to raise its productivity in response to the increasing scarcity of this factor and heightened competition for it.

As a result, the investor expected a higher return on investment and higher shareholder value. Pressure of competition caused pressure for returns, which drove an increase in capital productivity since higher capital returns could be achieved in other locations around the world. Other financial centers offered increasing opportunities for capital investment, once again heightening the expected returns on the factor of capital. The more numerous opportunities for investment in the global market also raised the opportunity costs for those whose capital was inefficiently invested. All advanced economies came under pressure, on the capital side and on the labor side, from the burgeoning options for investing capital and from the expansion of the supply of labor following the opening of new markets for investment and labor, particularly in China and East Asia.[31] Since the capital demanded by these countries created new investment opportunities, competition for capital in the advanced economies grew more intense.

The second cause of the interest in the shareholder-value principle was the relationship between the capital-owners and management. The heightened opportunities for investment also placed the dispositive factor, management, under pressure of competition. Due to the increased number of alternative uses, capital had more opportunities to migrate to other firms. Because of the increased opportunities for shareholder defection, shareholders could place management under greater pressure from takeover threats to generate higher capital returns or higher shareholder value than in the past. The shareholder-value debate became part of the discussion on corporate governance. Corporate governance was thought to be improved through greater emphasis on shareholder-value maximization.

Shareholder Value as the Control Instrument of the Firm

The orientation to shareholder value is a means of increasing the allocative efficiency of investment in the global market, because the shareholder-value principle is the instrument that prevents management shirking and indeed shirking throughout the entire firm. Managers and firms are in danger of growing slack. This is mitigated by a greater emphasis on the profit criterion and the need to increase shareholder value.

A firm's profit is the means by which members of the firm are prevented from shirking their responsibilities. According to the theory of Alchian and Demsetz,[32] the function of the owner is to be the one who prevents the firm's employees from slacking off their efforts. The firm's profit, in turn, is the means of preventing the owner from shirking his duty to prevent slacking by other members of the firm. The underlying principle is that the financing of a company implies control of it. If the owner fails to perform his control function, the residual profit declines and the owner is punished with lower profits or even losses, and thus forced into performing his function of preventing shirking within the firm.

---

[31] The financial market crisis can therefore also be seen as a consequence of this pressure for returns on a global scale. According to Angel Gurría, the Secretary-General of the OECD, the crisis is opening our eyes to the darker side of globalization. Cf. "Im Gespräch: OECD-Generalsekretär ANGEL GURRÍA: 'Wir entdecken die dunklen Seiten der Globalisierung' " (In conversation: OECD Secretary-General ANGEL GURRÍA: 'We discover the dark sides of globalization.'), *Frankfurter Allgemeine Zeitung*, No. 15 (19 January 2009), p. 13.

[32] A. A. ALCHIAN and H. DEMSETZ: "Production, Information Costs, and Economic Organization", in: A. A. ALCHIAN: *Economic Forces at Work*, Indianapolis (Liberty Press) 1977, pp. 73–110.

The shareholder-value principle, with its emphasis on the maximization of future cash flows, alters the way in which profit is understood. Profit is no longer measured in terms of the residual profit and the size of the dividend, but mainly in terms of share-price growth, growth in corporate value, i.e. capital gains. The firm must maximize future profit for the shareholder, which is made up of dividends *and* the uplift in the share price on the stock exchange. The objective of "profit and capital gains" requires management not just to generate a dividend but also to achieve growth in the share price.

The latter expectation puts management in the difficult position of having to guarantee something which depends not only on its own performance but also on capital-market speculation. If management is to fulfill this task, it must embrace a speculating role concurrently with its task of running the company, in order to perform the speculative role of maximizing corporate value on the stock exchange. Since the value of corporate shares is dependent on speculation in the capital market, over which the firm's management has only limited control, this presents the management with a difficult challenge.

The auxiliary hypothesis that the capital market always acts rationally and always determines corporate value correctly was an attempt to avoid this difficulty. If the hypothesized rationality of the capital market were true, the capital market would always determine the value of corporate shares correctly, i.e. exactly in accordance with the performance of the firm and its management. In that case, the management should not and could not practice any share-price management. The fact that share price management definitely happens, however, is an indication that ample scope exists for management to practice share-price management, and that the market clearly falls short of total accuracy in determining corporate value at all times. If the assessment of a firm's future earnings, along with all the problems attached to the prediction of a future return on investment, is a task that can be left to the capital market, then why is it also necessary to have such prodigious volumes of share-trading and professional speculation, which makes huge speculative gains but also huge losses? Here again, as with other problems concerning the less than perfect rationality of the market, the rational market hypothesis simply explains away the problem that management is forced de facto into a speculative role by the requirement to maximize shareholder value. In a perfect capital market, management would only have to perform its corporate governance function. If it does so, its performance is always correctly evaluated by the capital market. In reality, the management also engages in management of its firm's share price because the capital markets are not perfectly efficient after all.

Profit and shareholder value – from the perspective of the firm as a whole – are not the ultimate purpose of the firm but an instrumental goal. They are the means to prevent all employees of the firm from shirking responsibility, and to ensure that all members of the firm optimally perform their contractually agreed duties to the firm. Only for one group, the shareholders, is it true that the disciplining instrument of corporate profit and the share price are simultaneously their individual goal. For all other groups, this goal is only of interest as a means to ensure the success of the firm as a whole, but not as an end in itself which they can espouse as their own end.

Shareholder value can therefore only be designated the purpose of the firm in a roundabout way. It is principally the purpose of one group within the firm, the shareholders, and its primacy among the goals of the other groups within the firm can only be justified by its function of preventing the owners from shirking their responsibilities, which in turn prevents shirking by all other members of the firm. From the perspective of the firm as an organization, shareholder value cannot be seen as the ultimate purpose of the firm, but only as the principal criterion for the firm's success.

The Product as the Purpose of the Firm

If we want to distinguish a primary purpose or teleology of the firm, it is obvious that none of the goals of the different groups which make up the firm can be the sole purpose of the firm, because the other groups also have a right to pursue their purpose within the firm. If there is such a thing as a main purpose of the firm, this must be a purpose to which all groups within the enterprise could agree. For the main purpose to be capable of garnering a consensus, it must be useful to all members of the firm. Since all members of the firm and all members of society are consumers in one way or another, either directly as consumers of the products of the firm in question, or as demanders of its products as inputs for the demanders' production, we have to conclude that the purpose of the firm that can command the greatest universality is the purpose of realizing consumer benefits through its products.

All members of the firm are consumers, and therefore interested in the maximum productivity of the firm, which in turn leads to optimal products. Not all members of the firm are shareholders, however. The purpose of the shareholders will therefore not be the purpose of all the other members of the firm. From this we can conclude that the purpose of the firm is the production of optimal goods or optimal input materials for other goods, under the condition that the goals of the main groups in the firm, or of the groups affected by the work of the firm, are also taken into consideration. The purpose of the firm is the production of optimal goods under the condition that the goals of paying appropriate wages, appropriate dividends, and appropriate prices to suppliers are fulfilled at the same time as the purpose of producing optimal goods.

The necessary condition for the existence of the firm and the main purpose for which the firm came into existence is the production of goods, not the financial goals of generating profit and capital gains. This main purpose of the firm can only be realized if sufficient returns on investment are earned, and in this sense the realization of shareholder value is a condition for the realization of the main purpose of the firm; it is not, however, the prime condition. The main purpose of the firm, the production of optimal goods, requires the firm to be productive and efficient. How productivity and efficiency are to be achieved is a secondary question. The ultimate purpose of the firm is not the financial purpose but the production purpose: the financial purpose remains subordinate and does not take precedence, as it did prior to the financial crisis and the associated overemphasis on the purposes of and conditions imposed by finance.[33]

Since it is the purpose and the task of the industrial firm to supply society with the best products, manufactured at the lowest opportunity costs, the conditions that ensure the achievement of this purpose, namely secure financing and the profitability of the corporation, are also obligatory. The means to ensure that the firm fulfills its purpose are not, however, the primary purpose of the firm. If the purpose of the firm, the production of optimal goods, can best be achieved by means of market efficiency and the maximization of shareholder value, these are the required means to achieve this goal. If this goal can be achieved by other means, then those means must be utilized. Productivity is the duty of the firm, regardless of the efficiency of the market and the form of financing.[34]

The principle that the obligation is derived from the nature and the purpose of the matter or institution, and that the principal ethical and legal obligation of the firm arises from its main purpose and not from the conditions which ensure the realization of its purpose, tempers the idea of the primacy of shareholder value and the goals of the financial investors. The primary purpose of the firm is not the maximization of profit or of shareholder value in the capital market, i.e. the financing of the firm, but rather the production of optimal goods.

One of the merits of the *stake*holder approach is that it has restored to the theory of the firm an idea that was in danger of being forgotten amid the financial theory of the firm: that the firm is a multipurpose organization and not a single-purpose institution established solely for the purpose of maximizing the wealth of its shareholders. Yet the stakeholder approach provides no means of integrating the various goals of the stakeholders, but places them immediately alongside one another with parity of status. The question of how the goals of the different stakeholders can be integrated into the overall goal of the firm is not further elaborated in R. E. Freeman's[35] stakeholder theory.

---

[33] According to J. J. BROUWER, PIET MOERMAN: *Angelsaksen versus Rijnlanders: zoektocht naar overeenkomsten en verschillen in Europees en Amerikaans denken* (Anglo-Saxons and Rhinelanders: searching for agreements and differences in European and American thinking), Antwerpen (Garant) 2005, pp. 87 and 95, in the countries of Rhineland capitalism, particularly in Germany and the Netherlands, there is a greater emphasis on practical trades and the associated skills; in other words, employees and managers are observed to be more product- than finance-orientated than in American capitalism. Likewise, the managers more frequently come from production than in the USA, are more orientated to their profession and product, and therefore also feel a closer affinity with their staff.

[34] This fact is emphasized by LEE A. TAVIS: "Modern Contract Theory and the Purpose of the Firm", in: S. A. CORTRIGHT, MICHAEL J. NAUGHTON (eds.): *Rethinking the Purpose of Business. Interdisciplinary Essays from the Catholic Social Tradition*, Notre Dame, Indiana (University of Notre Dame Press) 2002, pp. 215–236.

[35] R. E. FREEMAN: *Strategic Management: A Stakeholder Approach*, Boston (Pitman) 1984, and R. E. FREEMAN: "The Politics of Stakeholder Theory: Some Future Directions", *Business Ethics Quarterly*, 4 (1994), pp. 413ff.

The goals of stakeholders are subordinated to the overall purpose of the firm, which means that their claims upon the firm's total yield are limited not only by their strategic power, which they can exercise in contention with the claims of other stakeholder groups, but these claims are primarily limited by their contribution to the purpose of the firm, by the extent to which they fulfill the demands that the firm must make on all its stakeholder groups for the sake of its own preservation as an institution over time. This principle also applies to banks, which cannot measure their success by shareholder value alone. The main criterion for the success of financial institutions, as in the real economy, is the product; in the case of banks, the financial service and its quality.

The purpose and condition of the firm's existence, consistently to produce first-class goods or services in response to market demand, constitutes the disciplining principle and the disciplining power in the strategic negotiations between the different stakeholder groups. It is the central disciplining principle alongside the disciplining instrument of profit or of shareholder-value maximization. Productivity as an obligation, and the product as the purpose of the firm, take pride of place as the main purpose of the firm and relegate the other purposes to the status of subordinate purposes. The effect of the "product as purpose" is that shareholder-value maximization is only the second-most-important purpose, a purpose that is subordinated to the productivity goal. Nevertheless, as a control principle, it carries the preponderant weight among the many other purposes that are pursued by the firm's stakeholders and ranked lower than the productivity goal in the hierarchy of the firm's purposes. The purpose of the firm is the production of its specific good, service or product, which amounts to its contribution to society.

When an entire industry so seriously jeopardizes its contribution to society as the banking industry did, by producing losses amounting to trillions of euros or dollars, it has not fulfilled its purpose, either in terms of product or service provision or in terms of shareholder value. Given that the banking industry constantly extolled shareholder value in the past, yet parts of that very industry subsequently consigned both its shareholders and its customers to de facto bankruptcy that was only avoided by the bailout from the state, it is now necessary to reappraise the purpose of financial institutions and the industry as a whole. The debacle that resulted from the primary pursuit of the purpose of shareholder value, the principle of shareholder primacy, forces the finance industry to think again.

The Dominance of the Shareholder-Value Orientation and the Holding Structure of the Firm

The overemphasis on the finance aspect and the financial purpose of the firm in industrial and banking businesses is particularly apparent from the rise of the holding company, a trend that has lost momentum recently, interestingly enough, despite the continuing pre-eminence of the shareholder-value principle.

In the transformation of the industrial firm into a conglomerate and into a holding firm which serves as a monitoring institution with oversight of the firm's investments in its different divisions, the corporate head office becomes a financing institution for the firm itself, modeled on a financial investor. Its role is to ensure that all divisions of the firm generate maximum shareholder value for the holding company, although the material purpose and product of the divisions themselves are of no great significance to the holding company's goals.

For the holding company, shareholder value is both the purpose and the product of the firm in the same way that, for investment funds, the maximization of their own firm's shareholder value and the shareholder value of investment clients is the firm's primary business purpose and its product. For the holding company, the products of the divisions are only a means of maximizing the holding company's shareholder value.

The holding company is a particularly good example of the inversion of means and ends. It implies that the purpose of the firm, the product, is appropriated as a means of increasing the share price, although share-price growth was originally just the means of controlling and ensuring that the firm was fulfilling its purpose of producing good products.

The most recent trends in business show the holding structure in a very much less advantageous light than just a few years ago. Industrial firms are turning back to their original strength and primary task, the production of goods in their core area of competence and are finding that this strategy is also the most profitable. They no longer see themselves as the portfolio for their own holding company's capital, or their divisions as mere investment opportunities for the holding company.

Understanding shareholder value as a control principle ensures that the holding company does not view shareholder value as its main purpose and, in this way, falls short of its optimal productivity, but rather that the firm ensures the optimality of the product and thereby its own optimal performance. The large firm can only maximize shareholder value if it regards this as a control principle and not as the purpose of its business activity.

As a control principle, the shareholder-value principle has the virtue that it is self-fulfilling insofar as it ensures that its purpose, the firm's success, is only guaranteed when it is not the main purpose of the firm, because it cannot realize maximum shareholder value if it views the employees only as a means to this end. There is no inherent tendency in the shareholder-value principle, of itself, to bring about the inversion of means and ends or its own transformation from a means of verifying success to the actual purpose of the firm. This transformation was caused by the outside influences of an unbalanced overemphasis on the financing of the company and exaggerated expectations of return on investment.

Perverse Incentives from Shareholder Primacy: Speculation Instead of Production

The subversion of the firm's purpose from the product as the primary purpose, to maximization of shareholder value as the primary purpose, alters the task of management: to the task of production is added the task of speculation. The idea that the overall orientation to shareholder value will automatically bring out the best in the firm, via the invisible hand of the market and the firm's contracts, is untenable. Admittedly, the industrial firm can only generate shareholder value if it produces useful goods and if it honors its implicit contracts, to a certain standard, with its employees and its customers. Nevertheless, it only realizes the common good of the firm "somehow" and "on the back of" shareholder-value maximization, because the new overall purpose of the firm, the maximization of shareholder value, is realized to a growing extent by capital market speculation.

Since share prices on the stock exchange do not reflect the real value of the firm's productivity exactly and at all times, but are also the result of speculation in the stock market, management has an interest in engaging in speculation and manipulation of its own firm's share price, and hence of its own shareholder value. This distraction of management's attention and intention away from the firm's principal task, the product, to the conditioning principle of the firm, the maximization of shareholder value which is made the main purpose, gives rise to two detrimental effects.

Firstly, it creates perverse incentives for management to take more interest in capital gains, road-shows etc., and thus in speculation on corporate value rather than in production, or at least to be overly interested in speculation instead of concentrating on the actual management task. Secondly, this leads to short-termism in corporate governance, and a blinkered focus on shareholder value in every quarterly report. Yet the "terror of the quarterly report" that is so characteristic of the American economy is rather less deserving of opprobrium than the focus on the share price. The demand that the firm should operate at a profit in every quarter is a perfectly justified requirement because a quarter-year is a long time in a human lifespan. The quarter-by-quarter scrutiny becomes problematic when, in every quarter, share price growth is viewed as the task for which management is held accountable.[36]

Incentives are central to every economic system, and it is one of the main arguments for the shareholder-value principle that it creates efficient incentives for management to maximize the total value of the firm measured in terms of shareholder value. However, incentives can also give rise to perverse incentives, which divert intentions to activities that are not in the firm's interest. If shareholder value becomes the overall purpose of the firm, the managers have strong incentives to devote their attention and time to finding possible ways of manipulating the share price of their firm in the capital market. The managers then allow their attention to be drawn to decision-making factors which are not in the interest of those members of the firm who are not shareholders. The possible perverse incentives that the shareholder-value principle is capable of exerting over management, when viewed as the sole purpose of the firm, are considerable.

The second effect of the perverse incentives that can stem from the shareholder-value principle, the short-termism of excessive attention to the day-to-day share price on the stock exchange, is not in the firm's long-term interest either if it inhibits

---

[36]BRANDEIS (1914), p. 140, has already pointed to the similar problem that arises when the bank appoints the directors of a firm and when these directors are more interested in the share price of the firm they direct than in the firm's product.

strategies for long-term profitability. It is nevertheless important to see that short-termism is not, in itself, an economically and ethically negative phenomenon. It can be economically necessary and ethically legitimate to liquidate an investment after only a very short time, if the original decision is found to have been mistaken or if, in the light of unforeseen new events, it is the right decision no longer.

The Inversion of the Control Instrument of Shareholder Value to the Purpose of the Firm, and the Role of the Employee in the Firm

The inversion of the principle of maximization of shareholder value from the control and financing principle to the primary purpose of the firm instrumentalizes the members of the firm's organization as means to the end of maximizing shareholder value. This practice of using the members of the organization as means to an end is not, in itself, reprehensible. The Kantian formula of the categorical imperative, that one should always act such that one never uses others as means to an end only, does not mean that one may never use another person as a means to a legitimate end. The firm that makes shareholder-value maximization its primary purpose need not necessarily use its members as means to this end *only*, but it is nevertheless in danger of acting in such a way and will give its members the impression that they are only means to this end, rather than also an end in themselves for the firm.

The stakeholder principle, in contrast, ensures that the interests of all stakeholders and groups of members of the firm are respected, but as mentioned earlier, it does not offer the firm any principle that helps it to arrive at a ranking of the "stakes" of the stakeholders, i.e. their particular concerns, in the negotiation process. Ultimately, the stakeholder approach leaves the stakeholders in the situation of an open battle for power and rewards within the firm. Whereas the shareholder approach only seems to acknowledge the interest of a single stakeholder group, the stakeholder approach acknowledges the many interests but supplies no principle of justice for the process of reconciling their interests; only a principle of strategic negotiation.

This is made apparent by the fact that during the negotiation process about the demands that the different stakeholder groups can justifiably expect the firm to satisfy, they must refer to some principle of justice. The principle of justice in business, and hence in the firm, is generally that payments and rewards for services rendered are determined according to the value that the party concerned has contributed to the purpose of the organization or firm.[37]

---

[37]On this principle, cf. G. SCHMOLLER: "Die Gerechtigkeit in der Volkswirthschaft" (Justice in the economy), *Jahrbücher für Gesetzgebung, Verwaltung und Volkswirthschaft im Deutschen Reich* (Yearbook for Legislation, Administration, and Economics in the German Empire), 5 (1881), pp. 19–54. – On the Historical School of National Economy cf. P. KOSLOWSKI: *Gesellschaftliche Koordination. Eine Theorie der Marktwirtschaft* (Social coordination. A theory of the market economy), Tübingen (Mohr Siebeck) 1991; P. KOSLOWSKI (ed.): *The Theory of Ethical Economy in the Historical School. Wilhelm Roscher, Lorenz von Stein, Gustav Schmoller, Wilhelm Dilthey*

The idea that rewards should be determined according to the contribution to the firm's purpose is expressed, albeit in different wording, in the old principle of Roman law *suum cuique tribuere*, to every man his due, as for example in Thomas Aquinas. Everyone should receive what they have contributed to the common purpose of the organization. This principle also forms the deeper justification for the theory that incomes and salaries should be based on the marginal productivity of the factors; that the production factors should be paid according to their marginal product.

The principle that all members of an organization should be paid according to their contribution to the firm's purpose is distinct from the shareholder-value principle, which tends to assume that the firm's task is to concentrate on the contributions of just one group, the shareholders, and on the investment income payments distributed to shareholders based on their contribution to the firm, their financing input.

The idea that the residual profit only belongs to the business owner and/or capital owner was criticized with the justification that the dispositive factor is not the only one responsible for the dispositive success of the firm, because there can also be dispositive elements in the contribution of employees to the firm's success. However, since the employees are not usually prepared to bear their share of any residual loss, the award of the residual profit to the owners is justified.

There are a series of disciplining principles in the firm, and a sequence of controls which reinforce one another as a fail-safe system: the shareholders prevent the members of the firm from shirking their responsibilities; the stakeholders exert discipline over the shareholders and their expectations of returns on capital, constantly reminding them that this purpose of theirs is not the firm's only purpose; the firm's purpose, i.e. the product, and the principle of justice, that every member of the firm should be rewarded according to his or her contribution to the firm's production process and product, exert discipline over the stakeholders. The shareholder-value principle and the shareholders exert discipline over the firm; the stakeholder-value principle and the stakeholders exert discipline and restraint on the shareholders; and finally, the purpose of the firm exerts discipline and restraint on the demands of stakeholders and shareholders.

Does the Shareholder-Value Principle Lead to a Fusion of Shareholder and Manager Interests?

The principle of shareholder value is not just a principle of greater control over management performance. In fact, the overemphasis on shareholder value by the firm can also lead to a fusion of managers' interests with those of shareholders,

---

and Contemporary Theory, Berlin, New York, Tokyo (Springer) 1995; and P. KOSLOWSKI (ed.): *Methodology of the Social Sciences, Ethics, and Economics in the Newer Historical School. From Max Weber and Rickert to Sombart and Rothacker*, Berlin, New York, Tokyo (Springer) 1997.

which end up being inimical to the interests of other stakeholders. If shareholders and managers form a single stakeholder group with the common interest of increasing their income by means of the firm's share price, the managers will be tempted to make decisions in their own and the shareholders interests to drive up the share price at a cost to the firm and to the detriment of the other stakeholders. The upward trend in executive pay in British state-owned enterprises after these were privatized and reorganized as joint-stock or limited liability companies speaks volumes. The most prominent consequence of the privatization of these firms was the escalation of their managers' salaries to multiples of their previous levels. Equally, the high bonuses of the finance industry can be seen as a result of a one-sided fusion of shareholder and management interests.

Nevertheless, blame for the hyper-speculation in recent decades and the resorting to risk-laden business strategies cannot be laid at the door of the managers alone. They were spurred on and "incentivized" by their shareholders. The one-sided emphasis of shareholder value seemingly legitimized the shareholders in imposing their ideas of profit maximization and high-risk strategies on the managers, who in turn relied on the shareholder primacy principle to justify their strategies. That principle can indeed be credited with primacy in the genesis of false incentive structures. It is therefore necessary to change the system of rewards, not only for managers but also for shareholders.[38] If, based on the shareholders' limited liability[39] for the firm, they are incentivized to expect a high level of management risk-taking, any negative consequences of which cannot affect them beyond the amount of their share capital, i.e. liability is limited, whereas they participate fully in the high profits, they will always demand a strategy involving (unduly) high management risk-taking. If both shareholders and managers also know that the state will bail them out of a banking insolvency, they will entertain even higher risks. An increase in the liable capital of banks, i.e. in shareholders' equity capital, is therefore an indispensable imperative for improving the corporate governance and for stepping up the liability of shareholders and managers. If the shareholders stand to lose more equity capital, if they bear a higher risk themselves, they will encourage the managers to tone down their business risk-taking. If the shareholders bear minimal risk and minimal liability for losses, the managers will be unable to stand up to them, even if the managers themselves are more risk-averse.

The demand to maximize shareholder value created incentives for management to pay more attention to speculative gains in their company's share price than to the profit from superior productivity and products. These incentives can become perverse incentives because the value of shares on the stock market is not the perfect

---

[38] The same is demanded by SINN (2009), p. 307.

[39] Sinn attributes the principle of limited liability a pivotal role among the causes of the financial crisis. He talks about the bacillus of limited liability ("*Bazillus der Haftungsbeschränkung*"; SINN [2009], p. 290). He argues that the limitation of liability creates incentives among those involved to take excessive risks, and claims that this process was exacerbated by diminishing liability further through deregulation and the reduction of the equity to balance sheet total ratio or capitalization requirement.

and infallible result of the actual performance of the manager and the firm, but the result of their performance as *perceived* by the stock market and of their policy of intimating their own success in their communications with the stock market.

Equally, the speculative element in share prices and hence in shareholder value makes it problematic to make executive remuneration too dependent on the development of the firm's share price.

If a firm's shares register a gain in value due to pure stock-exchange speculation about the firm's share price, the enhancement in income that management receives from share options and similar arrangements, as a result of such speculation, is unjustified since they are not the ones who caused the increase in the share price. Another question is whether or not it is justified to reward an average rise in a firm's share price with an above-average uplift in income for management by the mechanism of executive equity plans.

One of the most important effects of shareholder value as a control principle and disciplining method is to ensure that the firm makes profits in every period, which effectively regulates the time-structure and time-preference of investments. Rappaport[40] demonstrates this effect of the shareholder-value principle, which can be seen as one of the principle's main beneficial effects with regard to corporate performance and dividend policy. The shareholder-value criterion forces the firm to ensure, each and every year, that the year's investments in the firm have been profitable, and this requirement in turn ensures that a dividend is paid each and every year.

Rappaport points out that if the firm is going to generate positive capital gains above the market interest rate in the future periods, theoretically, it would make sense not to pay any dividend at all in the present. In that scenario, all profits should be retained within the firm because they will guarantee higher earnings in the future if they accumulate in the firm rather than being paid out as dividends.

However, the shareholder-value criterion prohibits this option by countering the proposition that profits should be retained within the firm for the purposes of self-financing and equity accumulation with a very simple argument: if the firm stops paying dividends, the shareholders will go elsewhere. But this outward impression of shareholder disloyalty masks a deeper insight: whatever management says about its plans for future earnings and dividends that are retained in the firm rather than distributed, the shareholders can never be certain that it is true; nor can they be certain whether it will come true, since the overall economic situation can change over the subsequent 3 years, with the result that profits retained in the firm for 3 years may suddenly vanish in year four. In either case, no gain will accrue to the shareholder – nor, indeed, to the firm – from agreeing to wait.[41]

---

[40] A. RAPPAPORT: *Shareholder Value. Wertsteigerung als Maßstab für die Unternehmensführung*, Stuttgart (Schäffer-Poeschel) 1995, pp. 27ff. Original: *Creating Shareholder Value. The New Standard for Business Performance*, New York (The Free Press) 1986.

[41] Cf. GÜNTER H. ROTH: "Shareholder Value und Dividendenausschüttung" [Shareholder value and dividend distribution], in: P. KOSLOWSKI (ed.): *Shareholder Value und die Kriterien des Unternehmenserfolgs*, Heidelberg (Physica-Verlag) 1999, pp. 128–145.

The emphasis of the shareholder-value approach, on the idea that shareholder value must be realized in each and every year, corresponds to the shorter time-horizon for reaping a return on investment that is characteristic of capitalist democratic societies. This shorter time horizon also seems desirable from an ethical perspective. Although *prima facie* it may seem counter-intuitive to prefer a short-term strategy, because decision-makers are usually inclined toward short-termism in any case, and therefore everything that supports long-term investment seems to have a higher ethical value, it is rational to insist that investments pay returns in every period. The study of undemocratic, non-capitalist societies shows that the population in these societies has often been deceived into sacrificing welfare in the here-and-now on the promise of a more prosperous future. One example was Stalin, who ordered the execution of the engineers who told him that certain longer-term capital projects in northern Russia or in Siberia could never be profitable. Their predictions were not what he wanted to hear, so he opted to shoot the messenger.

Leaving aside this tendency to demand and impose sacrifices for the future by means of cruelty and terror, the fact that long-termism causes losses is of interest with regard to the time-perspective of investments, the sacrifices that individuals are expected to make for their own investment, and the ethical relevance of this question. In a democratic, capitalist society, the population and investors calculate their expected returns on investment over a comparatively short time period. An investment that cannot prove its profitability in the short term will not find any takers. This recommendation justified by the shareholder-value criterion is not only economically efficient but also ethically legitimate for prosperous economies. Whether this judgment also applies to societies that are in the process of economic development and have to achieve higher savings rates is a question that must be left open for the time being.

The other positive side-effect brought about by the shareholder-value criterion, via this compulsion to declare a dividend each and every year, is that it increases the difficulty of building up a monopoly or market-dominating position in the given market. If the shareholders can compel the management to distribute dividends rather than accumulating profits within the company in the form of reserves or equity capital, then the shareholders can spend these profits on consumption or reinvest them in the shares of other firms. Either way, without retaining profits it will be more difficult for the firm to grow sufficiently to gain market dominance or control.

Chapter 10
Financial Overstretch: The Epochal Disturbance of the Invisible Hand of the Market by the Financial Industry

The overstraining of the shareholder-value principle, and the inversion of means and ends from the shareholder-value orientation as the means of controlling the firm's performance to the delivery of shareholder-value as the firm's sole purpose, resulted in overextension of the speculative side of the management remit in the lead-up to the financial crisis. Management was presented with the essentially unrealizable task of maximizing share-price growth.

The financial theory of the firm and the rise of the shareholder-value principle heralded the unleashing of corporate self-interest, which monumentally disturbed and threatened to annihilate the invisible hand of the market. Contrary to widespread belief, the invisible hand of the market, which transforms self-interested actions into economic optimality and efficiency, is not as robust as it needed to be to withstand the unleashing of such rampant self-interest.

The Disturbance of the Compatibility of the Acting Person's Aim with the Firm's Aim

At the center of the theory of the invisible hand of the market is the simple insight that the *finis operantis* and the *finis operis*, the intention of the acting person and the intention of the result of the action are not always the same, but can complement one another. There is a difference between the firm's purpose and the motives for action within the firm. In the language of older ethics this can be described as the difference between *finis operis* and *finis operantis*. The firm's members have their own intentions, which are to maximize their utility or profit. The firm has its own purpose, its own work-task (*opus*), which is the efficient production of a product or work. The "business firm" brings these two purposes together in such a way that both purposes are realized: both the good product and the maximization of utility or profit for the employees and owners. This coincidence is the deeper meaning of Adam Smith's metaphor of the invisible hand of the market.

But the invisible hand is neither so invisible nor so very mysterious as some of its critics believed. The *finis operantis* and the *finis operis*, the intention of the person acting and the intention of the action's result, can complement one another if the

P. Koslowski, *The Ethics of Banking*, Issues in Business Ethics 30,
DOI 10.1007/978-94-007-0656-9_10, © Springer Science+Business Media B.V. 2011

acting individuals in pursuit of their interests are forced, by competition, to accept the condition that if they fail to take consumer interests very seriously or to satisfy consumer demand, they will be squeezed out of the market. Competition and the market force the individual into behaving in such a way that the *finis operantis*, the intention of the person acting, coincides or at least very closely matches the *finis operis*, the intention of the firm's product for the consumer.

The purpose that the firm has to fulfill is to produce a product or a work (an *opus*). So the firm exists for a *finis operis*; for the sake of a product. Individuals have their own purposes, usually the purpose of earning as much money as possible. In the business world they can pursue this purpose much more vigorously than in politics, public administration or the academic world. The organizations of the business world, i.e. firms, must somehow bring together these two purposes in a way that makes them compatible. They do so by means of incentivization. Because business firms can make better use of income-based incentives than other fields of endeavor, they are very efficient. Financial institutions can offer even better financial incentives than industrial firms. By achieving their own purpose of income maximization, pursuing their *finis operantis*, employees simultaneously fulfill the purpose of the firm, the *finis operis*. Incentives do not always work, however, and can even steer efforts in the wrong direction, as has already been shown.

Hyper-Incentivization and the Hubris of the Financial Manager

The hyper-incentivization of financial managers had set the incentives in such a way that they were no longer compatible with the purpose of the finance industry, its *finis operis*, and were steering the efforts induced by the incentives in the wrong direction. The reward systems of the banks were tending to encourage an infinitely high degree of indebtedness,[1] because if bank customers and bank competitors were infinitely deeply indebted, bank employees and shareholders could theoretically earn infinitely high rewards. The remuneration structure geared towards rapid profits taught brokers to lose all sense of the correlation between risk and liability. A higher bonus focuses executive minds on business expansion, sidelining financial stability as a factor in their decision-making. Bonuses should be replaced with a bonus/malus system so that employees also bear a share of the loss occasioned by their excessive risk-taking and a penalty mechanism is built in to cover default risks. The question is how much performance-related pay, how many incentives the financial system can bear. There are considerable differences between the West and Japan in the reliance

---

[1] Thus GÜNTER FRANKE: "Gefahren des kurzsichtigen (internationalen) Risikomanagements des Bankkredits, der Collateralized Debt Obligations (CDO) sowie der Structured Products und die Finanzmarktkrise" [Risks of short-sighted (international) risk management of bank credit, CDOs and structured products, and the financial market crisis], presentation at the conference "Einsichten aus der Finanzmarktkrise für das Bank-Compliance" (Insights from the financial market crisis for bank compliance) of the "Working Group on Compliance and Ethics in Financial Institutions, German Business Ethics Network", held in collaboration with Bayerische Hypo- und Vereinsbank AG on 29 May 2009 in Munich.

on bonuses. According to Franke, the proportion of performance-related pay in the remuneration of financial industry employees in Japan is below 70% whereas in the USA and Europe it is over 85%.[2]

When salaries are extremely high, there is a strong suspicion that the appetite for risk is also extremely high. Excessive salaries fuelled the risk-taking mentality. When even the shareholders are fixated on rapid financial returns above all else and have a high appetite for risk, they appoint people to the head of the firm who seek out these risks. Both shareholders and managers want to see the share price rise and both think, "If it goes belly up, we'll make a fast exit" – the investor can ditch the share, the manager can ditch the firm. Shareholders with an eye on a quick buck appoint managers with an eye on a quick buck.

The consequence is that the risks taken are unduly high. For financial brokers or managers, these are made bearable by the fact that they can pocket their bonuses and leave the firm they have ruined, on the "Take the money and run!" principle, without being ruined themselves. It is therefore necessary to limit executive salaries and reassess the bonus system in the light of the link between managers' inflated pay and their extreme appetite for risk. Nevertheless, essentially it remains a valid principle that the firm has the right and the duty to decide on its own executive remuneration scheme. It normally works well, because a firm does not have money to give away.[3] But in the light of the financial crisis, we must conclude that this way of thinking – that the finance industry will not pay excessive sums to traders and financial brokers, if for no other reason than that salaries and bonuses represent costs – is too simple.

The costs argument is too simple because the bonuses, despite their staggering size, are often negligible in comparison to the revenues generated and the profits that can be earned on such volumes. One example concerns probably the most massive loss ever caused by a trader, the case of Jérome Kerviel of Société Générale bank. Before the disaster, in 2007 Kerviel had made profits of 43 million euros for his bank. That year, he put in a request for the bank to pay him a bonus of 600,000 euros. But the bank only awarded a bonus of half the amount he requested, 300,000 euros. That is a requested bonus of 1.395% and an awarded bonus of 0.697% of the profit generated by the employee – hardly a rate of commission to get worked up about in any other circumstances.[4] On the other hand, all Kerviel did was what his employment contract demanded of him. He just happened to do it successfully, which is what is generally expected under an employment contract and, what is more, without the incentive of a bonus in other industries. So why should he earn a bonus at all? The next year, Kerviel made a loss of 4.9 billion euros on behalf of the bank. He told the press that he had not done it out of any personal greed but for

---

[2]Ibid.

[3]If the only people appointed to a supervisory board are those who are known not to make any trouble over manager pay rises, the firm can still pay excessive salaries contrary to its own self-interest as an institution.

[4]JAMES B. STEWART: "The Omen. How an Obscure Breton Trader Gamed Oversight Weaknesses in the Banking System", *The New Yorker* (October 20, 2008), pp. 54–65, here p. 60.

the sake of the bank. He wanted to do well: "Truly, my goal was just to increase activity."[5]

In view of the high turnovers and the colossal sums of money involved in the banking business, the only possible solution is probably to ban bonuses altogether and confine payment to the contractually agreed salary. Exaggerated bonuses are an overextension of the principle of incentivization, as if financial services providers – unlike professionals in other fields – can only deliver peak performance if every decent idea bumps up their pay by an extra thousand. There is no excuse for the financial sector to act as if it were governed by completely different rules from other spheres of society. A Prime Minister cannot turn around at the end of his or her term of office and say, "Look at everything I've done to take the country forward – I deserve an extra five million." Unduly high bonuses encourage a harmful entitlement mentality, as if to say, "If I don't get an extra million, I'll give up thinking." This is untenable, firstly because there is an employment contract which stipulates the contribution of work for a fixed salary, and secondly because it contravenes the principle of shareholder value, since wrongly set incentives do not increase the value of the firm. When managers are over-incentivized by bonuses, their first thoughts are always about the bonus and the financial markets – and not about the firm. The effect of the incentive is counterproductive, a distraction from the actual task in hand.

The state, in itself, has no right to rein in executive salaries. But if bank executives have driven their banks into insolvency, and the state rescues these banks, the treatment of executives must reflect that they now work for bankrupted institutions. For the state, it would have been better to have let the rescued banks formally declare bankruptcy; in other words, to have let them slip into insolvency before steering them out of it. Since the state had stepped in to cloak the technical insolvency of a bank and allowed it to remain in business, its contracts and contractual bonuses remained in force, for better or worse, and the fact that executives sued for their bonuses should not have come as any surprise. In a certain way, by rescuing the banks in question from bankruptcy, the state was complicit in *Konkursverschleppung* (unlawfully delaying the initiation of insolvency proceedings).

A mentality dominated by share prices and shareholder value favored the taking of excessive risks, which were rewarded with excessive salaries. When excessive salaries are paid, this very fact points primarily to a disturbance of the market mechanism, of competition. This weakness of competition ought to be addressed by a long-term policy to reduce executive salaries in the finance industry while conforming to free-market principles. The crucial question is, was there sufficient competition throughout the echelons of banking? And if so, why did so few come forward to earn such extremely large sums of money? Why was the market for bankers and brokers not overrun by every highflier – as a consequence of which, salary levels in this market would have fallen? It is tempting to suspect that the bankers, and above all the investment bankers, simultaneously expanded

---

[5] Ibid., p. 65.

their business and artificially restricted supply, adopting oligopolistic practices to create a kind of financial oligopoly. Furthermore, the shareholder-value principle attempted to turn the manager into a speculator who must manage speculatively in order to secure speculative capital gains from his firm's shares, of which he in turn receives a share. If the managers in the financial industry refuse to give up consistently excessive returns on investment – i.e. returns consistently above the average for successful industries in the real economy – nor their excessive bonuses, then the legislator should amend tax law and tax the incomes and profits of the financial industry at a higher tax rate than the rest of the economy. In this particular case it would not violate the principle of equality, since the financial industry itself fails to acknowledge such a principle but, as an industry, insists on a special right to rewards and incomes that are not achievable under the conditions of normal market competition. And if the state were actually to concede this special right, it could apply a special rate of taxation as well.

The banks must return to "serving" the economy and the people. Financial capitalism has largely lost sight of the doctrine of service. But it still has a meaningful role to play. It belongs to the idea, rooted in capitalism, that the producer serves the consumer. The finality of the economy is the consumer, not the financial service provider. At the same time, it is important to know that the producer's motivation is rather different: the producer wants to make a profit. If a bank manager is driven solely by shareholder-value and loses sight of the principle of service to the firm as a whole, he has misunderstood his job and is destroying the invisible hand of the market. The duties listed in his employment contract are far wider-ranging than merely generating good yields for shareholders. In some circumstances, he must even put the interests of the firm above those of the shareholders.

For the invisible hand of the market to function, the doctrine of service and the profit motive, the *finis operis* and the *finis operantis*, must work in interaction; in fact, they must become two sides of the same coin. The invisible hand of the market, or of capitalism, consists in the fact that the entrepreneur can only make a profit by serving the consumer – and in the emergence of a kind of pre-stabilized harmony between entrepreneur and consumer. Without that, there is no functioning market. The doctrine of service makes sense when it is accompanied by benefits for the consumer and for the service provider. The business community must not overplay the idea that people's only motivation is to maximize profit. By virtue of their money-creating role, banks have an ancillary public function, and for that reason they cannot behave like sheer self-interest maximizers, any more than doctors can be driven solely by the maximization of their own self-interest when they are treating a patient.

Human beings are motivated by a variety of factors in everything that they do. They constantly have both selfish and altruistic motives. It is impossible to do well in any profession by thinking purely and simply about one's own profit. The same is true for banks. A manager whose mind is solely on his profit cannot be a good manager, because he is not sufficiently orientating himself to the nature of the matter of his or her task. Nothing prevents us from saying: in industry, the profit motive is more predominant than in the church. And yet even in industry, the manager's employment contract alone obliges him to act in the interest of the firm and not in his own interest. The employment contract "buys" the manager's loyalty and fiduciary duty to the firm, just as the consultancy contract buys the consultant's loyalty and fiduciary duty to his clients. The payment of a fee for a consultancy appointment covers not just the time taken for the consultation but also the loyalty of the advisor to the client.

The constricted logic of the shareholder-value principle persists to the point of absurdity, because it calls upon the manager to act primarily in the interest of shareholders, and not in the interest of the firm as his employment contract with the firm requires of him. In the permanent latent conflict of interest that exists between the interest of the firm and the interest of the shareholder, who holds the shares for anything from a few hours to a few months, the principle of shareholder value is constantly in danger of tipping the balance unfairly towards the shareholder, although it is the manager's task to withstand this conflict and to balance it rationally. Furthermore, it is absolutely impossible for a manager to assess every step of every decision he makes, e.g. in the course of product development, in sufficient detail to determine the impact upon the firm's shareholder value and to be sure that it is maximized by that decision compared with any of the alternatives. If the manager wants to do something well, he must first take his bearings from the matter at issue – and then ask himself whether this matter will also yield returns for the shareholders.

The purpose of the firm is not primarily to generate profits but to make good products. From Daimler to Siemens to Microsoft, the same holds true: these firms have always been far more than a loose association of people maximizing their own utility, as the financial theory of the firm would have us believe. All major corporations are centered around a product. To that extent, shareholder value is only a constraint upon their purpose. A firm does not exist purely to produce returns on investment for shareholders – even if the latter are within their rights to see things that way. The purpose of the firm, its *finis operis*, is to create an optimal product for the consumer – under the double restriction that, in the process, the purpose of the acting persons, their *finis operantis*, is also fulfilled. To the shareholders, that is the purpose of getting a good return on their investment, and for the employees it is the purpose of earning good rewards while achieving their own aims as well. A firm must generate profits, it need not maximize them. The shareholder-value principle is justified as a control function, as a means whereby shareholders can make their interests clear to management. What is wrong is shareholder value as an end in itself.

Even the head of Deutsche Bank, Josef Ackermann, explained the emphasis on shareholder-value mainly in terms of the pressure of competition in his industry. It was competition from other major banks, he said, that forced him to seek higher returns. After the financial crisis this argument no longer holds water, since the competitors of the major banks have largely gone bankrupt, despite or indeed because of the shareholder-value principle, and that itself did the very opposite of maximizing shareholder value.

From this we can conclude that it is obviously wrong to seek returns of 20% per annum over a period of three years instead of 5–10% per annum over a period of 30 years. Banks are not allowed to adopt a drug addict's outlook on life: "I'll take heroin for three years, have a great time, spend half my life getting high –

and then I'll be dead." A short-term strategy of that kind is also proscribed by law: the wording of the German Stock Corporation Act (*Aktiengesetz*) affirms that the continuity of the business is an interest. A private speculator may hope to make a fast buck and risk bankrupting himself in the process; the manager of a major bank most certainly may not.

In fact, because of the existing incentive systems in the finance sector, such high-risk, maximum-return strategies were pursued in spite of the existing stock corporation legislation, so that in the end, bankruptcies were almost inevitable. They were pursued because the shareholder-value principle had been made immune to criticism. It had been propagated with the justification that as long as the shareholders are making money, everyone is better off. But that is a non sequitur, an unjustified inference, which is only valid for adherence to the illusion of the perfect market in which all other stakeholders are better off if managers maximize the share price, because the share price reflects the value of the firm with complete accuracy and rationality. In this scenario, however, as the financial crisis demonstrated, there is no pre-stabilized harmony between the shareholder interest and all the other interests, because there is no pre-stabilized harmony or even identity between the firm's stock market value and its actual value at all times, on any trading day. After years of high returns, most of the world's major banks were plunged into bankruptcy, from which they only emerged with the help of state bailouts and hence with the help of taxpayers' money. In some cases, the market capitalization of these firms collapsed dramatically. So what happened to the perfect rationality of the market when it came to discerning the overvaluation of firms?[6]

The pursuit of self-interest mediated by the invisible hand of the market only results in an efficient solution if it does not completely lose sight of the interests of others. Can we call it "greed" when the banking sector, which also fulfills a public or at least an intermediary function by virtue of its role in money-creation through lending, succumbs to the exclusive pursuit of self-interest? For the moment, that question can be left hanging. But outright denial of the relationship between greed and excessive bonus entitlements, as Posner[7] resorts to, is taking the easy way out.

---

[6]Due to the imperfect rationality of markets, investing in shares remains a wager. Wagers are fundamentally uncertain. There are no safe bets, not even with shares. Going long, betting on rising prices, is a wager. Going short, betting on falling prices, is also a wager. Both wagers can be supported by blogs, but not guaranteed. To give an example: on November 24, 2008 the NASDAQ 100 index rose by approximately 6%. Practically all prices went up except for Google, which fell by about 4%. At the same time there was a flurry of blog-postings about Google – which took the tenor, "Google is worthless, overvalued, will be worst hit by the recession. Sell Google!" The originators of these blogs were probably short sellers needing to cover their positions. Their strategy came good. Counter to the market trend, the price dropped by 4%. The next day, November 25, 2008 the NASDAQ 100 fell by approximately 1.5% and Google climbed by about 10% – again, counter to trend. The only verified report issued by Google in these 2 days was a brief comment on November 25, 2008 by Eric Schmitt, CEO of Google, to the effect that business was pretty good. By and large, the price movements of Google were pure (chance-driven) wagers, which did not and could not have any basis, or very little, in information or known fact. Source: own observation.

[7]POSNER (2009), pp. 78, 100, 107.

Posner argues in defense of the finance industry, that "We want them (business people) to be profit maximizers."[8] Of course we want them to be profit maximizers, but not the kind who will maximize their own profit instead of the firm's and then, after a few years of maximizing their own profits, drive their institutions into bankruptcy. Here, as elsewhere, the complicated relationship between the self-interest of the manager, the self-interest of the shareholder and the self-interest of the firm is unacceptably oversimplified.

It would also seem that the misguided motivation structure of many actors in the finance industry before the crisis can most usefully be characterized not as greed but in terms of the vice of hubris.[9] Hubris is a complex behavioral and attitudinal constellation of exaggerated pride combined with unrealistic perceptions of the outside world. Not the least of the pitfalls of hubris is that excessive extrinsic praise and rewards may lead the affected individual to indulge in pride, self-overestimation, and hence, disproportionate risk-taking including a certain loss of reality. The overblown admiration and rewards and the absence of outside criticism can, in turn, stem from the admirers' narcissistic impetus and desire, perhaps as members of the same "stellar firm", to indulge in self-admiration. The admirers and their admiration may, themselves, be motivated by hubris and self-congratulation. Of course, hubris is not restricted to one profession alone. It is very common in politicians and film stars, who are subject to the same forces of adulation and exaggerated attention from the world around them.

Over time, hubris engenders a sense of unqualified superiority over others.[10] The longer the constellation is sustained, the greater the hold of the hubris and the more unlikely it becomes that the hubris-sufferer will break free of the blinders of hubris and recognize reality for what it is. Hubris leads to declining performance because the sufferer is not only blinded to reality, but afflicted by a hubris-induced inability to cooperate with others and find joint solutions to new challenges – a necessity for coping with changes in the organizational context, i.e. changes in the firm in the manager's case, and changes in the state in the politician's case. Extrinsic rewards reinforce the hubris. Here, too, the bonuses of financial managers have an adverse effect by reinforcing hubris and self-aggrandizement while diminishing the realism of their perceptions of the outside world.

---

[8]POSNER (2009), p. 107.

[9]Hubris is a pivotal concept in Greek tragedy, in the *Oresteia* by Aeschylus, for example. In Greek, hubris can also mean greed, an intemperate craving.

[10]Cf. MICHAEL LEWIS: "Self-Conscious Emotions: Embarrassment, Pride, Shame, and Guilt", in: MICHAEL LEWIS, JEANNETTE M. HAVILAND-JONES (eds.): *Handbook of Emotions*, New York (Guilford) 2nd edn. 2000, pp. 623–636; JUNE PRICE TANGNEY: "Perfectionism and the Self-Conscious Emotions: Shame, Guilt, Embarrassment, and Pride", in: G. L. FLETT, P. L. HEWITT (eds.): *Perfectionism: Theory, Research, and Treatment*, Washington, DC (American Psychological Association) 2002, pp. 199–215; and JESSICA L. TRACY, RICHARD W. ROBINS, and JUNE PRICE TANGNEY (eds.): *The Self-Conscious Emotions: Theory and Research*, New York (Guilford) 2007.

Easy Credit and the Hubris of the Consumer

Wanting more, as even Plato knew, is a human characteristic and therefore a quality common to almost all people, not just bankers and financial intermediaries. Greed has to be differentiated from "wanting more" or non-satiation. Greed is wanting more without regard to others and to the rules of business. Muhammad speaks of it as the greatest temptation for humankind; he came from a merchant family, and ought to know. In contrast, Christianity emerged from a skilled manual labor context – Christ was the son of a carpenter – and first gained traction amid the agricultural economy of late Antiquity and early Medieval times.

Easy credit does not initially encourage greed but carelessness. Carelessness leads to over-consumption, to people living beyond their means and neglecting the need for prudent money management. Easy money and easy credit also create more scope for fraud because the entire business environment becomes more careless and less cautious.[11]

With easy credit, nothing seems easier than having everything today rather than tomorrow. Deferring consumption, putting it off until tomorrow, seems pointless. Added to this, advances in cognitive psychology have placed even better and more refined instruments of persuasion in the hands of marketers and advertisers, with which to coax the consumer into buying consumer goods and durables. The hubris of the consumer is also encouraged by the producer, who subtly motivates the consumer into consumption and makes saving seem nonsensical or unnecessary.[12] This interdependency causes great concern. If the methods of marketing are able to motivate the consumer to over-consume and to take excessive credit in order to do so, a permanent spiral of over-consumption, over-indebtedness in private consumer credit, and excessive credit-enhancement on the part of the banks will be the consequence.

If a country's central bank sets an interest rate of 1%, as the Fed did in the United States in the lead-up to the financial crisis and has done again since, the difference between present and future utility is virtually wiped out: the individual really can have everything today, without having to pay extra for it over time in the form of interest. This leads individuals to act under the "debt illusion": the individual forgets that the loan must be repaid and tends to consume too much in the here and now. The result is over-consumption in the present time.

This individual acting under the debt illusion will have to save punishing amounts in future so as to be able to repay the debts for excessive present consumption,

---

[11]Pointed out by ANTONIO ARGANDOÑA: "Understanding the Financial Market Crisis – Improving the Financial Market Performance. From a Business Ethics Point of View", presentation at the conference "Einsichten aus der Finanzmarktkrise für das Bank-Compliance" (Insights from the financial market crisis for bank compliance) of the "Working Group on Compliance and Ethics in Financial Institutions, German Business Ethics Network", held in collaboration with Bayerische Hypo- und Vereinsbank AG on 29 May 2009 in Munich.

[12]The connection between the new possibilities of cognitive psychology and the plummeting savings ratio are pointed out by POSNER (2009), p. 109.

even if interest rates are low. This will pose difficulties for the individual, who has become accustomed to present consumption but now has to start saving twice as hard. Downward corrections of disposable income will have to be made. If the individual is unable to keep up repayments, and if many others find themselves in the same position, house prices will fall, and the falling house prices will drive more and more loans into default. A downward spiral sets in. The banks have to write down asset values. Capital is destroyed. Consumption has to be reined in. Stagnation and deflation follow.

The policy of easy money and easy credit enabled an unprecedented expansion of consumption, and of the banking and finance sector that brokered the consumer credit. But it also enabled the emergence of special finance and investment institutions on the investment side, such as private equity firms and hedge funds. The private equity firms and hedge funds owe their extra profits and indeed their very existence to easy credit. Thanks to the low interest rates, they were able to borrow money cheaply for leveraged corporate acquisitions and "corporate raiding", and are still able to do so today. Private equity firms not only accepted private equity from private investors, but also borrowed themselves, taking loans amounting to billions of dollars at 3% interest from the banks. The banks, for their part, were equally over-leveraged because, thanks to imaginatively structured products like CDOs, they were lending money far beyond the regulatory capitalization limits. The private equity firms bought corporations on the never-never, put management under pressure, improved corporate governance – or not, and then resold the corporations on the stock exchange after a year with a premium, an agio, of 10–20% on the capital deployed for the purchase, and made between 7 and 17% profit on the borrowed billions used to make the investment. When private equity firms sold firms after owning them perhaps for just 1 year, at a profit of only 6% on the acquisition price which they had financed by borrowing billions at 3%, the profit was huge.

This is where low interest rates facilitated greed, as evidenced in the pursuit of mere agiotage, the practice already described whereby a premium is levied although no value has been added. If lending rates are between 7 and 10%, and the resale of the firm acquired with borrowed capital is delayed for several years by a weak stock market, and the firm has gained little or no value in the intervening years, this business plan starts to look very different. In some cases this leads to losses amounting to billions, which these firms cannot absorb and dump on their banks, who are also unable to absorb them and therefore become insolvent, and seek a reprieve from the state. For an imprudent speculation, the state has to stump up billions from funds that belong to taxpayers – who ultimately take the loss. When the conditions that favored easy money no longer apply, easy profits are no longer a prospect whereas huge losses certainly are.

Mention must also be made here of the unfairness of the situation created by those who engaged in financial wagers, who amassed huge debts when these failed, and who then put an equal share of the burden of paying their wager debts upon those who detest wagers and might even think the state should not allow them. The elements of the population who oppose wagers find themselves having to accept that not only does the government allow such wagers; it even steps in with their money and pays the wagerers' debts if these wagers fail on a grand scale.

The policy of easy money led to extra profits and extra commissions, because the markets for credit and finance reached gargantuan volumes. It was a policy that exposed real-estate agents and consumers to hubris, which manifested itself as over-consumption of houses and consumer goods, but also in credit-financed amateur speculation on the most colossal scale. The overextension of mortgage credit in the USA was immense: "In 1949, mortgage debt was equal to 20% of total household income; by 1979, it had risen to 46% of income; by 2001, 73% of income."[13] The policy of easy mortgage lending in the USA led to an over-consumption of houses. Easy mortgage credit was made possible in the United States by the state guarantees for the US mortgage agencies Fannie Mae and Freddie Mac and their low-cost loans, and by the creation of tax incentives for home ownership.[14] Cheap mortgage credit was partially used for the credit financing of speculative financial deals, particularly in shares. In 2005, the government of the Netherlands had to reduce the ratio of mortgage lending to collateral which had previously allowed borrowing of up to 120% of a house's market value, in order to clamp down on the use of mortgage borrowing for purchasing shares.

Green and Wachter warned of the necessity for a big state bailout back in 2005, which they did not consider possible: "Funneling lower-than-market rate financial capital raises the risk that society will invest an inefficiently high amount in housing, and also that the risks of that investment are being underpriced by the market." However, they thought it unlikely that it would ever come to an actual bailout by the state: "No one wants to find out if the federal government would really pay off tens of billions of dollars if Fannie Mae and Freddie Mac became bankrupt."[15] The extent to which the state encouraged the take-up of mortgages even by those on low incomes in the USA becomes apparent from the rise in bad mortgage risks, sub-prime and near-prime loans, from 9% of newly securitized mortgages in 2001 to 40% in 2006.[16] The hubris of the finance industry was mirrored, if on a less extravagant scale, by the hubris of consumers, mortgage borrowers, and amateur speculators.[17]

---

[13]RICHARD K GREEN and SUSAN M. WACHTER: "The American Mortgage in Historical and International Context", *Journal of Economic Perspectives*, 19 (2005), pp. 93–114, here p. 93. The authors note that the American mortgage is decidedly different than in the rest of the world, but also remark that this securitization of loans protected the borrower against changes in the lending rate and therefore made it considerably easier for borrowers to take out mortgages (Ibid., p. 100).

[14]Cf. W. SCOTT FRAME and LAWRENCE J. WHITE: "Fussing and Fuming over Fannie and Freddie: How Much Smoke, How much Fire?", *Journal of Economic Perspectives*, 19 (2005), pp. 159–184.

[15]GREEN and WACHTER (2005), pp. 108/9.

[16]DANIELLE DiMARTINO and JOHN V. DUCA: "The Rise and Fall of Subprime Mortgages," *Economic Letter – Insights from the Federal Reserve Bank of Dallas*, Vol. 2, No. 11 (November 2007), Online: http://www.dallasfed.org/research/eclett/2007/el0711.html

[17]Cf. also MARKUS K. BRUNNERMEIER: "Deciphering the Liquidity and Credit Crunch 2007–2008," *Journal of Economic Perspectives*, 23 (2009), pp. 77–100.

Credit and *Credo*, Economic Success and "Manifest Destiny"

The connection between placing faith and trust in someone and giving them credit is obvious even linguistically in the common root of the word in the Latin verb "*credere*", to believe. To be trusted with credit, an individual must be believable, credible. There is a relationship between financial capitalism and religion, not in the sense that capitalism itself is a religion – which is a nonsense because nobody but fools could regard capitalism as divine – but in the sense that the religious interpretation of life and the world has repercussions for the interpretation of business, finance and economic action, and vice versa.

If credit is given to someone whom one believes able to repay the debts, believers will more readily believe this of people who share their own religious convictions. Therefore, in the past, credit was often given only to members of the same religious community. This again highlights that a globalized credit market which lacks any close proximity to the communities in which business takes place ought to have less of a basis for trust, and give less credit, than smaller, less complex societies with more uniformity of religious persuasion.

However, it is not only religion that matters to the credit market in this context, but also faith in the future and the interpretation of economic success. In a society with universal or at least widespread confidence in the future and a belief in constant growth, there is also a greater belief that loans will be repaid in due time.

The USA as a country is particularly credit-friendly and has great faith in credit. In part this goes back to America's Calvinist tradition. Switzerland's reformed Christianity and American Calvinism, which came together as one denomination, are the first Christian denomination and probably the first religion of any kind to view and approve of credit and lending at interest as something positive. The Swiss theologian Heinrich Bullinger was the first to defend interest.

Bullinger approves of economic activity, but also seeks to find the right yardstick for financial and credit transactions. All economic activities must be for mutual benefit. Taking undue advantage must be prevented. Mutual benefit and the prohibition of theft are the criteria of economic activity. Cheating and fraud ("*Beschiss und Betrug*") are forms of theft, in Bullinger's view, and need to be prevented.[18]

He therefore distinguishes two types of interest: the unconscionable, usurious kind and the "honest" kind. He begins to use the word "usury", which had previously always been synonymous with "interest", for the harmful form only, whereas in Scholastic theology any interest-taking was usury. Even the lender's sacrificed utility, an argument that Scholastic thinkers and most notably Thomas Aquinas[19]

---

[18]Thus MARTIN HOHL: "Heinrich Bullinger als Ökonom" [Heinrich Bullinger as an economist], *stab. Stiftung für Abendländische Bildung und Kultur*, Rundbrief 149 (2006), online: http://www.stab-ch.org/index.php?page=rundbrief-149. – Cf. also WILHELM A. SCHULZE: "Die Lehre Bullingers vom Zins" [Bullinger's theory of interest], *Archiv für Reformationsgeschichte*, 48 (1957), pp. 225–229.

[19]Cf. P. KOSLOWSKI: "Ethische Ökonomie und theologische Deutung der Gesamtwirklichkeit in der Summa Theologiae des Thomas von Aquin" [Ethical economy and theological interpretation

certainly understood, was not accepted as a justification for charging interest. In Scholastic theology, the debtor only has the duty to repay the loan in full, with the proviso of preservation of its value. Compensation for inflation would therefore be perfectly legitimate, for Scholastic thinkers, but no payment in excess of the amount of the loan, the principal, and the amount to compensate for inflation.

Bullinger, on the other hand, recognizes the "good" form of interest as economically useful. He develops the first ideas towards a theory of interest: interest is compensation for sacrificed utility. "He who lent the money could have bought some good with it, of which he would have had all the use." (21st Sermon, 116b own trans.).[20]

As early as 1531, Bullinger was the first reformer who allowed interest-taking within bounds laid down by authority. In Zurich, these bounds remained in the region of between five and six percent per annum until well into the nineteenth century. Bullinger's influence in the Calvinist world was considerable. During Holland's golden age in the seventeenth century, it is reported, the texts read aloud to sailors on board Dutch ships were the Bible and Bullinger.

From this historical sketch, it is clear what a turnaround preceded the financial crisis. For centuries, interest and later the rate of interest was the central question of economic and business ethics. With the easy money of recent decades, the problem is no longer the rate of interest but rather the conditions on which lending is approved and low interest rates are granted, and above all the structured products in which credit is packaged. It is no longer the case that too little credit is available, but too much.

In the USA, great value is traditionally attached to creditworthiness, but also to the principle of not giving credit too lightly. Calvinists set great store by a good "credit history". In the USA, taking on and paying off debts – establishing a "credit history" – is a necessary part of everyone's biography. The reason is simple: how can anyone know whether a borrower will repay his debts or not without looking into his track record? Someone who has repaid debts in the past will probably do so in future, although this is not certain. The criteria for acceptance by a credit card organization are one example. In 2002, the most important qualification for receiving a credit card, in the eyes of the issuing bank, was not the size of the applicant's income

---

of the whole of reality in Thomas Aquinas's Summa Theologiae], in: P. KOSLOWSKI: *Die Ordnung der Wirtschaft. Studien zur Praktischen Philosophie und Politischen Ökonomie*, Tübingen (Mohr Siebeck) 1994, pp. 64–88.

[20]Original source: "*Der das gält vssgliehen, hette mögen ein gout darumb kauffen, von welchem er alle nutzung gehabt hette.*" HEINRICH BULLINGER: Sermons 21 and 22 from the decades (1549–1551), after the German translation by Johannes Haller, Zurich 1558: "*Die Ein vnd zwentzigste Predig. Von dem vierdten gebott der anderen Tafel/welches in der Ordnung der Zehen geboten das achtet ist/Du solt nit stälen. Bey wölchem geredt wirt von der eygenschafft zeitlicher güet-teren/vnd wie man die recht vnd mit Gott überkommen sölle. Auch von mancherley geschlächten vnd gattungen dess diebstals.*" [The twenty-first sermon. Of the fourth commandment on the other tablet/which in the order of the ten commandments is the eighth/Thou shalt not steal. Which talks about the ownership of temporal goods/and how one shall transfer it rightly and with God. Also of many kinds of theft. Own trans.]

but his credit history. Newcomers to the United States could not obtain an American credit card, however high their income, unless they could prove their credit history – which is impossible for someone who has just arrived in the United States, since a credit history in a foreign country does not count. Likewise, a bounced check or any other problem in the credit history could make it impossible to obtain a credit card or severely delay the prospect.

Uncertainty about the repayment of credit in the future can only ever be reduced by the credit history, but never completely eliminated. The individual may suddenly become a wastrel from one day to the next, and gamble away a small fortune in Las Vegas. For that very reason, a high income is no insurance in the bank's eyes. High earners have more means of turning into big spenders than low earners do, so if anything, customers with high incomes are somewhat riskier for the bank.

The belief in credit in the USA has evolved over a long period of time, in stark contrast to continental Europe. In Austria, for instance, it is still necessary to pay a credit tax of 0.8% of the credit sum on any loan taken out. The credit tax, as a tax on income that one does not have but owes to somebody else, is highly paradoxical. It is Maria-Theresian statism. Perhaps part of the difficulties of the financial crisis lie in the fact that in the USA, the ready availability of credit was no longer matched by the strict Calvinist ethos that debts, once entered into, must be serviced. Calvinism also supports a balance between the affirmation of economic success and the demand for frugality in consumption. This balance, too, seems to have been shaken in the period before the financial crisis.

According to Max Weber, the Calvinist entrepreneur is motivated to creativity and to outstanding business achievements by incentives of an economic (the enjoyment of being successful in business) and a religious (proof of being in a state of grace with God) nature. Weber's *The Protestant Ethic and the Spirit of Capitalism* (1905/1958) shows that religious, cultural and economic incentives and motives overlap in capitalist entrepreneurship, and create an impetus for economic creativity and performance.

The Calvinist theory of justification undergoes a revision in Calvin's successors. The religious good of justification and predestination is partly redefined in terms of economic success by the emerging entrepreneurial class. The Protestants' uncertainty about their "state of grace" with God is alleviated by the idea that economic success is a sign of divine favor toward the individual concerned.

For in puritanical Calvinism, even "faith" itself is not a sufficient sign that the believer is chosen by God. According to the *Westminster Confession* of 1646, God elects those destined for eternal life "out of his free grace and love alone, *without any foresight of faith or good works* [emphasis added by the author] or perseverance in either of them, or any other thing in the creature, as conditions, or causes moving him thereunto;"[21] so neither faith nor good works give assurance that man is in

---

[21] *Westminster Confession*, Chapter III. Of God's Eternal Decree, § 5: "Those of mankind that are predestinated unto life, God, before the foundation of the world was laid, according to his eternal and immutable purpose, and the secret counsel and good pleasure of his will, hath chosen in Christ, unto everlasting glory, out of his free grace and love alone, without any foresight of faith or good

a state of grace. The sole proof of predestination for the state of grace, as Weber showed in his analysis, is that somebody is successful in business (ergo: benefiting from a particular form of divine favor). This reinterpretation of economic into religious success is probably one of the most powerful and subtle incentives and amplifiers of motivation and creativity ever experienced by humankind.

The difference in impact between the Calvinist and the Lutheran theory of justification cannot be overestimated. While the Lutheran is justified by faith alone (*sola fide*),[22] the Calvinist is unsure even of his justification by faith and therefore tends to seek visible signs of his justification. That is why economic success can acquire such great significance in certain historically influential expressions of Calvinism.

In Lutheran theology, visible (good) works have never attained a comparable status. Although they are appreciated as expressions of faith, they do not assure people of their justification in any way. The lesser importance of visible works in German Lutheranism influenced attitudes to economic activity with consequent implications for business success. Perhaps the weakness of economic thought in the German intellectual tradition may be traced back to this aspect of Lutheranism. For the success of actions is irrelevant to the justification of humankind in the theories developed from Luther's thinking; instead, justification is seen purely as a gift of grace. If this idea is transferred into a theory of business ethics, its ultimate consequence could be used to justify every person's right to any service or every good – also to be provided by the state – since no good can really be earned by means of good works.

But the distinctively Calvinist motivation to pursue economic success is not counterbalanced by any similar, religiously heightened motivation to engage in consumption. On the contrary, the Calvinist entrepreneur is supposed to reinvest his profits and lead a lifestyle that is frugal rather than ostentatious, freeing up resources for reinvestment to secure further investment success. If this second element of Calvinist interpretation of life and lifestyle, frugality, is left aside and only the element of economic success is taken up as "manifest destiny", as a manifested sign of predestination and a place among the chosen ones, then the business ethos is thrown off balance. Prior to the financial crisis, particularly in the financial sector, conspicuous consumption was also viewed as manifest destiny and led to inflated salary claims and bonus demands. The old Calvinist balance of hyper-motivation

---

works, or perseverance in either of them, or any other thing in the creature, as conditions, or causes moving him thereunto; and all to the praise of his glorious grace." Quoted after the online version of the text at: http://www.reformed.org/documents/index.html?mainframe=http://www.reformed.org/documents/westminster_conf_of_faith.html

[22] *Augsburg Confession* (1530), Article IV: Of Justification: "Also they teach that men cannot be justified before God by their own strength, merits, or works, but are freely justified for Christ's sake, through faith, when they believe that they are received into favor, and that their sins are forgiven for Christ's sake, who, by His death, has made satisfaction for our sins. This faith God imputes for righteousness in His sight." Quoted after the English translation published online at http://www.projectwittenberg.org/pub/resources/text/wittenberg/wittenberg-boc.html

to be successful in production coupled with modesty in personal consumption had
ceased to be the orientation of action.

Separating the Financial Services from the Value Creation
for the Customer: Self-Dealing of the Banks as Shady Dealings

The major banks that went into insolvency had hurt their customers by making total
losses on CDOs and certificates – for which clients had already incurred heavy costs
in the form of commissions and fees. In the case of the CDOs, the banks were also
discovered to have been engaging in forms of self-dealing, by acting vis-à-vis the
investor in the dual role of seller of securitized debts and broker of the transaction
via special-purpose vehicles. It has already been pointed out that transactions of
this kind cannot be classified as arbitrage but only as agiotage, pure pocketing of a
premium.

The same is true of the banks' involvement in the execution of IPOs (initial public
offerings), where they act as adviser and trustee of the seller of the firm going to the
stock exchange, and as trustee to the buyer of these shares. The allocation of the
new shares is largely at the bank's discretion, and remains anything but transparent
to outsiders.[23] It is striking that the IPO business, which was especially lucrative for
the investment banks and accounted for the bulk of their profits, is concentrated in
the hands of very few investment banks. The IPO business, because it is conducted
by a very select number of major banks, has a pronounced oligopolistic structure.[24]

---

[23]On IPOs, cf. THIELEMANN and ULRICH (2003), pp. 63–71.

[24]Even the head of Deutsche Bank and the Swiss National Bank warn of the danger of a global
oligopoly of major banks. Ackermann sees the oligopoly as a consequence of the mergers brought
about by the financial crisis, whereas the view is taken here that it existed even before the financial
crisis. Cf. "Ackermann warnt vor einem Banken-Oligopol. Der Chef der Deutschen Bank macht
sich Gedanken über ein krisenfestes Bankensystem" [Ackerman warns of a banking oligopoly.
The CEO of Deutsche Bank contemplates a crisis-proof banking system], *Frankfurter Allgemeine
Zeitung*, 18 June 2009, No. 138, p. 13: "The Chairman of the Management Board of Deutsche
Bank, Josef Ackermann, has warned that the world's major banks are forming 'more and more
of an oligopoly'. This not only affects competition but increases the systemic risks. 'After the
crisis there will be a few large banks slicing up the global cake – which gives rise to a danger
of oligopolistic structures.' These are dangerous if they collapse. In the crisis, mergers of stricken
financial institutions are taking place, explained Ackermann. The result is increasing concentration
in the banking sector. 'The question in future will be this: how big can banks be in relation to the
strength of the national economy, without becoming 'too big to fail' [...] The Americans say, if a
bank is too big to fail, then it is too big.'" (Own translation from the German).
   Cf. also the Swiss National Bank's call for the subdivision of the two major Swiss banks, UBS
and Credit Suisse: "'Banken notfalls zerschlagen'. Forderung der Schweizerischen Nationalbank
überrascht" ['Break up banks if need be'. Surprising demand from the Swiss National Bank],
Frankfurter Allgemeine Zeitung, 19 June 2009, No. 139, p. 13. "Break up" is not the appropriate
term to use for taking steps to split up an oligopoly.

The Financial Market Crisis as a Crisis Caused by Excessive Trust: Credit Enhancement and Excesses of Trust

Credit enhancement as an expansion of credit capacity by circumventing the minimum equity requirement led to an overextension of lending and a policy of easy money. It camouflaged the net risk of the banking sector and relieved the banks of their duty of debtor monitoring. The banks wanted to trust debtors because it was politically desirable in the USA to encourage the less well-off to take out home mortgages, and because it reduced the banks' debtor monitoring costs.[25]

This policy of easy lending contradicted the functional conditions of the financial system. The financial system is not based on trust. Nor is finance based on love, but on infidelity. If the share falls in value, it has to be ditched. As Jim Cramer said in his "Mad Money" show on CNBC in August 2008: "Don't fall in love with your share, it does not love you."

The non-functionality of trust and love in the lending business is a clue to the tension between religion and finance. The theological virtues of "faith, hope and love" are not the virtues of the finance industry. Its virtues are closer to "systematic mistrust, skepticism and objectivity". If it relies on trusting debtors, which means placing blank hope or blank trust in borrowers and giving them loans out of kindness, the finance industry collapses, exactly as came to pass during the American mortgage crisis of 2007–2009. The non-functionality of the theological virtues of "faith, hope and love" in the financial sector is no disavowal of the theological virtues, just as the virtues of the financial sector, "systematic mistrust, skepticism and objectivity", are not disavowed by the theological virtues.

The financial system is not built on trust but on collaterals, on secured credit. The banks do not trust their customers, nor should the customers trust the banks. Both must provide collaterals in order to be given credit or to be trusted. Strictly speaking, secured credit is the antithesis of trust. It carries no implication of faith and trust in the debtor, but faith and trust in the posted collateral. Trust is not the starting point

---

[25] Barney Frank, Democrat member of US Congress and positioned towards the Left of American politics, believes that there are people who are not equipped to deal with the duties and responsibilities of a mortgage. Giving them mortgage credit causes them more difficulties than benefits. Cf. JEFFREY TOOBIN: "Barney's Great Adventure. The Most Outspoken Man in the House Gets Some Real Power", in: *The New Yorker* (January 12, 2009), pp. 37–47, here p. 38: "According to Frank, at the root of the real-estate crisis was a misguided notion that homeownership should be available to all people – what President Bush has called 'the ownership society'. [...] 'Homeownership is a nice thing but it is not suitable for everybody', Frank said at Boston College. 'There are people in this society who don't have enough money to be homeowners, and there are people whose lives are not sufficiently integrated for them to take on the responsibility to be a homeowner. And we did too much pushing of people into inappropriate mortgages and into homeownership.' He said that many people would always be renters, and that there was nothing wrong with this. 'We need to get back into the business of building rental housing and preserving the housing we have,' he said." Cf. also GILLIAN TETT: "How Greed Turned to Panic", *Financial Times*, May 9/10, 2009, p. 17: "One particularly pernicious aspect of these defaults was that when this new breed of subprime borrowers walked away from their homes, they often left them in such a bad state that is was hard for lenders to realise any value from the repossessed properties."

for everything. In the economy, it all starts with mistrust, mistrust in the solvency and reliability of the borrower, mistrust in schemes and projects, mistrust in the future. A stranger who tried to strike up a business relationship by insisting on being trusted would rightly be viewed with mistrust. The instant reaction would be, "Aha, a confidence trickster." It then takes another step before suspicion can be overcome by trust. Demonstrable certainties remain the basis of trust. "In God we trust" is written on every dollar bill; "everyone else brings data to the table," the bankers used to add, in the days before collateralized debt obligations in the mortgage sector came into existence.[26]

Some posed the question during the financial crisis: "Why should we trust the banks anymore, when they no longer trust each other?" It is a reasonable question, because the financial crisis has chipped away at institutional trust. If the banks no longer give each other credit, why should the private individual give the banks credit in the sense of trust in their reliability and solvency. During the financial crisis, the state is trying to give the banks the certainties they need so that they can provide their banking colleagues with certainties and restore institutional trust.

The problematic issue with this is that even the state does not really know why it should still trust the banks, after their managers made such a total and utter mess.

The term for this policy coined in America is the "bailout" policy, the policy of financial rescue. Some say we are living in the "age of bailouts". In legal usage, bailing someone out means standing surety for someone suspected of a crime. Normally the bail bond is paid out of the assets of the suspect or his family and, particularly in the latter case, entails a show of confidence that the suspect is innocent. The present bailout of bank debt amounting to billions by the state is problematic, from this view, because the errors made by the suspects are clear beyond doubt, and because the bond is being posted not by those who made the business mistakes, out of their own assets or those of their family, but by the government with taxpayers' money and from national wealth. The liability for the economic failure is transferred to the taxpayer, with the immense consequence that asset losses are transferred from the business people who failed to the taxpayers of those nations whose net wealth is now required to underwrite the billions of losses. The bailout is also problematic because it is argued that it will prevent or camouflage the bankruptcy of the bad banks and thereby restore trust in the banking system. Restoring trust by camouflaging bankruptcy is like fighting fire with fire.

If the glut of money in the market engendered excessive trust before the financial crisis, the perception of reality will not be made more realistic and less credulous by pumping more state money into the market. On the contrary, it diverts attention from business failure, and fails to reinforce the lessons learned. For confirmation of this, we need look no further than the managers who, having driven the banks into bankruptcy and been bailed out by the state, promptly repressed all thoughts of bankruptcy, and undeterred by their de facto bankruptcy, sued their state-rescued firms for their bonuses.

---

[26]The alternative version goes: "In God we trust – all others pay cash." Cf. also JAMES SUROWIECKI: "The Financial Page: The Trust Crunch", *The New Yorker*, October 20, 2008, p. 36.

At the moment the whole world trusts the state to step in, as the great savior of the economy in times of trial and tribulation. The state's role as the helper of last resort implies that the government is the creditor of last resort, the insurer of last resort, the breadwinner of last resort. Trust in the state as the savior of last resort is an idea of the modern era, and one that is very seductive. Trust and hope in the state is problematic because it combines legitimate elements of state assistance for the development of society with the worship of state power and the willingness of citizens to delegate responsibilities to it.

Hegel says that the state is God made real, or words to that effect.[27] The religious faith in God is also a faith in the savior of last resort, but according to Hegel, that kind of help is not real in this world – whereas the state is real, in this world, and really able to help. It can give. On the other hand, the state in this world can only give by virtue of also taking. Like anyone else, unless it takes, the state cannot give. In this respect, the state is not God made real but a God who always has to take in order to give. It takes taxes from the citizens in order to give subsidies, such as bailouts to the banks. It also takes from corporations in order to help the socially disadvantaged. It keeps taking, in order to give. In the necessity of having to take in order to give, the state is not God made real. It may be real, but it cannot give without taking. Hegel's words on the state as God made real are therefore economically and theologically incorrect.

This fact does not increase trust in the present situation. It would be fairer to say that, in view of the high indebtedness of the state, the economy comes back to the message on the dollar bill: the more we trust the state in the present situation, the more we are trusting de facto in God. We have no alternative: in order to restore trust in the financial system, institutional trust must be restored. But this is only possible through the state and through trust in its action. On the other hand, as we have seen, the state is not God made real. It does not always know better, and there is a great likelihood that it will make the same or at least similar mistakes as the bankers, whose intellects were so extraordinarily well paid. Hope springs eternal, however. In his show on 2 April 2009, Jim Cramer announced the end of the Depression. But he added that the recession would continue for a while. The end of the Depression means the continuation of the recession. Can you trust someone who calls his show "Mad Money"? Or is someone like that the only one worth trusting nowadays?

---

[27]Cf. G. W. F. HEGEL: *Vorlesungen über die Philosophie der Geschichte*, Werke in zwanzig Bänden, ed. by Eva Moldenhauer and Karl Markus Michel, Frankfurt a. M. (Suhrkamp) 1970, Vol. 12, p. 57: *"Der Staat ist die göttliche Idee, wie sie auf Erden vorhanden ist."* [The state is the divine idea as it exists on earth.] HEGEL, *Grundlinien der Philosophie des Rechts*, § 270, loc. cit. Vol. 7, pp. 418 f.: *"Der Staat ist göttlicher Wille als gegenwärtiger, zur wirklichen Gestalt und Organisation einer Welt entfaltender Geist."* [The state is the divine will, in the sense that it is mind present on earth, unfolding itself to be the actual shape and organization of a world.] Ibid., § 272 Zusatz [Addition], p. 434: *"Man muss daher den Staat wie ein Irdisch-Göttliches verehren und einsehn, dass, wenn es schwer ist, die Natur zu begreifen, es noch unendlich herber ist, den Staat zu fassen."* [One must therefore venerate the state as a secular deity, and observe that if it is difficult to comprehend nature, it is infinitely harder to understand the state.] English translations from the hypertext versions of Hegel's General Introduction to the Philosophy of History and Philosophy of Right at http://www.marxists.org/reference/archive/hegel/index.htm

Conflicts of Interests and Conflicts of Disinterest: Having an Interest in Credit Enhancement and No Interest in the Monitoring of It

In past decades, the business ethics and business law discourse was determined by the thesis of the necessity of avoiding conflicts of interest. Conflicts of interest still play a major role, as is demonstrated by the danger of self-dealing and the conflicts between the bank's interest in obtaining a high launch price for its IPO customers and its interest in providing its investor advisory clients with the optimum advice. Firewalls between the divisions of the bank are a means of averting such conflicts, although the fact remains that the board of the bank has and must have access to all details from all divisions of its bank, and can never be completely free of conflicts of interest, because the conflicting interests of divisions of the bank remain the interests of the bank as a whole.

The expansion of lending and the sale of securitized loans shows, nevertheless, that banks are not only caught up in a conflict of interests, but also in a conflict of disinterest.[28] If there is an incentive for the bank to sell its borrowers' mortgages due to interest in the proceeds of sale and an interest in reducing the minimum equity, the collateralized debt obligation (CDO) creates an indirect incentive for disinterest in the collateral. It encourages disinterest in the mortgage collateral, and hence in the bank's debtor. The salability of mortgage-backed securities and mortgage loans to investors by means of CDOs carries the inherent risk that the bank will subsequently lose interest in monitoring its debtors and the security of the loans it has brokered. Thus, a conflict arises between the interest of the finance system in systematic debtor monitoring and the disinterest of the bank in carrying out this monitoring. Debtor monitoring is a burdensome duty for the bank, and one in which it has a disinterest or lack of interest if it sells the risk from the loan. If it can sell it, it will sell it. The investor, in turn, has a self-interest in carrying out the debtor monitoring, but he has neither incentives nor means of actually doing so. He does not possess the same resources and experience to carry out debtor monitoring as a bank whose primary role is to mediate between savings and investment, deposits and loans.

In the case of CDOs, the financial system faces the difficulty that they do not seem to permit the invisible hand of the market to bring about convergence of the bank's self-interest and the financial system's efficiency interest. Instead, a conflict arises between the interest of the financial system in diligent debtor monitoring and the disinterest of the bank in undertaking such monitoring in relation to the CDOs. Yet debtor monitoring matters not only to the lender, but also to the borrower as an aid to efficiency and self-control. So the net result is a coalescence of disinterest,

---

[28]Cf. BAKER (2008), p. 731: "In the new financial system, the link between lender and borrower has become increasingly tenuous. How else could mortgage loans emerge with no income documentation and dramatic interest rate resets built in? How else could leveraged loans appear with so few covenants?"

a fusion of the bank's disinterest in subjecting the debtor to monitoring, and the psychologically understandable but economically harmful disinterest of the debtor in being subjected by the lender to monitoring of his performance and servicing of the loan.

The function of the bank to exert discipline over the debtor lapses due to the conflict between both parties' disinterest in monitoring the debt and the interest of the economic system in doing so. This "conflict of disinterest" is caused by the disinterest of both lender and borrower in any monitoring of the loan actually taking place. Both sides have a disinterest in the kind of disciplining that is necessary for the efficiency of the credit industry and of capital allocation. The efficiency of the credit system as a whole is damaged by the conflict between the bank's and the debtor's disinterest in monitoring and the interest of the financial system in such monitoring. If we agree with Hans Albert that the price system of the goods market can be seen as a disciplining system,[29] this applies all the more to the interest-rate system of the credit market. Interest is a disciplining instrument, which disciplines both creditor and debtor. Without it, credit discipline is dealt a severe body-blow. If too much of this is meted out, it will cripple the efficiency of the financial system. The policy of easy money with extremely low interest rates and lax debtor monitoring leads to indiscipline and inefficiency in the credit market. It gives banks and debtors undue license for self-indulgence.

From Big Bang Deregulation to Big Bailout, or: How Deregulation Ended in the Largest State Bailout of Banks in History

The financial crisis led to the biggest state bailout in history, or at least the biggest ever state bailout of distressed banks.[30] The liability for the economic failure, particularly of the American banks, was transferred to the taxpayer. The repercussions for the understanding of liability in business will be considerable. The disappearance of the banks from the market was prevented by the state bailout, in a situation in which the banks were de facto bankrupt. The result of this bailout policy is that the full extent of the business failure and its full consequences did not become visible, and hence the lessons were not learned to their full extent, because the state covered up the business failure of banks by stepping in with the bailout.

The state bailouts of the banks are not bail bonds posted by the accused themselves, but bailouts that the state, effectively the prosecutor and judge, is paying for the accused, the insolvent banks. To some degree these bailouts imply that the

---

[29] HANS ALBERT: *Marktsoziologie und Entscheidungslogik* [Market sociology and decision logic], Neuwied (Luchterhand) 1967, pp. 66 f.

[30] Although perhaps the German unification project was and is an even bigger state bailout – for the eastern part of the country.

state is taking over the banks' debts in their entirety. The prevention of bank insolvencies by means of state intervention also means that the management that caused the crisis is not dismissed, or that if it is dismissed, it can still sue for the bonuses to which it is contractually entitled. Since the bankrupt employers are still in business, for the most part they must comply with their contractual obligations as if no bankruptcy had taken place. This is particularly the case in continental Europe where the civil law system, unlike American and English common law, means that retrospective legislation and adjudication are neither possible nor constitutional. Even a special tax on the bonuses still being paid by the state-rescued firms cannot be imposed retrospectively. In this respect, common law is more flexible than continental civil law.

On the other hand, it is apparent that desirable as it may be to replace the management of all banks, there is no other group of bankers or managers waiting in the wings to take over the banks from their colleagues who failed. The renewal of the financial industry must therefore be carried out by more or less the same people who ruined it. The greatest systemic risk is that the semi-nationalized financial system must be reformed and renewed by people who ruined the old system, and the majority of whom rejected more state and regulatory influence in the financial sector.

The experience of this risk is well-known in the political context from the distasteful necessity of having to accomplish the transition from dictatorship to democracy with the same administration and the same staff of senior civil servants, and even ministers etc., who had previously held positions of influence in the dictatorship.

The big bailout was spawned by the Big Bang deregulation of the finance industry, as the Ancien Régime spawned the revolution, or perhaps more appropriately, as revolution spawned counterrevolution. The Thatcherite deregulation certainly conceived of itself as a deregulatory revolution, and the "Big Bang" epithet was self-chosen. The front page of the *Wall Street Journal Europe* of 31 March 2009, ahead of the G20 summit of finance ministers on 2 April 2009 in London, carried an article with the headline, "'Big Bang' architects now have misgivings. The radical set of market reforms known as Big Bang, turning the city into ground zero of a revolution that begat today's buckling global financial system."

The metaphor of the Big Bang is a shocking one in relation to deregulation. It seems unconscionable to describe the politically-driven reform of a well-established industry as an explosion out of nothingness. The idea of a deregulatory Big Bang betrays a Jacobinist attitude to institutions and a contempt for continuity and institutional trust. This attitude also seems to be at odds with the bulk of the tradition of British political theory. It certainly resulted in another disastrous outcome of a revolution, because like any other industry, the financial services sector cannot be revolutionized from a zero-moment in time, since history does not admit of a zero-moment.

The architects of the Big Bang in the British finance industry maintain today that the consequences of the "Big Bang policy" – as they themselves describe it – of the 1980s were not foreseeable. Nigel Lawson, the former Chancellor of the Exchequer

(Treasury Chief) and the other architect of the Big Bang, Cecil Parkinson, the former Secretary of State for Trade and Industry, both cabinet ministers under Margaret Thatcher, have since become members of the House of Lords. Nigel Lawson maintains that, "The notion that banks would get as big and bloated as they did was totally unexpected."[31] The assertion that the financial crisis is only a crisis about the size of the banks which could have been avoided if banks had been smaller, is another vain attempt to justify the theory that a revolutionary, big-bang-like reorganization could have been appropriate as a policy for deregulating the finance industry. A vital reason for the adoption of the Big Bang theory of total deregulation of the finance industry was the hoped-for strengthening of the City of London as a world financial center.[32] Great Britain obviously pursued this strengthening of the City at the cost of stability of the international financial system. The idea of lifting financial regulation with a Big Bang in order to prime the pump for economic growth, to create advantages for London as a financial center, and to strengthen it through the deregulation revolution in the financial industry of the 1980s and 1990s, was confounded by reality – a fate that befalls most revolutions.

The consensus that underlay Big Bang deregulation was that markets are practically infallible if they are left to operate undisturbed by state regulation. The error of this position was either an error of economic theory, a failure to perceive the functional conditions of financial institutions realistically, or an error of will, a refusal to look reality in the eye. It was not a mistaken political consensus, as the British Prime Minister at the time of writing, Gordon Brown, assumed.[33] Consensus does not, as Jürgen Habermas and certain democratic politicians seem to think, constitute truth. Markets are the best way to coordinate the supply and demand of economic goods and services, but they are a very long way from producing perfect rationality or even infallibility or truth, because the individuals that make up markets are not infallible in their economic decisions. The herd instinct, adverse selection, moral hazard, etc., are well known constraints on the rationality of behavior in the market.

To take the example of the Catholic doctrine of papal infallibility as a comparison with the idea of the infallible market: neither the Pope's sense of reason nor the consensus of Catholics could justify the claim to infallibility. This could only happen

---

[31] *The Wall Street Journal Europe*, Vol. 27, No. 42, Tuesday, March 31, 2009, p. 1 and 32, here p. 32.

[32] The American policy of deregulation to strengthen their financial centers put pressure on regulatory authorities in other financial centers such as Paris and Frankfurt to reduce regulation in their own centers so that regulatory bureaucracy did not become a competitive disadvantage. This can be seen as a deregulation competition between financial centers which led to ever lighter regulation of the financial markets. SINN (2009), p. 175, calls it a "laxity contest" ("*Laschheitswettbewerb*"). He reports that a high-ranking official from the French regulatory authority commented at a conference in October 2008 that the authority had made it a principle not to approve anything that could not be understood by at least one person on his staff. They had not been able to abide by this policy, however, because they feared that any delay in authorization would cause a competitive disadvantage vis à vis the British or Germans (Ibid.).

[33] Cf. "Kurswechsel in Großbritannien. Wetteifern um harte Regulierung" [Political U-turn in Great Britain. Vying for tough regulation], *Frankfurter Allgemeine Zeitung*, (March 18, 2009), No. 65, p. 13.

through a higher principle that transcends human rationality and consensus. In the Catholic context, this principle is the power of the Holy Spirit which is not subject to any human constraints. Without the assumption of the divine higher principle which guarantees the infallibility of the lower principle, the claim to infallibility would be unjustifiable.

In relation to the market, this kind of recourse to a higher order principle that supposedly endows the market with perfect rationality and therefore justifies the assumption of perfect market rationality, had never been attempted up to the 1980s. Belief in the infallibility of the market does not render the market infallible. Even if all Catholics believe that the Pope is infallible, this does not guarantee that he really is. Infallibility cannot originate from a belief in it. Even if all bankers believed that the markets in which they worked were infallible, that would not ensure that the markets really were. It only proves that all bankers have an interest in believing, and especially making others believe, that the markets are infallible. Because of the conflict of interest between the bankers' interest in belief in the truth conditions of this thesis and the "interest" of the conditions of economic reality, which requires that this thesis is not only believed to be true but is in fact true, the thesis that the market realizes perfect rationality, which is primarily informed by the interests of financial actors, should be treated with great skepticism.

The thesis that the market is the best possible access to economic coordination and rationality, better than central planning for instance, has been empirically under-pinned since the end of Communism and has not been refuted by the financial crisis. The thesis of the market as the best possible form of coordination is not, however, identical with the thesis of the perfect rationality of the market and does not jus-tify any Big Bang policy of complete deregulation. The latter thesis was merely the ideology of market Jacobinism. The market economy is not a revolutionary or Jacobinist concept but an evolutionary one.

It is therefore no surprise that the German government demanded regulation of the finance industry even prior to the crisis, and refused during the crisis to embark on a bailout, a rescue, of the bankruptcies of Anglo-American banks[34] caused by the Big Bang policy, with a colossal injection of state support for failed firms after the Big Bang policy of deregulation had definitively misfired. When eco-nomics Professor Paul Krugman of the USA criticized the then (early 2009) German Finance Minister Peer Steinbrück for not doing enough to stimulate consumption in Germany, he might aptly have replied[35] that it cannot be the task of the (continental)

---

[34]The crisis in the major American banks is put into perspective somewhat if we take into account that the largest bank in the world, Citigroup of New York, made losses of approximately $27 billion in 2007, after having made a $27 billion profit the previous year, 2006.

[35]As reported in *Stern* magazine, No. 12, 2009. Cf. also P. KRUGMAN: "The Economic Consequences of Herr Steinbrueck", *The New York Times*, 11 December 2008. Cf. SINN (2009), p. 236, who is somewhat more diplomatic: "The constant jibes from Nobel prize winner Paul Krugman are somewhat incomprehensible, accusing Germany of not doing enough to combat the global economic recession, and garnering considerable attention for his view worldwide." German politicians would say that it is not the first pilgrimage to the shrine of San Marco (the Blessed

Europeans to support the American state bailout of American firms by launching a bailout of the American state by continental European states.

On the contrary, the question that has to be asked is whether the German government is not doing too much towards the bank rescue, whether it is not over-rescuing, and bearing too large a share of the international bank rescue packages in comparison to the rescue of American banks. According to the figures given by Sinn, the USA is bearing a 32.1% share of bank rescue packages, whereas Germany is bearing a share of 14%, the second-largest rescue package of the USA.[36] In relation to the populations of both countries, the share of the German rescue package of 43.61%, against a German population of 82.310 million – which is just 27.57% of the population of the USA, which numbers 298.444 million people – is hugely disproportionate and, if anything, too high rather than too low, in view of the fact that the crisis started in the USA and its banks are affected to a far greater extent. Krugman must therefore be challenged as to whether his attacks are scholarship and not part of an effort inspired by American power politics to co-opt Germany into joining a more comprehensive bailout of failed American banks, into cross-subsidizing them, in fact. Such an effort would be doubly suspect because, prior to the crisis, the American banks had been making larger profits than the German banks – and here we are talking mainly about the public German regional banks – which were sold the CDOs that turned out to be distressed.[37]

The superiority of the market as a coordination system does not, however, justify a policy of re-regulation of the finance industry, which would be detrimental to the financial markets in any situation. A further drawback of this policy is the lack of a pool of people equipped with superior knowledge to the financial industry's existing staff and capable of implementing an optimal form of regulation. Politicians – unless they happen to be Minister-President of a German regional state – cannot run large businesses and states simultaneously. Regulation is only justified as a policy which is based on the assumption that markets, and not political direction, are the basic

---

Mark, or nowadays the proverbial San Euro della Germania) and is unlikely to be the last. POSNER (2009), p. 285, talks about Krugman's "orgy of recrimination against Wall Street", but the Social Democrat Steinbrück can hardly be called a Wall Street man.

[36] SINN (2009), p. 216.

[37] Just as dubious, in its own way, is the German reproach leveled at Washington by no lesser dignitary than the head of the German Lutheran Church, Bishop Wolfgang Huber of Berlin, (cf. *Wallstreet Journal Europe* of 31 March 2009), who accuses Washington of letting the Lehman Brothers bankruptcy happen in September 2008 solely because the affected investors were mainly Germans, who were invested especially heavily in the bank, having been drawn by the German origin of the name Lehman. This same attribute would apply to Goldman Sachs, which was not left to go bankrupt. It seems a more likely explanation that the then US Treasury Secretary, Henry M. Paulson, who took the decision (term of office 3 July 2006 – 20 January 2009) was CEO of Goldman Sachs prior to his appointment to head up the US Treasury. This possible conflict of interest between his affiliation with Goldman Sachs and his duty of neutrality on competition as American minister of finance must at least set alarm bells ringing.

form of economic coordination; but that markets in certain particular situations, and only in these, mainly when they become irrational or exuberant, need support from the state and must get it from the state in accordance with the subsidiarity principle.

After the American Financial Overstretch – Have We Reached the End of the Washington Consensus?

The gigantic bailout of the financial system that emerged from the deregulatory Big Bang of the 1980s calls into question the foundations of a humane economic system, because it casts doubt on the relationship between work and reward and between work and liability[38] which underpins a capitalist system based on private property. Whitewashing over failure with state bailouts and rewarding bad financial services with high salaries and bonuses breach the fundamental tenet of capitalism that production factors are paid according to the added value they contribute.

For the past two decades since the fall of the Berlin Wall in 1989, it was the Washington Consensus that gave direction to all the moves. But since the failure of radical deregulation and the bailout of the financial system in the aftermath, it is a consensus no more. Gordon Brown, Chancellor of the Exchequer of the United Kingdom from 1997 to 2007 (the height of the deregulation era) and British Prime Minister from 2007 to 2010, publicly stated in mid-March 2009 that the Washington Consensus no longer held good: "The 40-year-old prevalent orthodoxy known as the Washington Consensus in favour of free markets has come to an end." He continued, "Laissez-faire has had its day. People on the centre-left and the progressive agenda should be confident enough to say that the old idea that the markets were efficient and could work things out by themselves are gone."[39] From what the former Prime Minister says, the Washington Consensus encapsulated the view that markets are rational, markets provide perfect information, and markets are therefore as good as infallible. That consensus no longer exists.

---

[38]PAUL KIRCHHOF: "Der Schaden der anderen. Unsere Wirtschaftskrise besteht darin, dass die Beteiligten für ihr Produkt und ihre Schuldner kaum noch verantwortlich sind. Eigentum kann es nur noch in begrenzter Freiheit geben" [The woes of others. Our economic crisis is that financiers have divested almost all responsibility for their products and debtors.], *Frankfurter Allgemeine Zeitung*, 28 May 2009, No. 122, p. 31, discerns in the crisis a perversion of the principle of liberty: "Liberty is being used to harm others. But a right of liberty never justifies causing harm to others. The risk of structural irresponsibility is the core problem of our crisis scenario. The banker loses interest in the creditworthiness of the borrower, withdraws [via CDOs] from the responsibility for his original choice of debtor." (Own translation).

[39]GORDON BROWN, quoted in the article: "Kurswechsel in Großbritannien. Wetteifern um harte Regulierung" [U-turn in Great Britain. Vying for tough regulation], *Frankfurter Allgemeine Zeitung*, 18 March 2009, No. 65, p. 13, reporting comments made by Brown to the *Guardian*. The original comments can be found at: http://www.guardian.co.uk/politics/2009/mar/17/gordon-brown-recession-banking-regulation.

Whatever one may believe about the details of the Washington Consensus[40] – and some of its elements undoubtedly remain valid today – it is odd for the former British premier to have believed in infallible markets, based on a consensus reached in the 1980s, only to decide they are not, based on a new consensus in 2009.

It is also remarkable that the British premier believed he could continue in office as his country's leading politician even as he turned tack from supporting yesterday's consensus, which turned out to be wrong, and embraced a new consensus diametrically opposed to it. In response to the ease with which someone can give up one political consensus that he supported only yesterday and switch allegiance to another, it is tempting to say that of course people are free to change their minds; they are not free to alter the fact that only yesterday, they held a different opinion, which is wrong today.[41]

Gordon Brown's statement is disconcerting. It implies that members of the political elite only follow the general consensus of an era; when that consensus no longer prevails, they change their views and line up behind the next consensus with great

---

[40] The term was coined in 1990 at a conference in Washington DC. It also describes the position of the International Monetary Fund and the World Bank regarding the conditions that should be met by debtor countries. The Consensus requires debtors to implement the ten following structural adjustment policies:

– fiscal discipline,

– public expenditure priorities towards education, health and infrastructure, reduction of subsidies,

– tax reform to lower tax rates and broaden the tax base,

– market-determined, positive interest rates to prevent capital flight and attract foreign capital,

– competitive exchange rates to promote exports,

– trade liberalization to open up national markets to foreign suppliers,

– openness and improvement of conditions for foreign direct investment,

– privatization of public corporations and institutions,

– deregulation and de-bureaucratization and a reduction in state intervention,

– legal protection of private property.

Deregulation is only mentioned here in ninth place. This condition was especially important for the development of financial markets, however.

[41] During his term of office as chancellor, Brown had failed to respond to warnings from the British Financial Services Authority (FSA) that tighter regulation of the financial services industry and, most importantly, a better British deposit guarantee scheme was needed. After the severity of the financial crisis, Brown told the Guardian that, in retrospect, he wished that he had pushed harder over the past 10 years for more responsible worldwide market regulation. In this interview, Brown took "full responsibility" for all his actions, but refused to give in to demands from the Conservative opposition for an apology. Reported as per the article "Kurswechsel in Großbritannien. Wetteifern um harte Regulierung" [U-turn in Great Britain. Vying for tough regulation], *Frankfurter Allgemeine Zeitung*, 18 March 2009, No. 65, p. 13.

alacrity; and they have no sense of responsibility for the mistakenness of the consensus they were long-time supporters of, because they were only following the consensus, after all.

The ex-Prime Minister's statement further implies that such a switch can be accomplished without being held accountable for having defended a mistaken consensus for a long period of time and caused the problems that his own nation now faces, in no small part because the actions of the political elite were following the original, now mistaken, consensus. Nor is the British political elite held to account, worse still perhaps, for the harm done beyond the confines of their own nation, to continental Europe and to other nations that never supported the first consensus.

It is obvious that nations which were skeptical about the implications for the financial industry of what Gordon Brown called the "Washington Consensus" but which, in relation to the financial industry, could more accurately be described as the "Washington and City of London Consensus", were reluctant to assist governments that had pursued the so-called Washington consensus policy with their bailouts. If the question of who should bail out whom is not resolved fairly, a huge potential for conflict will build up within the Western world. The continental European governments cannot support the American and the British governments unconditionally. American criticism of Germany's hesitation to spend yet further trillions of euros on subsidizing bankrupt firms and stimulating private consumption must therefore be met with equanimity.

The dominance of the Washington Consensus has been ended by the financial crisis and the big bailout amounting to trillions of dollars. The loss of value of American market-listed shares amounting to 8 trillion dollars (i.e. 8 million million dollars), together with losses of 2 trillion dollars incurred by American banks since 2007[42] and the 2 trillion dollar costs of the bailout and the US stimulus package, financed by government borrowing, do nothing to keep the main proponents of the Washington Consensus in good standing, particularly as the rest of the world was substantially invested in American shares. A track record of bankruptcy is no recommendation, even if it need not mean the end of a career.

The gigantic bailout rescued and underwrote a banking industry that had welcomed Big Bang deregulation and boasted, especially in the Anglo-American economies, that it could not only survive but flourish without the state's help; indeed, without the state. Therefore the greatest bank rescue operation in the history of the world calls into question the past system of a fully deregulated financial market,

---

[42]Figures according to POSNER (2009), pp. 14f. and 190. – A US billion (one thousand million) is known in continental Europe as a milliard; a European billion equals a US trillion (one million million). For comparison, the gross domestic product of the USA amounts to 14 trillion US dollars. German GDP seems almost modest by comparison. Cf. SINN (2009), p. 11: "The state-controlled banks ran up some 27 milliard [USA: 27 billion] euros in losses, which will overwhelmingly have to be borne by the taxpayer. [...] in total some 580 milliard [USA: 0.580 trillion] euros were made available by way of assistance and guarantees for the banks as well as 100 milliard [USA: 100 billion] euros in guarantees for private companies and 81 milliard [USA: 81 billion] euros for two economic stimulus programs." (Own translation from the German).

and forces the nations to rethink the principles of the social and humane market economy. Even the charisma of President Barack Obama cannot belie the fact that without state intervention, the majority of major American banks would be bankrupt. Moreover, the USA is under even more pressure than Germany because American retirement pensions are organized via pension funds, whereas German pension provision is better safeguarded by the pay-as-you go pension system of a social insurance scheme that acts as a built-in economic stabilizer. This means that the American government needs to stabilize share prices in order to guarantee the old-age pensions of the American population.

The financial market crisis was not caused by capitalism but by the American model of capitalism and its foremost protagonists, as even American academics will concede, the financial industry. Posner writes: "The Depression is a failure of capitalism, or more precisely of a certain kind of capitalism ('laissez–faire' in a loose sense, 'American' versus 'European' in a popular sense), and of capitalism's biggest boosters."[43] Baker concurs with John C. Bogle in identifying three points of criticism of "corporate, investment, and mutual fund America":

> "The first focuses on the misdeeds and excessive compensation of corporate managers. The second describes the misdeeds and excessive compensation in financial intermediation, including investment banking, equity research, and investment management firms. And, the third marks the misdeeds and excessive compensation of one type of financial intermediation [. . .]: mutual funds."

The defining influence on all three is:

> "An increasing distance between individual investors, the ultimate providers of capital, and corporate managers, the eventual users of capital. The consequence of distance is expropriation by a chain of middlemen and an individual investor who keeps less and less of the return to capital."[44]

The destruction of capital through big bank deregulation is so colossal that it must weaken America's reputation and power in the longer term. The dramatic decline in the wealth of the USA has also undermined its strategic capability to assert its global dominance in the world. The link between the American "imperial overstretch" following the end of the Cold War, and the subsequent "financial and fiscal overstretch" may be alluded to but cannot be analyzed here.[45] It is not in Europe's interest, however, for the USA to weaken itself through forms of overstretch – imperial, financial or otherwise. It would have been better if Europe had spoken out sooner against the American financial overstretch – and if its word had carried more weight within the Western world.

The financial market crisis forces the West to reconsider the principles of a humane and free economic system. Part of this reconsideration of the economic system must be an impartial and objective inventory of the shared and the divergent

---

[43]POSNER (2009), p. 260.

[44]BAKER (2008), p. 732, following on from JOHN C. BOGLE: *The Battle for the Soul of Capitalism* (2005).

[45]Cf. PAUL KENNEDY: "American Power Is on the Wane", *The Wall Street Journal*, 15 January 2009), http://online.wsj.com/article/SB123189377673479433.html

principles of the Anglo-American and continental European concepts of the market economy. The common goal should be a new synthesis of economic systems and a new and better business legislation and business ethics, not a micro-managed system of regulation and supervision. To this end, what is needed is not a new Big Bang consisting of re-regulation and a totally new corporate order for the finance industry, but an evolution of capitalism and its financial system.

In the kingdom of theory, there can be no hegemony except the hegemony of the better argument. The better argument is neither always nor never on the side of the strongest and mightiest actor in the given discourse. It is not always on the side of the American or Washington Consensus, as the crisis shows; but nor is it never on the side of this Consensus. Which side has the best argument is contingent upon which argument is the best, not on the greater or lesser power of the argument's proponent.

The Failure of Economics and Management Science

Much has been written about the incapability of economics and management sciences to foresee the crisis or warn that it was coming, let alone prevent it.[46] Two elements of this incapability to recognize the crisis come to the fore: firstly, the academics' difficulty in keeping pace with the development of financial instruments within financial institutions, and secondly, the academics' lack of critical distance towards the financial institutions. On the first point: the pace of financial innovations, and the sometimes hermetic way in which they were introduced, made it difficult for the academic world to become familiar with these new instruments at the time and to critically probe them and to examine their risks. It is not in the interests of the financial institutions that introduce financial innovations to have them audited by independent and public researchers, because this could undermine their competitive advantage as an innovator. For this reason, it seems advisable to set up a state authority which examines new financial instruments, like the authority that assesses and approves new drugs, but which is strictly bound to maintain confidentiality and protect the intellectual property rights to the innovation. That way, financial instruments capable of such far-reaching damage as CDOs would never have been introduced, or at least their worst impacts could have been abated.

On the second point of the academics' lack of independence, particularly that of corporate finance experts from their partners in the financial industry: the development of academic disciplines leads the universities into ever-greater dependency on external funding and external donors. This steadily erodes the "public" character of academic research and steadily shrinks the critical distance of disciplines from their object of study. Added to this, in the case of economics, is the development of business schools, which are even more dependent on corporate patrons and tuition

---

[46]Cf. JOACHIM STARBATTY: "Warum die Ökonomen versagt haben" [Why the economists failed], *Frankfurter Allgemeine Zeitung*, 4 November 2008, No. 258, p. 12.

fees than the conventional universities. It is sometimes difficult to discern the qualities of scientific independence and striving for scientific knowledge in the business schools. They appear to be entirely at the service of corporations. Industry often supports the business schools precisely because it expects less criticism from them than from the universities.

This objective is short-sighted because industry needs academia as a critical corrective or sparring partner, and not just as a producer and supplier of instrumental management know-how. The role of the university as a place of independent, unencumbered scholarship, in the sense that it cannot be annexed by any institution, be it state, church or corporation, has been weakened in recent decades. The result, in the case of economics, is a lack of distance from the object of study and from the actors in business, which manifests itself in a lack of capacity for criticism and early warning.[47]

So far the business schools have not succeeded in their original objective of establishing management as a profession on the model of the medical or the legal professions, as Harvard Business School Professor Rakesh Khurana, shows. He also shows that this had been the original intention of the American business schools. According to Khurana, the business schools largely capitulated in this struggle for "managerial professionalism", and have become suppliers of the mere product, the MBA, which treats the students as consumers. The business schools, according to Khurana are dominated by the idea that managers are mere agents of shareholders, and solely obligated to the matter of increasing shareholder-value. The MBA students, for their part, see the MBA primarily as a gateway to networks and contacts, and are more interested in these than in a rigorous academic training. Khurana pleads for an intellectual reinvigoration of the training of future corporate directors and managers.

In the case of corporate finance scholars, the danger of dependency on the financial industry is greatest because they can receive lucrative consulting assignments from the financial institutions. Their economic and scientific interest does not incline them to make themselves unpopular with their clients through critical thinking.[48]

---

[47]RAKESH KHURANA: *From Higher Aims to Hired Hands: The Social Transformation of American Business Schools and the Unfulfilled Promise of Management as a Profession*, Princeton (Princeton University Press) 2007. Despite its devastating criticism of the business schools, the book won distinguished awards: "Winner of the 2008 Max Weber Award for Best Book, Section on Organization, Occupations and Work, American Sociological Association" and "Winner of the 2007 Best Professional/Scholarly Publishing Book in Business, Finance and Management, Association of American Publishers." – According to Khurana, in the USA 20% of all undergraduate students enroll for degrees in business disciplines. However, the impacts of the financial crisis were starting to filter through into subject choices, and student numbers in business disciplines are declining, Khurana said in a presentation at the Annual Meeting of the Academy of Management in a joint session with the Society of Business Ethics on 7 August 2008 in Anaheim, California.

[48]POSNER (2009), p. 259. "The entwinement of finance professors with the financial industry has a dark side. If they criticize the industry and suggest tighter regulation, they may become black sheep and lose lucrative consultantships. [. . .] One does not expect economists employed by real estate companies or banks to be talking about housing and credit bubbles."

In the same way, it can be very awkward for banks' compliance officers to have to confront the management board with prospective critical warnings, evaluations or even prohibitions, because the board wields the ultimate authority over their position and determines how they must work. The consequence is that the banking compliance, which should also exercise a critical and anticipatory function, is generally confined to the question of conformity to rules, compliance with existing legal norms, and is not required to comment on new financial instruments.

Another reason why the USA was able to push through the deregulation of finance virtually unopposed in the global market was that the USA commands opinion leadership, and indeed dominance, in the domain of economics and management sciences. American scientific theories and approaches in economics and the management sciences can be promulgated virtually unopposed. Approaches from anywhere other than America are barely noticed because of the dominance of American economics and its organs of publication.[49] What is missing is the element of criticism and the presence of alternative approaches within scientific theory-construction.

After the end of the Cold War, what Posner writes about Alan Greenspan is all the more true of the most recent history of the USA and its economy: "The Duke of Wellington remarked that a great victory is a great danger. Success breeds complacence. Or as William Blake said, damn braces – bless relaxes. Greenspan's triumphs and laurels ill prepared him and his successor to confront a new crisis with fresh thinking".[50] The proverb that a great victory is a great danger applies just as much to nations. Blake's sentiment that "damn braces, bless relaxes" applies not just to the head of the US Federal Reserve but also to the USA as the victor of the Cold War and the sole remaining superpower after 1989. After 1989, there was virtually nobody in the fields of financial management, financial scholarship and financial legislation who contradicted the USA. Germany, in particular, did not fulfill its role as a place of independent institution-building, theory-construction and legislation during these years. Nothing was done to enhance the international financial system's efficiency and learning capacity in the years after 1989.

This experience shows that laws, rules and customs of the international financial system have another side, which can be described as dogmatic. The factual and dogmatic validity of rules is half manifest and half normative. If US institutions dominate because they are backed by the largest law community and the greatest economic and political power, the theories that underpin US law gain dogmatic significance. They become a self-fulfilling prophecy for the rules of international business. They are valid because they are valid in the vast majority of business transactions. This dogmatic side of international business law, which is largely determined by American law, is unavoidable to a certain extent. Nevertheless, it remains

---

[49]Cf. STARBATTY (2008), p. 12: "Anything that has no chance of being published in American journals is brushed aside." (Own translation) Starbatty views this phenomenon as one cause of the crisis in the discipline of economics as a whole.

[50]POSNER (2009), p. 282.

the task of the international discourse on law and legal theory to question this dog-
matism and to complement or replace it, as the case may be, with new and better
rules and justifications. This process has already been set in train by the financial
crisis. Alternative business models to the American model are increasingly being
discussed.[51]

"Wealth in the Hands of Others": The Outsourcing of Asset Management and the Growth of Financial Intermediation as Causes of the Financial Crisis

The outsourcing of asset management and the increase of financial intermediation
play their part in the higher proportion of speculative forms of investment, and hence
in the hyper-speculation that preceded the financial market crisis.

Two trends combined to produce higher expected returns on investment, which
in turn were only achievable with riskier and more speculative forms of investment. The first trend concerned the increased demand for capital that arose from
the opening of the global market. The opening of the global market, and above all
the opening of South-East Asian, Indian and Chinese markets as well as the markets
of Eastern Europe, of necessity, usher in a shift in the relationship of capital and
labor income in highly developed economies. Capital has become scarcer – despite
the phenomenon of greater inheritance of capital wealth which, for Germany in particular, represented an important historical turnaround after the substantial losses of
wealth during and after the Second World War. On a global scale, however, capital
scarcity has intensified despite lower interest rates. This scarcity was confirmed by
the high dividends and price rises on the stock market before the financial crisis.
Globalization, as has already been shown, is not only the cause but also the consequence of the expansion of the capital market, induced in turn by the demand for
capital in countries characterized by a high supply of labor and high demand for
capital investment from the developed economies.

In the global market, there has been a shift in the relationship between capital
income and labor income. Capital has become scarcer than labor, a development
that has repercussions on the globalized allocation of capital and capital investment.
The relative increase in capital income in relation to earnings before the crisis was
intensified by a phenomenon that is equally a consequence of heightened globalization: heightened capital mobility. Since the factor of labor is necessarily more
tightly integrated into a community and more location-specific, whereas the factor

---

[51]Cf. PETER CAPPELLI: "The Future of the U.S. Business Model and the Rise of Competition",
The Academy of Management Perspectives, 23 (2009) pp. 5–10; RICHARD WHITLEY: "U.S.
Capitalism: A Tarnished Model?", ibid., pp. 11–22; MAURO F. GUILLÉN, ESTEBAN GARCÍA-
CANAL: "The American Model of the Multinational Firm and the 'New' Multinationals From
Emerging Economies", Ibid., pp. 23–35.

of capital can roam freely around the globe, income streams from capital are less location-specific than earnings from employment.

Overall, income from capital rose more markedly than wages from labor. As a result, the expected returns on capital investments were also heightened. In the course of this process, there was increased demand for professional investment advice and greater outsourcing of investment management, with the consequence that the outsourcing of investment management led to the selection of more speculative and higher-risk portfolios than owner-investors would choose if managing the investment themselves. More speculative and higher-risk portfolios have to be selected when investment management is outsourced, in order to achieve average returns on capital for the investor's portfolio after deduction of the fees for the investment advice.

Heightened demands on the performance of investment advisors included demands for a high degree of professionalization. Investors were prepared to outsource investment management to others, in the hope that the outsourcing and financial intermediation would achieve a return in excess of what an individual taking autonomous investment decisions can achieve, despite the fees for the intermediation. The financial intermediation fees, for their part, forced the financial intermediaries to select more assumedly profitable, more risk-laden, and more speculative forms of investment.

Although the growth in financial intermediation may have increased the professionalization of asset management up to a point, it also raised the degree of risk and speculation in asset management. Furthermore, it has to be asked whether the financial intermediary did not tend to exhibit a greater appetite for risk than the investor on his own account, because ultimately the investor rather than the intermediary bears the investment risk. A higher degree of financial intermediation will therefore, *ceteris paribus*, lead to a higher appetite for risk and speculation.

The listed factors of increased financial intermediation, which was also encouraged by the advertising of financial intermediation by the banks, contributed to hyper-speculation in the financial markets. It did not reduce it, as one might expect based on the higher degree of professionalization.

The returns that bank customers expected of their bank in its capacity as financial adviser were also inflated because the banks were coming under competitive pressure from other, newer financial institutions which were not banks – such as online brokerage and pure financial consultancy firms – and were forced to promise higher returns and to achieve them by means of more speculative forms of investment. Moreover, the banks were forced by the pressure of competition to use a higher degree of leverage in the financing of their lending, because in their lending business too, they were placed under pressure by new financing providers, some of whom benefited from lower credit-financing costs because of their lower or nonexistent minimum capitalization and minimum reserve requirements. The banks had to respond to a new competition between financing firms which could penetrate the banks' business segments thanks to deregulation, and competed so vigorously that banks were compelled to promise and to generate higher returns. Deregulation and rising competition along with the investors' desire to outsource investment management combined to produce a higher degree of speculation and risk propensity in the capital and credit market.[52]

This desire on the part of investors for higher returns from the outsourcing of investment management might be characterized as investor "greed". But that would be to underestimate the systemic effects of the raising of average returns. It is natural for an investor who sees higher average returns in the market to strive to match them with his own portfolio. This is hardly a case of pathological greed. Nevertheless, perhaps it is fair to criticize investors for being too greedy for systemic reasons because they amplify the dynamic which leads to an increasingly speculative and risk-laden capital and credit market, and which must ultimately culminate in the financial market crisis, and because the desire for convenience, wishful thinking, and the expectation of higher returns makes them more trusting of financial intermediaries than they should be.[53]

The idea that others, even if well-paid, want nothing more than to make rich people's wealth grow as much as possible is unfounded. Financial intermediation is constantly allied with the risk of being exploited by the financial intermediary. The growth in outsourcing increases this individual risk, and along with it, the systemic risk of undue risk-propensity in the capital and credit market, with the consequence that hyper-speculation takes hold of the financial markets. A lesser degree of outsourcing would diminish this risk.

When capital owners fully outsource the investment risk, legitimation problems of capitalism also arise, because if all property owners left the management of their capital assets to others, it would nullify the argument that an owner's interest in looking after his property and managing it with due diligence is one of the main benefits of the economic system of private property. If the management of capital assets were turned over entirely to financial intermediaries, any such constellation of income-generation from capital ownership would hark back to the "workless income" from capital and land ownership that has been much criticized in the past, especially in the nineteenth century. The relationship between the outsourcing of investment management, a higher appetite for risk and speculation among financial intermediaries, and hyper-speculation culminating in a financial crisis, makes it clear that the

---

[52]The higher pressure of competition is most apparent, as Posner shows, in the USA where deregulation did away with the former division between investment and savings banks. POSNER (2009), p. 130: "Notice the pernicious effect of competition, and ultimately of deregulation, on bank safety. Deregulation increased competition in banking by allowing other financial firms to offer close substitutes for banking services." This increasing competition put the banks under pressure, affecting not only their advisory arms but also their credit business: "Increased competition in turn compressed the margin between the interest rates that banks paid to borrow capital for lending and the interest rate they charged their borrowers. The narrower the margin, the more leverage banks need in order to obtain enough revenue net of their borrowing costs to cover other expenses and provide a return to their shareholders."

[53]One can also interpret this problem as an instantiation of the more general problem that the middleman causes costs, and that middlemen try to extend their services beyond the useful. BRANDEIS (1914), p. 97, wrote of the banking industry's tendency, like any other intermediary's, to over-extend its services: "Eliminate the banker-middleman where he is superfluous."

link between property ownership and dispositive control over property by its owner should be tenaciously preserved.

On the Way to Lesser Inequality in Wealth Distribution? Distributional Effects of the Financial Crisis Towards Greater Equality

The assessment that the outsourcing of asset and investment management led not to its improvement but rather to its deterioration is confirmed by the fact that the financial crisis harmed the wealthy more than the less wealthy. The redistributive effect of the financial crisis does not, as many observers assume, regressively favor the rich. In fact, the picture that emerges is that of a redistributive effect to the detriment of owners of equity assets, which therefore works progressively relative to greater wealth and brings about greater overall equality of wealth distribution.[54]

Those hit by the huge losses in value of exchange-listed securities, but also CDOs, are the heavily-invested, wealthy investors. The financial crisis and the stock market crash triggered a massive redistribution in which the rich lost mega-fortunes. Admittedly, their losses do not turn into direct gains for the not-so-wealthy classes, but nevertheless, they shift the distribution of wealth in the direction of a more even-handed share-out. After all, government consumer stimulus programs such as car-scrappage schemes do not directly benefit the wealthier classes, either. It seems rather as if, having witnessed the inflation of huge fortunes in recent years, government policy is now consciously – and up to a certain point, understandably – staked on fiscal measures that bring about a more equal income distribution. The asset bubble built on share price growth and rising property prices that benefited the wealthy has burst.

The crisis is by no means unjust. The losses are greatest for those who had profited most from the stock market and property market booms. It must be noted that even those in the USA who obtained mortgages without the corresponding collateral and proof of income, and subsequently lost their homes, benefited from a progressive redistribution; for the homes they lost in the crisis had never really been theirs. Anyone who obtained a loan without satisfying the lending criteria, and then failed to service it, was effectively being gifted free money by the bank for a number of years, and living in a borrowed house. One day, those who stayed longest in their homes without paying interest on their mortgages might look back on the period between the two bubbles as a relatively good time.

Unfortunately, those who partook in amateur financial market speculation will not remember things that way. When the structured financial products bubble burst,

---

[54]It is estimated that the wealthy in the USA lost, on average, 1/5 of their assets. Cf. "Reiche verlieren ein Fünftel ihres Vermögens" [Rich lose one-fifth of their wealth], *Frankfurter Allgemeine Zeitung*, 25 June 2009, No. 144, p. 19. Those affected by the Madoff fraud case were also for the most part rich private investors. Cf. "Der tiefe Fall des Bernie Madoff" [The deep downfall of Bernie Madoff], *Frankfurter Allgemeine Zeitung*, 20 December 2008, No. 298, p. 18.

the redistributive effect on amateur speculators was terrifying. While financial inter-mediaries earned handsome fees for these products, many inexperienced individual financial investors lost their pension funds, their children's college funds, and other savings that they had placed in these products.

The state's assumption of liability for losses from mortgages must not benefit the banks alone; it must also help the normal earner. A sign of a step in the right direction is that consideration is being given in the USA to support for credit card debtors as well as the banks. The banks cannot be the sole concern; consumers also need help out of the liability that drives them towards insolvency. A bailout should be available not just to the banks but also to mortgage borrowers, over-indebted homeowners. The state should become the owner of the mortgages guaranteed by it, and subsequently sell these back to their currently insolvent owners or offer them on the open market and use the proceeds to repay the taxpayer or reduce public debt.

Likewise the share price losses on share options suffered by the main culprits of the financial crisis, the managers of major banks, are immense. It is not the case that those responsible, as for example the CEO of Lehman Brothers, Richard Fuld, were not punished by the crisis. After the Lehman bankruptcy, Fuld's share options were worthless. If we look at the asset losses of the directors of major American banks that became insolvent, it is clear that these sometimes ran into billions of dollars.

The widespread view that managers are never economically punished for their failure is not tenable. If the director is not permitted to sell his shares from company options schemes for a year after his departure, if he has run the company badly, these shares will lose their value in the year after his departure so that his share options are also of lesser value. It is different if the corporate crisis he induced only comes to light in the second year after his departure and affect the share price then. In such a case, however, it is also difficult to track the company's loss of value solely to his management errors.

Due to the distributional effects of the financial market crisis, it would not be astonishing if the crisis actually contributed to the resurgence of the middle class, and redressed some of the inequality of income distribution as well as asset dis-tribution.[55] The financial market crisis might turn out to be a period of wealth redistribution, a kind of an unintended "jubilee year" as it is called in the Bible, where it denotes a periodically recurring year of debt cancellation once every 25 years.

The Financial Crisis – Systems Crisis or Action Crisis?

Purely economic economists generally take the view that the financial market crisis is a systemic crisis and the consequence of systemic flaws. If we follow this interpre-tation, strictly speaking the crisis is nobody's fault except the politicians' because

---

[55]Cf. MICHAEL PERSSON: "De crisis als de grote gelijkmaker. Door de economische neergang zal de welvaart beter worden verdeeld." [The crisis as the great leveller. Through the economic decline, welfare will be distributed better], in: *de Volkskrant* (Amsterdam), 10 January 2009, p. 11.

they "did not set the system levers correctly". But it is not the politicians' fault either; they are not experts in the system, and therefore could not be expected to do any better. The politicians' excuse is not entirely wrong because the system does not actually have levers that are readily adjustable, nor a user manual with instructions for adjusting the levers that the politicians might have been able to adhere to. The upshot of the system idea is simply that the spokesmen of the financial sector and politicians can pass the blame and the excuses back and forth.

The system conception must be severely criticized if it is used for such imputations of non-responsibility. In every system, those acting within it, especially those endowed with power, carry responsibility for the system as a whole, for actions in it, and for the development of the system over time. If the system takes a turn for the worse, the responsibility rests primarily with the acting persons with decision-making power, who presided over the downturn. Consensus reigns that the ethos and the action-orientation before the crisis did not improve, but shifted in the direction of an untrammeled egotism and striving for enrichment among financial actors. For this, the financial market actors bear responsibility.[56]

In the classic style of "purely economic economics", Posner defends the motivation structure of the finance industry before and during the financial market crisis, pointing the finger at the inevitably Darwinist nature of capitalism. Moral condemnation of the bankers for the financial market crisis for which they are to blame, according to Posner, is as futile as morally condemning a lion for eating a zebra.[57] It is normal and natural for lions to eat zebras. If it is equally normal and in their nature for bankers to maximize their bonuses without regard to the sustainability of their results, to drive their banks into bankruptcy and the financial system into the most serious crisis, it is legitimate to reflect on the possibility that something is very wrong with their nature, that the incentive-effort system of the finance industry is not tenable and that its "nature" needs to be reformed. Posner's position is characterized by the contradiction that while Posner recognizes the financial industry as the cause of the crisis, he insists on holding tight to its fundamental constitution and motivation structure. His social Darwinism wants to defend the system, but turns on itself and against the economic system. On the one hand, he is analytically correct in insisting that the financial system is the cause of the crisis, and on the other hand, he is wrong in thinking that the action-orientations of those who caused the crisis, and who must be held accountable for it, are both unalterable and borne of their nature. If the action-orientations in the system are unalterable and if the system caused the crisis, the system is untenable and ought to be changed. Posner's position is questioning the financial system to a much greater extent than he himself assumes. If the market economy and its financial system are to be kept, there must be reason for the positive hope that the action-orientations of those operating the financial system can be changed. If this is not possible the system will not survive.

---

[56]Cf. also the "Berliner Rede" [Berlin speech] of 24 March 2009 by Germany's then head of state, Federal President HORST KÖHLER: "Der Markt braucht Regeln und Moral" [The market needs rules and ethics], *Frankfurter Allgemeine Zeitung*, 25 March 2009, No. 71, p. 8.

[57]POSNER (2009), p. 284f.

Likewise in Hans-Werner Sinn's analysis of the crisis, the idea of systemic error is in the foreground. The search for the guilty parties makes little sense, "because misconduct became the normality."[58] The system conception dominates the interpretation of business in economic theory. It can find no place for personal ethical responsibility and therefore denies it. The importance of the system perspective is not disputed here. What can be disputed, however, is whether it is the sole perspective. Two objections spring to mind: first, why did not all the banks follow the perverse incentives with which the system, according to Posner and Sinn, was riddled? Second, what were the historical roots of such a massive unleashing of the enrichment motive in the finance industry, on a scale hitherto without precedent in a capitalist financial system? The answer to both questions must be that the idea of "purely economic economics" created a new, previously unknown model and system of the financial sector, which was and is the opposite of an ethical economy in which those doing business within the system feel bound by ethical orientations to "good conduct" in pursuit of the industry's purpose. "Good" means, here, good in an encompassing way that includes not only the private but also the public interest.

The new model of the deregulatory Big Bang of the finance industry cast the financial market in an even more egotistical light than the old "selfish system" of the market. It legitimated uninhibited self-interest – in contrast to the enlightened self-interest of classical market theory – and transformed the "selfish system" into an "ultra-selfish system" in comparison to the previous theory of the regulated financial market. The ultra-selfish system went beyond the old laissez-faire school and created the stereotype of a financial manager and intermediary pursuing only his own self-interest and that of the shareholder; not bound by any criteria concerning the good of the firm or the customer, whose fiduciary duty is devoid of normative content and follows nothing but considerations of advantage. The ultra-selfish system had a new ferocity. It had been the objective of financial market reforms to create a new financial system without any ethical or welfare orientation out of the nothingness of a deregulatory Big Bang; a system in which the general equilibrium of the egotism of actors in a perfect market was expected to produce optimality. It signaled a jettisoning of any orientation to business ethics, although the market system in no way compelled this and not all actors chose to go along with it. Not all banks went bankrupt even in the USA. They did not pursue the courses of action which Posner and Sinn consider to be in keeping with the system imperatives and unavoidable within the framework of the system. The system clearly leaves room for ethical decisions and for strategies that are not dominated by the idea of making the fast buck.

Certainly, some of the causes of the financial market crisis lie outside the sphere of influence and ethical responsibility of financial actors, and cannot be fully remedied by business ethics alone.[59] Not all trends in the financial sector, then

---

[58]SINN (2009), p. 99.

[59]A balanced combination of business ethics, reputational pressure on the banks and state regulation is necessary. Cf. BAKER (2008), 734: "How do we get the intermediaries – corporate

or now, are consequences of intentional actions. The theory of financial crises can come up with multiple causes for financial crises. Multiple causes can also interact. Allen and Gale specify the following theoretical approaches for the explanation of financial crises:

1. Crises arise from the financial sector's function to provide consumers with insurance that they will constantly have sufficient liquidity. Crisis-like impacts on this function may be caused by spontaneous panic among banking customers who fear for their liquidity and start a run on the banks. Financial crises, according to Kindleberger,[60] the most prominent advocate of this approach, are the result of spontaneous panic.
2. The economic cycle approach: In the economic downturn when the economy is entering a recession or depression, the yields on bank lending decline due to increasing credit defaults. When the banks have fixed obligations and liabilities for bank deposits and bonds, however, they can find themselves in a situation in which solvency is no longer possible, and slip into insolvency. This can lead to a run on bank accounts.

---

managers, investors, and mutual funds – to be more efficient and keep less for themselves? The first option is conscience. [...] But, appealing to Wall Street to 'make a decent profit decently' – as Edwin Gay, the first dean of Harvard Business School, once said – seems unlikely to work.

The second option is reputation. Consumers put companies with bad products out of business, and voters toss out corrupt politicians. The main prescription [...] is to facilitate this process in the financial system, to tilt the playing field toward longer-term active investors and away from managers and intermediaries, by improving independent governance, encouraging proxy fights, and increasing disclosure. The key ingredient for democracy and markets to work is intelligent participants, who aggressively pursue their own economic interests. [...] But, how smart are the participants? Not very, it seems. Individual investors overpay for active investment management, paying high fees for below average performance. Individual investors chase returns, moving aggressively into technology at just the wrong time. Why aren't investors smarter? The process of learning in financial decisions is not very efficient. A defective refrigerator is immediately apparent when milk spoils. Bad investment advice is hard to recognize and even harder to prove. Businesses fail for legitimate reasons all the time, so poor investment performance is not, on its own, a reason to fire your investment advisor. [...] The upshot of an uninformed herd is speculative bubbles. These can get started quite easily, whether in tulips, technology stocks, or Florida real estate. And this, more than anything else, is what allows corporate managers and entrepreneurs to sell overvalued stock, investment bankers to pocket underwriting fees, and mutual funds to profit in spite of mediocre performance. [...] And, as long as capital is distributed across millions of people, developing real wisdom and skill at investing is not going to be a worthwhile proposition for the typical individual investor. [...]

The third option and the last resort is more heavy handed regulation. Sarbanes-Oxley is a move in this direction. And, there are now calls for similar oversight of mortgage banking. No doubt, regulation can help restore trust, and prevent a spiral from excessive optimism to pessimism. The concern is an intervention that has unintended consequences and delivers measurable costs for immeasurable benefits. [...] Should the Fed, the Treasury, and the SEC be more activist regulators, attempting to stop bubbles before they start? There is no easy, quantifiable answer here." Baker concludes.

[60]CHARLES P. KINDLEBERGER: *Manias, Panics, and Crashes: A History of Financial Crises*, New York (Basic Books) 1978.

3. The asset price approach: One of the most dramatic causes of crises is the sudden plummet in the price of assets such as shares and real estate due to the fact that future cash flows are falling. The price crash in asset values leads to an increasing demand for liquidity by borrowers and banks, which the banks cannot meet. As described in Theories 1 and 2, this leads to liquidity crunches and insolvencies.[61]

It can be seen that the present financial crisis is best explained by Theory 3 and the fall in house prices engendering the insolvency of mortgage banks.[62] Even if this systemic cause is acknowledged, the question is why the banks' lending policies supported the formation of an asset bubble in the first place, especially in the housing market; why did they persist with credit enhancement through opaque securitization and stoke an excess of financial bets on derivatives, through financial wagers between banks, which created no added value?

The observer must be conscious of the variety of reasons for a financial crisis and must guard against hasty moralizing and criminalization. The ethical perspective, however, is not one of moralizing but of determining the personal responsibility of actors in the systems within which they were acting. The systems of the economy are still action systems and not physical systems of mechanical cause and effect. The actors can respond positively or negatively to the imperatives of the system.

The fact that it is difficult, and perhaps not even desirable, to criminalize those who bankrupted the banking system, because misconduct had become more or less commonplace, can be conceded without ethically excusing the actors. When what is wrong behavior has become commonplace, those who behave that way cannot be declared guilty of a criminal act, because if all citizens are conforming to the same behavioral norms, they cannot be accused of deviant behavior. Deviant behavior is the precondition for criminalization, because non-deviant – i.e. "normal" –

---

[61]FRANKLIN ALLEN and DOUGLAS GALE: *Understanding Financial Crises*, Oxford (Oxford University Press) 2007, paperback edition 2009, pp. 19–21. Cf. also FREDERIC S. MISHKIN: "Global Financial Instability: Framework, Events, Issues," *Journal of Economic Perspectives*, 13 (1999), pp. 3–20, here p. 6: "Four factors can lead to increases in asymmetric information problems and thus to financial instability: deterioration of financial sector balance sheets, increases in interest rates, increases in uncertainty, and deterioration of non financial balance sheets due to changes in asset prices."

[62]CARMEN M. REINHART and KENNETH S. ROGOFF: "Is the 2007 US Sub-Prime Financial Crisis So Different? An International Historical Comparison", *American Economic Review*, 98 (2008), pp. 339–344, ask whether the current crisis in the USA is unique or follows a general pattern. They come to the conclusion that in many respects, the crisis follows the pattern of previous financial crises, e.g. in that the majority of financial crises in history were preceded firstly by a rise in public borrowing and secondly a liberalization of financial markets (p. 342). In comparison with the other five major financial crises in the recent past, the USA's budget deficit is particularly high, running at over 6% of gross national product (p. 341). The authors conclude in their pre-crisis paper: "The United States should consider itself quite fortunate if its downturn ends up being a relatively short and mild one."

behavior can only be criminal in extreme situations.[63] This is a valid legal argument, but not an ethical one. In terms of business ethics, the fact remains that almost the entire finance industry had become accustomed to forms of behavior which no longer served the purpose of the financial industry, only that of the brazen, unbridled enrichment of financial actors. Furthermore, rather than the taxpayer, it is the financiers at the helm of the industry who failed to prevent the debacle as a whole but it is the taxpayer who must now pay compensation for the damage done to the economy. Liability for the damage caused by the financial crisis must also take the form of repaying the state support and paying interest on the state loans and guarantees taken out at the time.

The financial system can only be preserved if each one of its attributes that became a cause of the financial market crisis can be modified. Among these attributes are the development of hyper-speculation, the upsurge in derivatives wagers, the excessive bonuses, and the inversion of the shareholder-value principle from a control to an ultimate-end principle of the firm. Nothing compels Western societies to cling to these attributes of hyper-finance capitalism, and nothing stops financial intermediaries from acting in accordance with the laws of simple morality once again, e.g. that when one enters into a fiduciary contract, one must also fulfill the fiduciary duty. The described attributes of hyper-finance capitalism, including neglect of the fiduciary duty, are not necessary attributes of capitalism. Capitalism will still function with that degree of speculation that is necessary to maintain financial market liquidity, and with the expedient level of derivatives betting that is necessary for hedging. It will function with normal employment contracts instead of with bonus systems, and with the shareholder-value principle as a principle of control instead of an ultimate end in itself.

The hyper-finance capitalism of the period before the financial market crisis was a kind of impostor capitalism. Like all impostors, it made the most of its opportunities until time was called on the charade. The astonishing thing about the time before the financial crisis was that almost everybody was better off for the duration; or more precisely, everyone felt better off than they had been in periods of normal capitalism. Since the 1990s, there was a kind of impostor economy – and parts of the banks were worse impostors than most, that is all. When the first bubble burst in 2002, it would not have been unreasonable to have thought: "Okay, that was that; now things have to change." But then the ingenious US Federal Reserve chief Alan Greenspan arrived on the scene, evaded the recession and inflated the next bubble – which inevitably burst.

---

[63]More important than penal prosecution is the personal, civil liability of those responsible for the bankruptcies of the financial institutions. Cf. also ROGER PARLOFF: "Wall Street: It's Payback Time," *Fortune*, January 19, 2009, pp. 37–45, here p. 45: "Criminality is about deviance, so the more widespread undesirable conduct turns out to have been, the harder it is to treat it as criminal."

The Way Out of Financial Crises

Behind the individual causes of the financial market crisis lie the tendency and deliberate aim of modern industry to push production capacity to its limits and to achieve the maximum domestic product by means of optimum capital allocation. The finance industry plays an important role in meeting this objective through its function of financial intermediation. Through its defining role in the credit market and its mediating function in the markets for capital and derivatives, it serves the optimal allocation of capital and hence the efficiency of the economy as a whole.

Investment credit creates new opportunities for economic growth. For that reason, we will keep on needing the financial industry in future. Nevertheless, the crisis shows that a failure of financial institutions is as much of a negative multiplier as their sound functioning is a positive multiplier. Financial crises, with their inefficient allocation of capital, lead to shrinkage of the real economy. It is therefore necessary to avoid any failure or malfunctioning of the financial sector. Even if the financial sector does not always achieve the production-possibility frontier in its financial services to the real economy, a slightly suboptimal allocation of capital is preferable to a full-blown financial crisis, which results from unduly risky allocation of capital by means of excessive credit provision and total depletion of the banks' equity. If less creative and risk-laden financial instruments mean that we lose 0.5% of growth in the economy as a whole, this has to be better than a financial market crisis with substantial capital destruction and negative growth of −5% in the national economy. Taking the frequency of financial crises to be once every 30 years, and a loss of growth of 0.5% per year over 30 years, the calculation looks different again. In this case, it would be better to put up with one financial crisis every 30 years. We would then be talking about rational financial crises, which it is more rational to tolerate than to forego the endeavor for optimal capital allocation.[64] The choice between risk-laden capital allocation and possible financial crises is no longer so clear-cut, if a substantial loss of growth over a number of years caused by less-creative financing instruments is countered by the risk of a relatively modest and infrequent crisis. The frequency of financial crises is critical.

With reference to the relationship between the efficiency of capital allocation, the efficiency of the financial industry, and growth in the real economy, it is evident that risk assessment for financial instruments is difficult, and when it comes to the question of what risks the financial system should enter into as regards its choice of instruments, consensus is virtually impossible. Finance ethics must therefore be circumspect, and reluctant to reject these instruments as a whole and to declare them ethically problematic. Even for the assessment of risky financial instruments, ethics does not seek to counter the reality of the financial industry with an abstract principle, but rather, setting out from the purpose of the finance industry and the

---

[64]MICHAEL THIEL: *Eine Theorie der rationalen Finanzkrise* [A theory of the rational financial crisis], Frankfurt/M. (Peter Lang) 1996, discusses the approaches which explain financial crises from the rationality of the actors.

restrictions of human rights, it develops ethical normativity out of the nature of the matter of the finance industry. The obligations thus derived, from the principle of adequacy for the purpose of an institution or the principle of obligation arising out of the nature of the matter, are certainly normative, even if they are not perhaps as comprehensive and strict as those who were harmed by a financial market crisis might hope. From the ethical principle that the obligation arises out of the nature of the matter, we can infer that we must reject utterly inflated instruments which deliver no benefits for the customer or superficial solutions which reap micro-economic benefits for the financial institutions but have no macro-economic merit.

According to this principle, certain forms of securitization are also ethically problematic. When Posner, for instance, writes, "The opacity of complex securities to investors on one side, there is nothing improper about securitizing debt – that is transforming a debt into a security",[65] it is a self-contradictory statement. The opacity of complex securitized financial instruments cannot be left aside. It is the central economic and ethical problem of securitization. From the viewpoint of a theory of ethical economy, it is indefensible to create securitized instruments that are not understood and consequently cause enormous damage. It would be like allowing racing cars on the public highway – most drivers could not handle them safely even though there will always be a few who can. The conditions for securitization must be modified and made more stringent.[66] And banks must be prepared to explain the economic benefit for capital allocation of securitized bonds like CDOs, which are only constructed and sold in order to circumvent the banks' capitalization requirements and which thereby increase the economic or systemic risk and trigger crises.

The question of limiting derivatives wagers has already been discussed. When it comes to derivatives, the same question applies as to securitization. Do the vast majority of derivatives have any functional benefit other than to generate commissions and fees for the financial institutions? On ethical grounds it is also worth demanding that the number of derivative contracts is not inflated and is not decoupled from the hedging and arbitrage function, so as to lead to economically harmful speculation. The objective of avoiding hyper-speculation makes it necessary for derivatives contracts to be made more responsible and transparent through registration and the deposit of capital than is the case today. As a general principle for financial markets speculation, it is required on ethical grounds that speculation does not escalate out of control and exceed the necessary level to ensure market liquidity.

The most effective way out of the crisis is to instill an awareness among the actors in financial institutions and financial markets that the finance industry is not just a playground for financial geniuses and speculators, but that banks, the stock exchange and financial advisers have a service function. They serve the real

---

[65]POSNER (2009), p. 54.

[66]This demand is also voiced by SINN (2009), p. 314: "So multi-tiered securitization should be prohibited. [...] A multi-tiered securitization of often six and up to 24 tiers is absurd and fulfils no economic function whatsoever. It is nothing other than trickery to exploit the highly lax and loophole-ridden rules of the system." (Own translation from the German).

economy by improving the allocation of capital, which in turn is necessary for the efficiency of the economy as a whole.

Part and parcel of the service mentality of the finance industry is respect for the bank's fiduciary duty towards the customer. This duty is not only an external legal duty but also an inner, ethical duty or self-commitment. The conscious knowledge that the finance industry also has an ethical self-commitment, and not just externally justiciable duties, is a point of central importance for overcoming the financial market crisis. The financial industry must realize that it is operating in a domain of the utmost ethical sensitivity. An ethical self-commitment by financial advisers and financial institutions is indispensable for the simple reason that the state cannot underwrite every consultation with a financial adviser. The banks must understand that they are financial service providers, that their job is to serve the customer, and that they should therefore feel bad every time they sell somebody something or advise them to do something that later leaves them worse off. They have a duty to act in the customer's interest, a duty of allegiance to the customer. The impression we are given by many financial intermediaries is that if anything goes wrong, it is a result of the general risk or market sentiment, but certainly not the result of their bad advice.

Unlike doctors, financial services providers have no malpractice insurance, but sometimes the financial advice they give is akin to malpractice. Financial service providers do not assume the role of a guarantor, as doctors do, which entails a heightened duty of care for the patient and which has stronger legal reinforcement than the warranties of other occupations. Doctors must have the feeling, based on their professional ethics, that if the patient is worse after treatment, something is wrong. Financial intermediaries prefer to shift the blame onto the market, seeing it as having turned against the customer. This betrays the continuing lack of a clear code of professional ethics for financial intermediaries.

The financial crisis, like all far-reaching historical crises, has not just one but several causes. Not all are relevant in terms of business ethics; that is, conditioned by shortcomings in business and corporate ethics. Some crisis phenomena, however, were caused by a lack of ethical motivation and of willingness to act ethically on the part of financial actors, or by defective institutional ethics in the financial institutions.

The causes are not exclusively the fault of the bankers, because everybody from politicians to bank customers clamored for and capitalized on the policy of easy money and universal access to cheap credit. In this sense, everybody played a part in the expansion and overextension of the finance sector. It is inappropriate to put the blame solely on the market economy and its specific components, the banks and the finance industry. The financial sector made big mistakes but was not the sole cause of the supply of unduly cheap credit. This policy initially broadened everybody's opportunities: major investments by major corporations, house building by the wealthy and the not so wealthy, and not least, the scope for state expenditure in excess of the restrictions of a balanced budget by means of public borrowing on the financial market. Added to that came a dramatic increase in the price of oil, which was exogenous to the financial industry. It reduced household disposable income and caused distress to the American automobile industry with its gas-guzzling SUVs that suddenly nobody wanted to buy.[67]

It was a social policy desideratum that even poorer people should be in a position to borrow in excess of their normal creditworthiness to buy their own homes. Cheaper home mortgage financing, particularly in the USA, was not invented by bankers but by politicians. It is also wrong to say that simplifying access to mortgages is bad per se. On the contrary, this reduction in the cost of mortgages was an element of the demands of nineteenth-century social reform, realized by the introduction of cooperative and mutual banks.

The policy of cheap money also had to help with the financing of Germany's extraordinary burdens, like German unification, or America's extraordinary burdens, like the Iraq war. Nobody wanted to impose consumer austerity on the German or the American populations to cover the bloating of these items of public expenditure, as would have been necessary in order to finance the extraordinary burdens entirely from taxation. Politicians chose credit financing, public borrowing, which contributed to the overstrain of the credit market. Public borrowing in Germany followed a dramatic trajectory, growing almost fourfold in the decade after German unification.[68] Such a steep rate of increase was bound to trigger an explosion in the financial sector.

Therefore the scale of the current crisis cannot be blamed solely on the greed of actors in the financial institutions. It is also a consequence of the fiscal and welfare state, which has to finance more and more tasks and expenditures, but on the other hand – not least due to international competition from tax havens – cannot crank the tax lever any tighter and therefore has to resort to public borrowing and call upon the market for credit.

After the collapse of major banks with illustrious histories, the word on everyone's lips is more control. Nevertheless, it is necessary to steer a course between the extremes of fully deregulated capitalism, on the one hand, and state control of the financial sector, on the other, along a third route of ethical self-commitment and self-control within the framework of a market system based on the model of the social market economy.

In the decade from 1997 to 2007, voluntary restraint and self-control in the financial sector were ideas that were out of sight and out of mind, replaced by the idea of the efficient market, with external competition which rendered voluntary restraint by market participants superfluous. Control by means of efficient markets was also the

---

[67]This connection between the dramatically rising oil price, reduced consumer income, and the crisis surrounding car models with better fuel economy in the American car industry, as causes of recession are pointed out by JAMES SUROWIECKI: "The Financial Page: Oil Check.", *The New Yorker*, June 22, 2009, p. 30. The causal factors resulting from the oil price hike in 2007/8 had nothing to do with the financial market crisis. The oil price can be a major downturn factor because, according to Surowiecki, it sends consumer confidence through the floor.

[68]Source: Bund der Steuerzahler (German Taxpayers Association), according to Statistisches Bundesamt (Federal Statistical Office) (1950–2007) and own calculations by Bund der Steuerzahler (2008–2009).

basis of the Washington Consensus which was deemed to apply to all countries and to the global financial market. In contrast to the Washington Consensus, the consensus of the theory of the German Social Market Economy rejects any such dogma of market infallibility and holds it to be permanently beyond the pale of rational discussion.

The Social Market Economy does not defend the thesis that markets infallibly produce correct information, but rather that they produce the best possible information while sometimes functioning inadequately or imperfectly. The Social Market Economy is cognizant of the limits of human rationality. In "social market economy", the attribute "social" should not therefore be understood to mean "redistributing", "equalizing" or "leveling", but rather, "having an attenuating influence on instabilities".[69] The effects of the limitations of human rationality in the market coupled with inordinate egotism in the market, cause instabilities, as the financial crisis shows. Attenuation of these instabilities is the goal of the social market economy. In taking cognizance that market instabilities will need to be attenuated time after time, the Social Market Economy is intellectually ahead of the harmony-credulity of shareholder-value capitalism, and is therefore superior in terms of the theory and practice of the market economy. Risks are not inherent only to the Anglo-American system, however. They are also inherent to the continental European systems, even if one system is sometimes the mirror-reflection of the other. Anglo-American capitalism is threatened by the pensions crisis due to the weakness of the capital market, while the European Social Market Economy's pension system is endangered by the demographic problem.

Another aspect of the theory of the Social Market Economy is the awareness that market instabilities are related to the problems people have in accurately gauging risk. People can take excessive risks in the market. Therefore the Social Market Economy attaches great value to strict adherence to the banks' capitalization requirements, which have been undermined since 1980.

---

[69]SIEGFRIED HAUSER, in: "Die ökonomische und soziale Dimension der Sozialen Marktwirtschaft – Komplementarität versus Konflikt" [The economic and social dimension of the Social Market Economy – complementarity versus conflict], lecture at the conference on "Die Perspektiven der Sozialen Marktwirtschaft" held by the Wirtschaftspolitische Gesellschaft von 1947 (WIPOG) in Wiesbaden on 6 April 2006. In his talk at the same conference, the author of the present book saw the future of Germany's Social Market Economy in a rather dismal light, in that the word "social" in "Social Market Economy" is increasingly shifting away from the sense of "attenuating instabilities" towards "redistributing" and "corporatist bargaining between major parties and associations", a mood exacerbated by Germany's demographic and pension problems. As an impact of the crisis in the financial market, the pension problems of American "pension fund capitalism", far from diminishing, have been rendered rather greater today by the financial crisis than the woes of Germany's pay-as-you-go pension insurance scheme; although this is no more than cold comfort for the threatened German pension system. The financial market crisis will force the Social Market Economy to revert to the original meaning of "social" as "attenuating instabilities", thereby restoring its vitality and appeal. – Cf. on the theory of the Social Market Economy P. KOSLOWSKI (ed.): *The Social Market Economy. Theory and Ethics of the Economic Order*, Berlin, Heidelberg, New York, Tokyo (Springer) 1998.

The Social Market Economy is equally cognizant that people in the market may be too risk-averse and not take big enough risks, which is an equally bad thing. So it is no use invoking the "social" attribute to reinforce demands for the German finance industry to adopt an unduly risk-averse strategy as opposed to the high-risk strategy of the Anglo-American finance industry, because this would not be social at all: such a strategy of the financial system would waste considerable macro-economic growth potential from which the economy as a whole would no longer stand to benefit.[70] The rise in the cost of finance in Germany would mean a loss of potential economic growth, and would leave Germany and other continental European countries to fall behind other members of the international community.

One great difference between the USA and Europe resides in the greater realism as well as a certain caution found in the model of the Social Market Economy, which draws partly on experiences of severe crises in the German economic system to arrive at a more realistic assessment of the market economy than the historical victors' perspective of American capitalism. The market economy is the best of all conceivable economic systems, but it is not infallible. Cognizant of the fallibility of humans and human institutions, it needs its regulatory framework. Germany in particular – in light of its history, the atrocities of the regression to Nazism, two World Wars and two additional stock market crashes – and continental Europe in general are more pessimistic and cautious than the USA and Great Britain.

In the 1920s, there was only one crash that hit all the Western countries, and that was the stock market crash of 1929, whereas Germany alone was affected by the earlier currency wipe-out and stock market collapse of 1923, which occurred largely as

---

[70]The same applies *mutatis mutandis* to regulation. If this produces higher costs than returns, it must also be hauled onto the dissection bench of criticism, according to HORST SIEBERT: "Ein Regelwerk für die Finanzmärkte" [A regulatory code for the financial markets], *Frankfurter Allgemeine Zeitung*, 25 October 2008, No. 250, p. 11. – JILL LEPORE: "I.O.U. How we used to treat debtors", *The New Yorker*, April 13, 2009, pp. 34–41, here p. 38f., points out in her essay on the history of the treatment of debtors and bankruptcy in the USA that the USA has a different, more forgiving and therefore more risk-embracing relationship to debt and bankruptcy than Europe:

> "Americans, though, came to prefer forgiving everyone's debts, on the ground that sorting debtors into two systems (bankruptcy for wheelers and dealers, debtor's prison for chumps) is, finally, undemocratic. Americans fought to provide the same debt relief for everyone because we believe in equality, and because bankruptcy protection makes taking risks less risky. Americans, Tocqueville wrote, 'make a virtue of commercial temerity'. We like risk. 'Hence arises the strange indulgence which is shown to bankrupts.' Our willingness to forgive – and forget – debt lies behind a good part of our prosperity [...]. Some Americans want traders to pay the risks we all took, as if traders *sinned* but we were merely *investing*."

Since the settlers in eighteenth century America were deeply in debt to traders in London, Lepore takes the view of the American Declaration of Independence as a fortunate reprieve:

> "Virginia planters like Jefferson and Washington were monstrously in debt to merchants in London [...]. Declaring independence was a way of cancelling those debts. The American Revolution, some historians have argued, was itself a form of debt relief." (Ibid., p. 36).

a consequence of the Treaty of Versailles war reparations[71] – the German currency fell to 400 billion Reichsmark to the dollar – and Germany alone saw its currency collapse once again after the Second World War. Therefore people in Germany are understandably more alarmed by the current crisis, and place more value on monetary stability – including during the present phase of crisis management – than those in charge of American monetary policy.

Especially compared to the currency collapse of 1923, we can afford to view the present financial crisis with greater equanimity. In comparison to the dimensions of Germany's historical financial crisis, the present one is considerably more modest in caliber.

The Social Market Economy considers the minimum equity requirement upon financial institutions not just from the perspective of the banks but of the financial system as a whole. In the past, this has often been at odds with the interests of Germany's *Mittelstand*, its small and medium-sized businesses, since they like to borrow as cheaply as possible. Sure enough, by June 2009 the German spokesmen for business owners were calling for a new kick-start to the securitized bond market in order to lower the costs of their corporate borrowing. All the criticism of securitized loans, especially collateralized debt obligations (CDOs), was making credit more expensive for businesses, they claimed.[72]

A risk assessment will have to be conducted in such a way as to strike an appropriate balance between the corporate interest in cheap finance and the public interest in the stability of the financial sector through the adequate capitalization of banks. This appeal for easy money, even in the very midst of the crisis, shows how difficult a thing financial discipline is to define and maintain. Barely is one crisis receding and the next is already in the making.

---

[71] Not forgetting that these, in part, were also a reaction to the – albeit substantially lower – French reparation payments following the Franco-Prussian war of 1870/71.

[72] "Der Staat soll den Verbriefungsmarkt ankurbeln. Sorge vor Kreditklemme im Mittelstand/ Banken brauchen Instrumente zum Risikotransfer" [The state should kick-start the securitization market. Fears of a credit crunch in small and medium-sized businesses/ Banks need instruments of risk transfer], *Frankfurter Allgemeine Zeitung*, 18 June 2009, No. 138, p. 22.

References

ALBERT, H.: *Marktsoziologie und Entscheidungslogik*, Neuwied (Luchterhand) 1967, p. 66f.

ALCHIAN, A. A and H. DEMSETZ: "Production, Information Costs, and Economic Organization", in: A. A. ALCHIAN: *Economic Forces at Work*, Indianapolis (Liberty Press) 1977, pp. 73–110.

ALLEN, F. and D. GALE: *Understanding Financial Crises*, Oxford (Oxford University Press) 2007, paperback edn. 2009.

ALTENDORFER, Ch.: *Insidergeschäfte. Rechtsgrundlagen und Sanktionen*, Vienna (Bank-Verlag/Orac) 1992.

ANDERSEN, K.: "The End of Excess. Why this crisis is good for America", *Time-Magazine*, April 6, 2009, cover-story, pp. 35–38.

ANDREAS, K.: "Denkansätze für eine Ethik im Bankwesen", in: P. KOSLOWSKI (ed.): *Neuere Entwicklungen in der Wirtschaftsethik und Wirtschaftsphilosophie*, Berlin, Heidelberg, New York, NY, Tokyo (Springer) 1992 (= Studies in Economic Ethics and Philosophy Vol. 2), pp. 177–193.

ANGER, D.: *Insiderregeln im Wertpapiergeschäft ausgewählter Länder*, Diss. (Erlangen-Nuremberg) 1981.

ARGANDOÑA, A. (ed.): *The Ethical Dimension of Financial Institutions and Markets*, Berlin, New York, NY, Tokyo (Springer) 1995 (= Studies in Economic Ethics and Philosophy Vol. 7).

ARGANDOÑA, A.: "Understanding the Financial Market Crisis – Improving the Financial Market Performance. From a Business Ethics Point of View", presentation at the conference "Einsichten aus der Finanzmarktkrise für das Bankcompliance" of the "Working Group on Compliance and Ethics in Financial Institutions, German Business Ethics Network", held in collaboration with Bayerische Hypo- und Vereinsbank AG on May 29, 2009 in Munich.

ART CARDEN and JOSHUA HALL: "Why are some places rich while others are poor? The Institutional Necessity of Economic Freedom", *iea Economic Affairs* (March 2010), pp. 48–54.

ASSMANN, H.-D.: "Das künftige deutsche Insiderrecht (I und II)", *Die Aktiengesellschaft* (1994), pp. 196–206 and 237–258.

ASSMANN, H.-D.: "Das neue deutsche Insiderrecht", *Zeitschrift für Unternehmens und Gesellschaftsrecht* (1994), pp. 494–529.

ATWOOD, M.: *Payback. Debt as Metaphor and the Shadow Side of Wealth*, London (Bloomsbury) 2008. In German: *Payback: Schulden und die Schattenseite des Wohlstands*, Berlin (Berliner Taschenbuch Verlag) 2009.

AUGSBURG CONFESSION.: (1530) English translation published online at http://www.projectwittenberg.org/pub/resources/text/wittenberg/wittenberg-boc.html.

BAETGE, J.: *Insiderrecht und Ad-hoc-Publizität*, Düsseldorf (IDW-Verlag) 1995.

BAKER, M.: "Review of John C. Bogle: The Battle for the Soul of Capitalism, New Haven, CT and London (Yale University Press) 2005," *Journal of Economic Literature*, 22 (September 2008), pp. 731–734.

BALZLI, B. et al.: "Der Bankraub", in: *Der Spiegel*, November 17, 2008, 47, pp. 44–73, online: http://www.spiegel.de/spiegel/0,1518,590656,00.html.

BATCHVAROV, A. (ed.): *Hybrid Products.Instruments, Applications and Modelling*, London (Risk Books) 2005.

BAUMANN, W.: "Bekämpfung der Geldwäsche: Banken an die Front", *Bankinformation*, 18 (1991), Issue 4, pp. 19–21.

BERKSHIRE HATHAWAY INC.: *2002 Annual Report: Chairman's Letter*, http://www.berkshirehathaway.com/2002ar/2002ar.pdf.

BEUTTER, F.: "Geheimnischarakter des Geldes und ethische Grundlagen der Geheimhaltungspflicht", *Acta Monetaria*, 2 (1978), pp. 9–17.

BLOND, PHILLIP: *Red Tory. How Left and Right have Broken Britain and How we can Fix It*, London (Faber and Faber) 2010.

BOATRIGHT, J. R.: *Ethics in Finance*, Malden, MA and Oxford (Blackwell) 1999 (Foundations of Business Ethics).

BÖCKLI, P.: *Insiderstrafrecht und Verantwortung des Verwaltungsrates*, Zurich (Schulthess Polygraphischer Verlag) 1989.

BÖHM, J.: *Der Einfluß der Banken auf Großunternehmen*, Hamburg (Steuer- und Wirtschaftsverlag) 1992.

BOGENSBERGER, W.: "Die Bestrafung der Geldwäscherei – Gefahr oder Chance für die Banken?", *Bank-Archiv*, 40 (1992), Issue 12, pp. 1049–1058.

BOGLE, J. C.: *The Battle for the Soul of Capitalism*, New Haven, CT and London (Yale University Press) 2005.

BORCHARDT, K.: "Einleitung," in: *MAX WEBER: Börsenwesen Schriften und Reden 1893–1898*, ed. Knut Borchardt, Tübingen (Mohr Siebeck) 1999.

BRADY, F. N.: *Ethical Managing: Rules and Results*, Upper Saddle River, NJ (Prentice Hall) 1989.

BRADY, F. N.: "Impartiality and Particularity in Business Ethics", in: P. KOSLOWSKI, Y. SHIONOYA (eds.): *The Good and the Economical. Ethical Choices in Economics and Management*, Berlin, Heidelberg, New York, NY and Tokyo (Springer) 1993 (= Studies in Economic Ethics and Philosophy Vol. 4), pp. 175–194.

BRANDEIS, L. D.: *Other People's Money and How the Bankers Use It* (1914), Boston, MA and New York, NY (Bedford/St. Martin's) 1995.

BRAUNBERGER, G.: "Credit Default Swaps. Das Produkt, das die Finanzkrise verschärfte", *Frankfurter Allgemeine Zeitung*, 3 (April 2009), Issue 79, p. 24.

BREMMER, IAN: *The End of the Free Market. Who Wins the War Between States and Corporations?* New York (Portfolio) 2010.

BRENNER, B.: "Das Bankgeheimnis – abschaffen oder stärken?", *Neue Zürcher Zeitung*, 242, (October 18/19, 1997), p. 9.

BREUER, R.-E.: "Die Deutsche Terminbörse als Vorreiter einer Börsenlandschaft der 90er Jahre?", *Zeitschrift für Bankrecht und Bankwirtschaft*, 2 (1990), Issue 3, pp. 101–103.

BROUWER, J. J. and P. MOERMAN: *Angelsaksen versus Rijnlanders: zoektocht naar overeenkomsten en verschillen in Europees en Amerikaans denken*, Antwerpen (Garant) 2005.

BRUNNERMEIER, M. K.: "Deciphering the Liquidity and Credit Crunch 2007–2008," *Journal of Economic Perspectives*, 23 (2009), pp. 77–100.

BRUNS, H.-G.: "Finanzpublizität nach Inkrafttreten des 2. Finanzmarktförderungsgesetzes – Zur praktischen Umsetzung bei Daimler-Benz", in: J. BAETGE: *Insiderrecht und Ad-hoc-Publizität*, Düsseldorf (IDW-Verlag) 1995, pp. 107–119.

BÜSCHGEN, H. E.: "Zur Diskussion um das Bankensystem in der Bundesrepublik Deutschland", *WSI Mitteilungen* (1995), Issue 7, pp. 362–374.

BULLINGER, H.: *Predigten 21 und 22 aus den Dekaden (1549–1551)* [Sermons 21 and 22 from the decades 1549–1551] after the German translation by Johannes Haller, Zurich 1558.

CAHL, D. and J. KLOS: *Bankgeheimnis und Quellensteuer im Vergleich internationaler Finanzmärkte*, Herne/Berlin (Neue Wirtschaftsbriefe) 1993.

CAPPELLI, P.: "The Future of the U.S. Business Model and the Rise of Competition", *The Academy of Management Perspectives*, 23 (2009) pp. 5–10.

CARTER, E. J.: "Breaking the Bank: Gambling Casinos, Finance Capitalism, and German Unification", in: *Central European History*, 39 (2006), pp. 185–213.

CASPARI, K.-B.: "Die Problematik der wesentlichen Kursbeeinflussung einer publizitätspflichtigen Tatsache", in: J. BAETGE: *Insiderrecht und Ad-hoc-Publizität*, Düsseldorf (IDW-Verlag) 1995, pp. 65–78.

CATRINA, C.: *Arms Transfers and Dependence*, New York, NY (Taylor & Francis) 1988 (=United Nations Institute for Disarmament Research. UNIDIR and Dissertation University of Zurich).

CHEW, D. H. JR.: *The New Corporate Finance. Where Theory Meets Practice*, Boston, MA (Irwin McGraw-Hill) 1999.

CLAPSON, M.: *A Bit of a Flutter: Popular Gambling and English Society, 1823–1961*, Manchester (Manchester University Press) 1992.

COPELAND, M. V.: "Intel's secret plan. This giant box contains a super-hush-hush project that promises to transform Intel's business. Can the company inside millions of PCs find a way to power billions of phones and other gadgets?", in: *Fortune*, May 12, 2009, http://money.cnn.com/2009/05/12/technology/copeland_intel.fortune/index.htm

CORBETTA, G.: "Shareholders", in: B. HARVEY (ed.): *Business Ethics. A European Approach*, Hemel Hempstead (Prentice Hall) 1994, pp. 88–102.

CORTRIGHT, S. A. and M. J. NAUGHTON (eds.): *Rethinking the Purpose of Business. Interdisciplinary Essays from the Catholic Social Tradition*, Notre Dame, Indiana (University of Notre Dame Press) 2002.

COVAL, J., J. JUREK and E. STAFFORD: "The Economics of Structured Finance," *Journal of Economic Perspectives*, 23 (2009), pp. 3–25.

CULP, C. L.: *Structured Finance and Insurance: The ART of Managing Capital and Risk*, New York, NY (Wiley) 2006.

DAHRENDORF, R.: "Europäisches Tagebuch (XII)", *Merkur*, 48 (1994), Issue 7, pp. 639–640.

DARRIN, W. SNYDER BELOUSEK.: "Market Exchange, Self-Interest, and the Common Good: Financial Crisis and Moral Economy", *Journal of Markets and Morality*, 13 (2010), pp. 83–100.

DAS, S.: *Structured Products and Hybrid Securities*, Hoboken, NJ (John Wiley) 2nd edn. 2001.

DAS, S.: *Structured Products 4: Equity, Commodity, Credit and New Markets: 2*, Hoboken, NJ (John Wiley) 2005 (Swaps & Financial Derivatives Library).

DEGEORGE, R. T.: "Ethics and the Financial Community: An Overview", in: O. F. WILLIAMS, F. K. REILLY, J. W. HOUCK (eds.): *Ethics and the Investment Industry*, Savage (Rowman & Littlefield) 1989, pp. 197–216.

DEGEORGE, R. T.: *Business Ethics*, New York, NY (Macmillan Publishing Company) 1990.

DE LUCIA, R. D., R. H. DIXON, D. T. FERRIS, J. PETERS and B. R. PLUMMER: *Commercial Bank Management: Functions and Objectives*, Wamberal (Serendip) 1987.

DENNERT, J.: "Insider Trading", *Kyklos*, 44 (1991), Issue 2, pp. 181–202.

DESSAUER, F.: "Dienst- und Verdienstwirtschaft. Ein Wort zur Wirtschaftsnot der Gegenwart", *Hochland*, 23 (1926), Issue 2, pp. 513–520.

DÍEZ-ALEGRÍA, J.: "El problema del fundamento ontológico de la obligación en la obra De iustitia de Luis de Molina", *Pensamiento*, 7 (1951), pp. 147–167.

DIMARTINO, D. and J. V. DUCA: "The Rise and Fall of Subprime Mortgages," *Economic Letter— Insights from the Federal Reserve Bank of Dallas*, 2 (November 2007), Issue 11, online: http://www.dallasfed.org/research/eclett/2007/el0711.html

DINGELDEY, TH.: *Insider-Handel und Strafrecht*, Cologne, etc. (Heymanns) 1983.

DRUCKER, P.: *The Unseen Revolution: How Pension Fund Socialism Came to America*, New York, NY (Harper and Row) 1976.

ENGEL, G.: "Zur Problematik eines gesetzlichen Verbots von Insider-Geschäften", *Jahrbuch für Sozialwissenschaft*, 42 (1991), pp. 388–407.

FRAME, W. S. and L. J. WHITE: "Fussing and Fuming over Fannie and Freddie: How Much Smoke, How much Fire?", *Journal of Economic Perspectives*, 19 (2005), pp. 159–184.

FRANK, J.: *Dostoevsky: The Stir of Liberation*, Princeton, NJ (Princeton University Press) 1986.

FRANKE, G.: "Inside Information in Bank Lending and the European Insider Directive," in: KL. HOPT, E. WYMEERSCH (eds.): *European Insider Dealing*, London (Butterworth) 1991, pp. 273–286.

FRANKE, G. and J. P. KRAHNEN: "Default risk sharing between banks and markets: The contribution of collateralized loan obligations," in: M. CAREY, R. STULZ (eds.): *The Risks of Financial Institutions*, National Bureau of Economic Research, Chicago, IL (University of Chicago Press) 2006, pp. 603–631.

FRANKE, G.: "Gefahren des kurzsichtigen (internationalen) Risikomanagements des Bankkredits, der Collateralized Debt Obligations (CDO) sowie der Stuctured Products und die Finanzmarktkrise," presentation at the conference "Einsichten aus der Finanzmarktkrise für das Bankcompliance" of the "Working Group on Compliance and Ethics in Financial Institutions, German Business Ethics Network", held in collaboration with Bayerische Hypo- und Vereinsbank AG on 29 May 2009 in Munich.

FREEMAN, R. E.: *Strategic Management: A Stakeholder Approach*, Boston, MA (Pitman) 1984.

FREEMAN, R. E.: "The Politics of Stakeholder Theory: Some Future Directions", *Business Ethics Quarterly*, 4 (1994), pp. 413 ff.

FREEMAN, R. E. and D. L. GILBERT: *Unternehmensstrategie, Ethik und persönliche Verantwortung*, Frankfurt am Main (Campus) 1991.

FREUD, S.: *Die Traumdeutung* (1900), Frankfurt am Main (S. Fischer) 1982 (Studienausgabe, Vol. 2). Title in English: *The Interpretation of Dreams*.

FRIEDMAN, B. M.: Article on "Capital, credit and money markets", in: *The New Palgrave. A Dictionary of Economics*, London (Macmillan), New York, NY (Stockton), Tokyo (Maruzen) 1987, Vol. 1, pp. 320–327.

FUNK, F.-X.: *Zins und Wucher. Eine moraltheologische Abhandlung mit der Berücksichtigung des gegenwärtigen Standes der Cultur und der Staatswissenschaften*, Tübingen (Laupp) 1868.

GAUGLER, E.: "Shareholder Value und Unternehmensführung", in: P. KOSLOWSKI (ed.): *Shareholder Value und die Kriterien des Unternehmenserfolgs*, Heidelberg (Physica-Verlag) 1999, pp. 175–186.

GAY, D. E. R.: Article on "Dividend Policy", in: *The New Palgrave. A Dictionary of Economics*, London (Macmillan), New York, NY (Stockton), Tokyo (Maruzen) 1987, Vol. 1, pp. 896–899.

GELINAS, NICOLE: *After the Fall. Saving Capitalism From Wall Street – and Washington*, New York, NY and London (Encounter) 2009.

Gesetz über den Wertpapierhandel und zur Änderung börsenrechtlicher und wertpapierrechtlicher Vorschriften (Zweites Finanzmarktförderungsgesetz) [German Act Governing Securities Trading and for the Modication of Regulations Governing the Stock Exchanges and Securities: Second Financial Market Promotion Act] of 26 July 1994.

GIERSCH, C. (ed.): *Money makes the world go round: Ethik als notwendiges Gestaltungsprinzip für Banken und Kapitalmärkte*, Mering (Hampp) 2007.

GLAHE, F. R.: "Professional and Nonprofessional Speculation, Profitability, and Stability", *Southern Economic Journal*, 33 (1966), Issue 1, pp. 43–48.

GORLIN, R. A. (ed.): *Codes of Professional Responsibility*, Washington DC (Bureau of National Affairs) 3rd edn. 1994.

GRABNER-KRÄUTER, S.: *Die Ethisierung des Unternehmens: ein Beitrag zum wirtschaftsethischen Diskurs*, Wiesbaden (Th. Gabler) 1998.

GREEN, R. K. and S. M. WACHTER: "The American Mortgage in Historical and International Context", *Journal of Economic Perspectives*, 19 (2005), pp. 93–114.

GRUNDMANN, St.: "The Prohibition of Insider Dealing in Germany", *Revue de la Banque* (1995), pp. 275–282.

GRUNEWALD, B.: "Neue Regeln zum Insiderhandel", *Zeitschrift für Bankrecht und Bankwirtschaft*, 2 (1990), Issue 3, pp. 128–133.

GUILLÉN, M. F., E. GARCÍA-CANAL: "The American Model of the Multinational Firm and the 'New' Multinationals From Emerging Economies", *The Academy of Management Perspectives*, 23 (2009), pp. 23–35.

HABERMAS, J.: "Die postnationale Konstellation und die Zukunft der Demokratie", in: J. HABERMAS: *Die postnationale Konstellation*, Frankfurt am Main (Suhrkamp) 1998.

HALDANE, A, A. TURNER and M. WOLF.: "What is the Contribution of the Financial Sector: Miracle or Mirage?", in: *The Future of Finance*, LSE Report, 2010, downloadable at http://harr123et.files.wordpress.com/2010/07/futureoffinance1.pdf

HARTMAN, L. P.: *Perspectives in Business Ethics*, New York, NY (McGraw Hill) 2004.

HAUSER, S.: "Die ökonomische und soziale Dimension der Sozialen Marktwirtschaft – Komplementarität versus Konflikt", lecture at the conference on "Die Perspektiven der Sozialen Marktwirtschaft" held by the Wirtschaftspolitische Gesellschaft von 1947 (WIPOG) in Wiesbaden on 6 April 2006.

HAUSER-GERHARTER, M.: "Die Umsetzung der EG-Geldwäschereirichtlinie in Deutschland", *Bank-Archiv*, 41 (1993), Issue 6, pp. 473–475.

HEGEL, G. W. F.: *Vorlesungen über die Philosophie der Geschichte*, in: *Hegels Werke in zwanzig Bänden*, edited by Eva Moldenhauer and Karl Markus Michel, Frankfurt am Main (Suhrkamp) 1970, Vol. 12.

HEGEL, G. W. F.: *Grundlinien der Philosophie des Rechts*, in: *Hegels Werke in zwanzig Bänden*, edited by Eva Moldenhauer and Karl Markus Michel, Frankfurt am Main (Suhrkamp) 1970, Vol. 7. English edition of Hegel's *General Introduction to the Philosophy of History* and *Philosophy of Right* at http://www.marxists.org/reference/archive/hegel/index.htm

HENDRIE, A. (ed.): *Banking Structures and Sources of Finance in the European Community*, London (The Financial Times Business Publishing) 1981.

HENRY, N. and C. SCHMITT (eds.): *Victorian Investments: New Perspectives on Finance and Culture*, Bloomington, IN and Indiana (Indiana University Press) 2008.

HERRHAUSEN, A.: "Zu den Vorschlägen der Monopolkommission zur Begrenzung des Anteilserwerbs von Banken an Nichtbanken", in: H. HELMRICH (ed.): *Wettbewerbspolitik und Wettbewerbsrecht. Zur Diskussion um die Novellierung des GWB*, Cologne (Heymanns) 1987, pp. 299–326.

HERRHAUSEN, A.: "Großbanken und Ordnungspolitik", *Die Bank* (1988), Issue 3, pp. 120–129.

HESSELBERGER, D.: *Das Grundgesetz. Kommentar für die politische Bildung*, Neuwied (Luchterhand) 8th edn. 1991, pp. 136ff.

HOHL, M.: "Heinrich Bullinger als Ökonom", *stab. Stiftung für Abendländische Bildung und Kultur*, Rundbrief 149 (2006), online: http://www.stab-ch.org/index.php?page=rundbrief-149.

HOPT, K. J and M. R. WILL.: *Europäisches Insiderrecht. Einführende Untersuchung – Ausgewählte Materialien*, Stuttgart (Enke) 1973.

HOPT , K. J.: "Europäisches und deutsches Insiderrecht", *Zeitschrift für Unternehmens- und Gesellschaftsrecht*, 20 (1991), pp. 17–73.

HOPT, K. J.: "Ökonomische Theorie und Insiderrecht", *Die Aktiengesellschaft* (1995), pp. 353–362.

HOPT, K. J.: "Das neue Insiderrecht nach §§ 12 ff WpHG – Funktion, Dogmatik, Reichweite", in: *Das Zweite Finanzmarktförderungsgesetz in der praktischen Umsetzung. Bankrechtstag 1995*, Berlin and New York, NY (Walter de Gruyter) 1996, pp. 3–34.

HOUSE OF REPRESENTATIVES/ARSÈNE P. PUJO.: *Report of the Committee Appointed Pursuant to House Resolutions 429 and 504 to Investigate the Concentration of Control of Money and Credit, Submitted by Mr. Pujo, February 28, 1913*, Washington, DC (Government Printing Office) 1913, p. 131

HÜFNER, M.: "Zur Wettbewerbssituation des deutschen Kreditgewerbes", in: H. HELMRICH (ed.): *Wettbewerbspolitik und Wettbewerbsrecht. Zur Diskussion um die Novellierung des GWB*, Cologne (Heymanns) 1987, pp. 261–276.

INTERNATIONAL SWAPS AND DERIVATIVES ASSOCIATION (ISDA): *Market Survey*, Year End 2008.

ITZKOWITZ, D. C.: "Fair Enterprise or Extravagent Speculation: Investment, Speculation, and Gambling in Victorian England," *Victorian Studies*, 45 (2002), pp. 121–147.

JACOB, A.-F. (ed.): *Bankenmacht und Ethik*, Stuttgart (Poeschel) 1990.

JACOB, A.-F. (ed.): *Eine Standesethik für den internationalen Finanzmanager?*, Stuttgart (Poeschel) 1992.

JANSEN, S. A.: *Mergers and Acquisitions. Unternehmensakquisitionen und –kooperationen. Eine strategische, organisatorische und kapitalmarkttheoretische Einführung*, Wiesbaden (Gabler) 3rd edn. 2000.

JAROSLAW, B.: *Ideal und Geschäft*, Jena (G. Fischer) 1913.

JAY W. R.: *Money, Greed and God. Why Capitalism is the Solution and Not the Problem*, New York, NY (HarperOne) 2010.

JENSEN, M. C.: "Agency Cost of Free Cash Flow, Corporate Finance, and Takeover", *American Economic Review*, 76 (1986), pp. 323–329.

JENSEN, M. C. and W. H. MECKLING: "The Theory of the Firm: Managerial Behavior, Agency Costs, and Ownership Structure", in: K. BRUNNER (ed.): *Economics and Social Institutions*, Boston, MA (Martinus Nijhoff) 1979, pp. 163–231.

JOHN DUNS SCOTUS: *Quaestiones in Lib. IV. Sententiarum*, Vol. 9, Lyon (Laurentius Durand) 1639, Reprint Hildesheim (Olms) 1968.

JOHNSTON, J. F.: "Natural Law and the Fiduciary Duties of Business Managers", in: NICHOLAS CAPALDI (ed.): *Business and Religion: A Clash of Civilizations?*, Salem, MA (M&M Scrivener Press) 2005, pp. 279–300.

JONES, C.: "Money laundering. What's in the suitcase?", *The Banker*, 140 (1990), Issue 770, pp. 12–14.

JUAN DE LUGO: *De iustitia et iure*, Lyon 1670.

JUNKER, K.: *Insidergeschäfte. Das heisse Geld an der Börse*, Munich (Langen-Müller) 1993.

KALDOR, N.: "Speculation and Economic Stability", *The Review of Economic Studies*, 7 (1939), pp. 1–27.

KANTOROWICZ, H.: *Der Begriff des Rechts*, Göttingen (Vandenhoeck & Ruprecht) 1963. Original: *The Definition of Law*, Cambridge (Cambridge University Press) 1958.

KANTZENBACH, E.: "Die Macht der Banken", *WIST Wirtschaftswissenschaftliches Studium*, 19 (1990), Issue 3, p. 105.

KASERER, C.: "Trends in der Bankenaufsicht als Motor der Überregulierung des Bankensektors – Anmerkungen aus einer politökonomischen Perspektive", *Perspektiven der Wirtschaftspolitik*, 7 (2006), pp. 67–87.

KAVANAGH, T. M.: *Enlightenment and the Shadows of Chance: The Novel and the Culture of Gambling in Eighteenth-Century France*, Baltimore, MD (Johns Hopkins University Press) 1993.

KAVANAGH, T. M.: *Dice, Cards and Wheels: A Different History of French Culture*, Philadelphia, PA (University of Pennsylvania Press) 2005.

KENNEDY, P.: "American Power Is on the Wane", *The Wall Street Journal*, January 15, 2009, http://online.wsj.com/article/SB123189377673479433.html

KHURANA, R.: *From Higher Aims to Hired Hands: The Social Transformation of American Business Schools and the Unfulfilled Promise of Management as a Profession*, Princeton, NJ (Princeton University Press) 2007.

KINDLEBERGER, C. P.: *Manias, Panics, and Crashes: A History of Financial Crises*, New York, NY (Basic Books) 1978.

KIRCHHOF, P.: "Der Schaden der anderen. Unsere Wirtschaftskrise besteht darin, dass die Beteiligten für ihr Produkt und ihre Schuldner kaum noch verantwortlich sind. Eigentum kann es nur noch in begrenzter Freiheit geben", *Frankfurter Allgemeine Zeitung*, 28 (May 2009), Issue 122, p. 31.

KLEINFELD, A.: *Persona oeconomica: Personalität als Ansatz der Unternehmensethik*, Heidelberg (Physica) 1998.

KNIGHT, F.: *Risk, Uncertainty, and Profit*, New York, NY (Houghton Mifflin) 1921.

KÖHLER, H.: "Der Markt braucht Regeln und Moral", *Frankfurter Allgemeine Zeitung*, 25 (March 2009), Issue 71, p. 8.

KOSLOWSKI, P.: *Zum Verhältnis von Polis und Oikos bei Aristoteles. Politik und Ökonomie bei Aristoteles* 1976, 2nd edn. 1979, 3rd revised and expanded edition published as *Politik und Ökonomie bei Aristoteles*, Tübingen (Mohr Siebeck) 1993.

KOSLOWSKI, P.: *Gesellschaft und Staat. Ein unvermeidlicher Dualismus*, Stuttgart (Klett-Cotta) 1982.

KOSLOWSKI, P.: *Ethik des Kapitalismus.* Mit einem Kommentar von James M. Buchanan, Tübingen (Mohr Siebeck) 1982, 6th edn. 1998. English translation: *Ethics of Capitalism,* in: P. KOSLOWSKI: *Ethics of Capitalism and Critique of Sociobiology. Two Essays with a Comment by James M. Buchanan,* Berlin, Heidelberg, New York, Tokyo (Springer) 1996, 142 pages (= Studies in Economic Ethics and Philosophy, Vol. 10).

KOSLOWSKI, P.: *Principles of Ethical Economy,* Dordrecht, Boston, MA and London (Kluwer, now Springer) 2001 (Issues in Business Ethics, Vol. 17). German original: *Prinzipien der Ethischen Ökonomie,* Tübingen (Mohr Siebeck) 1988, Reprint 1994.

KOSLOWSKI, P.: *Wirtschaft als Kultur. Wirtschaftskultur und Wirtschaftsethik in der Postmoderne,* Vienna (Edition Passagen) 1989.

KOSLOWSKI, P.: *Gesellschaftliche Koordination. Eine ontologische und kulturwissenschaftliche Theorie der Marktwirtschaft,* Tübingen (Mohr Siebeck) 1991.

KOSLOWSKI, P.: "Ethische Ökonomie und theologische Deutung der Gesamtwirklichkeit in der Summa Theologiae des Thomas von Aquin", in: P. KOSLOWSKI: *Die Ordnung der Wirtschaft. Studien zur Praktischen Philosophie und Politischen Ökonomie,* Tübingen (Mohr Siebeck) 1994, pp. 64–88.

KOSLOWSKI, P. (ed.): *The Theory of Ethical Economy in the Historical School. Wilhelm Roscher, Lorenz von Stein, Gustav Schmoller, Wilhelm Dilthey and Contemporary Theory,* Berlin, New York, NY and Tokyo (Springer) 1995.

KOSLOWSKI P. (ed.): *Methodology of the Social Sciences, Ethics, and Economics in the Newer Historical School. From Max Weber and Rickert to Sombart and Rothacker,* Berlin, New York, NY and Tokyo (Springer) 1997.

KOSLOWSKI, P. (ed.): *The Social Market Economy. Theory and Ethics of the Economic Order,* Berlin, Heidelberg, New York, NY and Tokyo (Springer) 1998.

KOSLOWSKI, P.: "Shareholder Value und der Zweck des Unternehmens," in: P. Koslowski (ed.): *Shareholder Value und die Kriterien des Unternehmenserfolgs,* Heidelberg (Physica-Verlag) 1999, pp. 1–32.

KOSLOWSKI, P.: Solidarism, Capitalism, and Economic Ethics in Heinrich Pesch, in: P. KOSLOWSKI (ed.): *The Theory of Capitalism in the German Economic Tradition: Historism, Ordo-Liberalism, Critical Theory, Solidarism,* Berlin, Heidelberg, New York, NY and Tokyo (Springer) 2000, pp. 371–394, especially Part III of the essay on Pesch's theory concerning interest, "The Legitimacy of Taking Interest", pp. 378–386.

KOSLOWSKI, P.: "The Theory of Ethical Economy as a Cultural, Ethical, and Historical Economics: Economic Ethics and the Historist Challenge", in: P. KOSLOWSKI (ed.): *Contemporary Economic Ethics and Business Ethics,* Berlin, Heidelberg, New York, NY and Tokyo (Springer) 2000, pp. 3–15.

KOSLOWSKI, P.: "The Limits of Shareholder Value", *Journal of Business Ethics,* 27 (2000), pp. 137–148.

KOSLOWSKI, P.: "Privatheit und Bankgeheimnis. Staatsphilosophische und wirtschaftsethische Überlegungen", in: KONRAD HUMMLER, GERHARD SCHWARZ (eds.): *Das Recht auf sich Selbst. Bedrohte Privatsphäre im Spannungsfeld zwischen Sicherheit und Freiheit,* Zurich (Verlag Neue Zürcher Zeitung) 2003, pp. 189–202.

KOSLOWSKI, P.: "Speculation and Insider Trading as Problem of Business Ethics," in: LAURA P. HARTMAN (ed.): *Perspectives in Business Ethics,* Boston, MA (McGraw–Hill Irwin) 2004, pp. 703–716.

KOSLOWSKI, P.: "Schuldverhältnisse", in: MARCO M. OLIVETTI (ed.): *Le don et la dette,* Padova (CEDAM e Biblioteca dell'«Archivio di filosofia») 2005, pp. 421–436.

KOSLOWSKI, P.: "The Common Good of the Firm as the Fiduciary Duty of the Manager", in: NICHOLAS CAPALDI (ed.): *Business and Religion: A Clash of Civilizations?,* Salem, MA (M&M Scrivener Press) 2005, pp. 301–312.

KOSLOWSKI, P.: "Some Principles of Ethical Economy", in: CHRISTOPHER COWTON, MICHAELA HAASE (eds.): *Trends in Business and Economic Ethics,* Berlin, Heidelberg, New York, NY and Tokyo (Springer) 2008, pp. 31–70 (Studies in Economic Ethics and Philosophy).

Revised and extended version of the author's inaugural lecture at the VU University Amsterdam on 9 December 2005. Available online at: http://www.springer.com/cda/content/document/cda_downloaddocument/9783540794714-c1.pdf?SGWID=0-0-45-572511-p173820940

KOSLOWSKI, P. and F. HERMANNI (eds.): *Endangst und Erlösung 1. Untergang, ewiges Leben und Vollendung der Geschichte in Philosophie und Theologie*, Munich (W. Fink) 2009.

KOSLOWSKI, P. (ed.): *Endangst und Erlösung 2. Rechtfertigung, Vergeltung, Vergebung in Philosophie und Theologie*, Munich (W. Fink), in press 2010

KRAHNEN, J. P.: "Der Handel von Kreditrisiken. Eine neue Dimension des Kapitalmarkts," *Perspektiven der Wirtschaftspolitik*, 6 (2005), pp. 499–519.

KRÜGELSTEIN, A.: *Über den begrifflichen Unterschied von Spiel und Wette. Ein civilistische Studie*, Leipzig (Fues' Verlag) 1869, p. 65.

KRUGMAN, P.: "The Economic Consequences of Herr Steinbrueck", *The New York Times*, (11 December 2008).

LAMBSDORFF, O.: "Banken und Unternehmenskonzentration – Muss der Bankeneinfluß zurückgeschraubt werden?", *Zeitschrift für das gesamte Kreditwesen*, 41 (1988), Issue 2, pp. 56–59.

LANDMESSER, F. X.: *Die Eigengesetzlichkeit der Kultursachgebiete (Wirtschaft und Staat)*, Cologne, Munich, Vienna (Oratoriums-Verlag) 1926.

LAHMANN, K.: *Insiderhandel: ökonomische Analyse eines ordnungspolitischen Dilemmas*, Berlin (Duncker & Humblot) 1994.

LEARS, J.: *Something for Nothing: Luck in America*, New York, NY (Viking) 2003.

LEE, J.: "Money laundering and payment systems", *World of Banking* (1990), Issue 5, pp. 14–15.

LEIBACHER, W.: "Ein facettenreiches Problem. Geldwäscherei: Wie weiter?", *Schweizer Bank*, 4 (1989), Issue 4, pp. 15–19.

LEISINGER, K. M.: *Unternehmensethik. Globale Verantwortung und modernes Management*, Munich (C. H. Beck) 1997.

LEISKOW, H.: *Spekulation und öffentliche Meinung in der ersten Hälfte der 19. Jahrhunderts*, Jena (Gustav Fischer) 1930.

LEPORE, J.: "I.O.U. How we used to treat debtors", *The New Yorker*, April 13, 2009, pp. 34–41.

LUHMANN, N.: "Kapitalismus und Utopie", *Merkur*, 48 (1994), Issue 3, p. 191.

LEWIS, M.: "Self Conscious Emotions: Embarassment, Pride, Shame, and Guilt", in: M. LEWIS, J. M. HAVILAND-JONES (eds.): *Handbook of Emotions*, New York, NY (Guilford) 2nd edn. 2000, pp. 623–636.

LUTTERMANN, C.: "Der Wahrheitsstandard einer Weltfinanzordnung", *Frankfurter Allgemeine Zeitung*, 10 (November 2008), Issue 263, p. 20.

LYNCH, J. J.: *Banken und Moral:die vierte Dimension im Finanzmanagement*, Wiesbaden (Gabler) 1996.

THE MAHABHARAIA, Book 2: *Sabha Parva of Krishna-Dwaipayana Vyasa*, translated by Kisari Mohan Ganguli [published between 1883 and 1896], online edition: http://www.sacred-texts.com/hin/m02/m02080.htm

MAIHOFER, W.: "Die Natur der Sache", in: A. KAUFMANN (ed.): *Die ontologische Begründung des Rechts*, Darmstadt (Wissenschaftliche Buchgesellschaft) 1965, pp. 52–86.

MANNE, H. G.: *Insider Trading and the Stock Market*, New York, NY (The Free Press) 1966.

MARTIN, D. W and J. H. PETERSON.: "Insider Trading Revisited", *Journal of Business Ethics*, 10 (1991), pp. 57–61.

MAYR, G. von.: *Die Pflicht im Wirtschaftsleben*, Tübingen (Laupp) 1900.

MCGEE, R. W.: "Insider Trading: An Economic and Philosophical Analysis", *Mid-Atlantic Journal of Business*, 25 (1988), pp. 35–48.

MCKIBBON, R.: "Working-Class Gambling in Britain, 1880–1939," *Past & Present*, 82 (1979), pp. 147–178.

MEIER, Ch.: *Wirtschaftsdelikte im Bankengewerbe. Eine empirische Untersuchung über Entwicklung, Erscheinungsformen, Schadensfolgen und Risikoursachen bankbezogener Wirtschaftsstraftaten*, Bern, Stuttgart (Haupt) 1986.

MESSNER, J.: *Das Naturrecht. Handbuch der Gesellschaftsethik, Staatsethik und Wirtschaftsethik*, Berlin (Duncker & Humblot) 1984.

MESSNER, J.: *Ethik. Kompendium der Gesamtethik*, Innsbruck, Vienna and Munich (Tyrolia) 1955, VII. Buch: *Wirtschaftsethik*.

MISHKIN, F. S.: "Global Financial Instability: Framework, Events, Issues," *Journal of Economic Perspectives*, 13 (1999), pp. 3–20.

MITCHELL, L. E.: *The Speculation Economy: How Finance Triumphed over Industry*, San Francisco, CA (Barrett-Koehler) 2007.

MOLINA, L. de.: *De justitia et jure*, Moguntiae (Madrid) 1602.

MOORE, D, D. LYELL, D. WHELLER, J. TONGZON and R. CRANE.: *Financial Institutions and Markets*, Wamberal (Serendip) 1988.

MOORE, J.: "What is Really Unethical About Insider Trading", *Journal of Business Ethics*, 9 (1990), pp. 171–182.

MÜLLER, KLAUS: *Globalisierung*, Frankfurt, New York, NY (Campus) 2002.

MÜLLER-MÖHL, E.: *Optionen und Futures. Grundlagen und Strategien für das Termingeschäft in Deutschland, Österreich und in der Schweiz*, Stuttgart (Schäffer-Poeschel) 5th edn. 2002.

MUNTING, R.: *An Economic and Social History of Gambling in Britain and the USA*, Manchester (Manchester University Press) 1996.

NEIDLINGER, K.: *Studien zur Geschichte der deutschen Effektenspekulation von ihren Anfängen bis zum Beginn der Eisenbahnaktenspekulation. Ein Beitrag zur Börsengeschichte*, Jena (G. Fischer) 1930.

NELL-BREUNING, O. von.: *Grundzüge der Börsenmoral*, Freiburg im Breisgau (Herder) 1928. Reprint, Münster (LIT) 2002.

NELL-BREUNING, O. von.: "Volkswirtschaftlicher Wert und Unwert der Börsenspekulation", *Stimmen der Zeit*, 114 (1928a), pp. 46–56.

OELLERKING, C. and M. HOLZGRABE.: *Sparkassen und Genossenschaftsbanken im Spannungsverhältnis zwischen Moral und Ökonomie. Strukturelemente, Organisationsgrundsätze und Geschäftspolitik*, Frankfurt am Main (Lang) 1990.

OTTO, H.: "Geldwäsche und das strafrechtliche Risiko von Bankmitarbeitern", *Zeitschrift für das gesamte Kreditwesen*, 47 (1994), Issue 2, pp. 63–68.

PALAZZO, B.: *Interkulturelle Unternehmensethik: deutsche und amerikanische Modelle im Vergleich*, Wiesbaden (Th. Gabler) 2000, Reprint 2001.

PARLOFF, R.: "Wall Street: It's Payback Time," *Fortune*, January 19, 2009, pp. 37–45

PAUL, J. CELLA III.: "The Financial Crisis and the Scientific Mindset", *The New Atlantis. A Journal of Technology & Society*, 26 (Fall 2009 Winter 2010), pp. 30–38.

PAUMGARTEN, N.: "The Death of Kings. Notes from a Meltdown," *The New Yorker*, May 18, 2009, (Annals of Finance), pp. 40–57.

PEILL-SCHOELLER, P.: *Interkulturelles Management*, Berlin and New York, NY (Springer) 1994.

PERSSON, M.: "De crisis als de grote gelijkmaker. Door de economische neergang zal de welvaart beter worden verdeeld", in: *de Volkskrant*, January 10, 2009, p. 11.

PESCH, H.: "Zinsgrund und Zinsgrenze", *Zeitschrift für katholische Theologie*, 12 (1888), pp. 393–418.

PETER, HANS-BALZ, H. RUH and R. HOHN.: *Schweizer Bankwesen und Sozialethik. Teil I: Einleitung. Sozialethische Erwägungen und Folgerungen, Teil II*, Bern und Lausanne 1981 (=Studien und Berichte aus dem Institut für Sozialethik des Schweizerischen Evangelischen Kirchenbundes, 31 und 32).

PETERS, TH. J. and R. H. WATERMAN JR.: *Auf der Suche nach Spitzenleistungen. Was man von den bestgeführten US-Unternehmen lernen kann*, Landsberg (Verlag Moderne Industrie) 1986. Original: *In Search of Excellence. Lessons from America's Best-Run Companies*, New York, NY (Harper & Row) 1982.

PICOT, A and H. DIETL: "Informations(de-)regulierung am Kapitalmarkt aus institutionenökonomischer Sicht", *Jahrbuch für Neue Politische Ökonomie* (1994), pp. 113–148.

PICOT, G.: *Handbuch Mergers & Acquisitions. Planung, Durchführung, Integration*, Stuttgart (Schäffer-Poeschel) 2000.

PODLINSKI, W.: "Insider – deutsch und europäisch", *Die Bank* (1981), Issue 8, pp. 382–386.

POSNER, R. A.: *A Failure of Capitalism. The Crisis of '08 and the Descent into Depression*, Cambridge, MA (Harvard University Press) 2009.

RACHEL, K, J. HALL and S. BEAULIER: "The Virtues of Business: How Markets Encourage Ethical Behavior", *Journal of Markets and Morality*, 13 (2010), pp.45–58.

RADBRUCH, G.: Rechtsphilosophie, Stuttgart (Koehler) 8th edn. 1973.

RAPPAPORT, A.: *Shareholder Value. Wertsteigerung als Maßstab für die Unternehmensführung*, Stuttgart (Schäffer-Poeschel) 1995, pp. 27 ff. Original: *Creating Shareholder Value. The New Standard for Business Performance*, New York, NY (The Free Press) 1986.

REBÉRIOUX, A.: "Does shareholder primacy lead to a decline in managerial accountability?", *Cambridge Journal of Economics*, Advance Access published online on May 15, 2007.

REED, E. W. and E. K. GILL: *Commercial banking*, Englewood CO (Prentice-Hall) 4th edn. 1989.

REINHART, C. M. and K. S. ROGOFF: "Is the 2007 US Sub-Prime Financial Crisis So Different? An International Historical Comparison", *American Economic Review*, 98 (2008), pp. 339–344.

REITH, G.: *The Age of Chance: Gambling in Western Culture*, New York, NY (Routledge) 1999.

RIEKEBERG, M.: "Banken und Ethik – Ethik durch Banken?", *Bank-Archiv*, 41 (1993), Issue 7, pp. 513–518.

ROCHET, J.-C.: *Why Are There So Many Banking Crises? The Politics and Policy of Bank Regulation*, Princeton, NJ and Oxford (Princeton University Press) 2008.

ROHATYN, F.: "World Capital: The Need and the Risks", *The New York Review of Books*, 41, (14 July 1994), Issue 13, pp. 48–53.

RÖLLER, W.: "Zum Selbstverständnis der Banken in einer offenen Gesellschaft", in: A.-F. JACOB: *Bankenmacht und Ethik*, Stuttgart (Poeschel) 1990, pp. 1–14.

RONALD, T. W.: *Whatever Happened to Thrift. Why Americans Don't Save and What to Do about It*, New Haven, CT and London (Yale University Press) 2008.

RÖPKE, W.: Article on "Spekulation", in: *Handwörterbuch der Staatswissenschaften*, 4th edn. Jena (Gustav Fischer) 1926, Vol. 7, pp. 706–710.

ROSE, P. S.: *Money and Capital Markets. Financial Institutions and Instruments in a Global Marketplace*, Boston, MA (McGraw-Hill) 7th edn. 2000.

ROSEN, R. J.: "The role of securitization in mortgage lending", *Chicago Fed Letter* (The Federal Reserve Bank of Chicago), 244 (November 2007), http://www.chicagofed.org/publications/fedletter/cflnovember2007_244.pdf

ROTH, G. H.: "Shareholder Value und Dividendenausschüttung", in: P. KOSLOWSKI (ed.): *Shareholder Value und die Kriterien des Unternehmenserfolgs*, Heidelberg (Physica-Verlag) 1999, pp. 128–145.

ROTH, W.: "Macht der Banken", in: *Tutzinger Materialen* No. 35, Tutzing 1986.

RYAN, PATRICK HANLEY: *Adam Smith and the Character of Virtue*, Cambridge (Cambridge University Press) 2009.

SCHACHTSCHNEIDER, K. A.: *Res publica res populi. Grundlegung einer allgemeinen Republiklehre. Ein Beitrag zur Freiheits., Rechts-, und Staatslehre*, Berlin (Duncker & Humblot) 1994.

SCHÄFER, H.-B. and C. OTT: *Lehrbuch der ökonomischen Analyse des Zivilrechts*, Berlin, New York, NY and Tokyo (Springer) 1986.

SCHERER, A. G., G. HÜTTER and L. MASSMANN (eds.): *Ethik für den Kapitalmarkt? Orientierungen zwischen Regulierung und Laisser-faire*, Munich (Rainer Hampp) 2003.

SCHERER, A. G.: *Die Rolle der Multinationalen Unternehmung im Prozeß der Globalisierung*, Heidelberg (Physica-Verlag) 2003 (= Ethische Ökonomie. Beiträge zur Wirtschaftsethik und Wirtschaftskultur, Vol. 7).

SCHIMMLER, J.: *Spekulation, spekulative Gewinne und Preisstabilität. Eine Theorie der Spekulation unter besonderer Berücksichtigung der Auswirkungen spekulativer Transaktionen auf die Preisstabilität*, Meisenheim am Glan (Hain) 1974.

SCHMID, N.: *Schweizerisches Insiderstrafrecht. Ein Kommentar zu Art. 161 des Strafgesetzbuches: Ausnützen der Kenntnis vertraulicher Tatsachen*, Bern (Stämpfli) 1988.

SCHMID, N.: "Insiderdelikte und Geldwäscherei – neuere und künftige Aspekte aus der Sicht der Banken", in: W. WIEGAND (ed.): *Aktuelle Probleme im Bankrecht, Berner Tage für die juristische Praxis 1993*, Bern (Stämpfli) 1994, pp. 189–215.

SCHMIDT, R.: "Neuere Property Rights-Analysen in der Finanzierungstheorie", in: D. BUDÄUS (ed.): *Betriebswirtschaftslehre und Theorie der Verfügungsrechte*, Wiesbaden (Gabler) 1988.

SCHMITZ, W.: "Währungsethik – eine tragende Säule der Wirtschaftsethik", in: HELMUT HESSE (ed.): *Wirtschaftswissenschaften und Ethik*, Berlin (Duncker & Humblot) 1988, pp. 373–400.

SCHMOLLER, G.: "Die Gerechtigkeit in der Volkswirtschaft", *Jahrbücher für Gesetzgebung, Verwaltung und Volkswirtschaft im Deutschen Reich*, 5 (1881), pp. 19–54.

SCHNEIDER, D.: "Wider Insiderhandelsverbot und die Informationseffizienz des Kapitalmarkts", *Der Betrieb*, 46 (1993), Issue 29, pp. 1429–1435.

SCHÖRNER, P.: *Gesetzliches Insiderhandelsverbot. Eine ordnungspolitische Analyse*, Wiesbaden (Gabler) 1991.

SCHULZE, W. A.: "Die Lehre Bullingers vom Zins," *Archiv für Reformationsgeschichte*, 48 (1957), pp. 225–229.

SCHUSTER, L.: *Macht und Moral der Banken*, Bern (Haupt) 1977 (= Bankwirtschaftliche Forschungen, Vol. 26).

SCHUSTER, L.: "Moral conflicts in commercial banking", in: S. F. FROWEN, F. P. MCHUGH (eds.): *Financial decision-making and moral responsibility*, Basingstoke etc. (Macmillan) 1995, pp. 73–77.

SCHUSTER, L.: *Unternehmungskultur in Banken*, Ingolstadt (Catherine University Eichstätt, WFI) 1997.

SCHUSTER, L. (ed.): *Wege aus der Banken- und Börsenkrise*, Berlin and Heidelberg, etc. (Springer) 2004.

SCHWARZE, H.-J.: "Ad-hoc-Publizität und die Problematik der Notierungsaussetzung", in: J. BAETGE: *Insiderrecht und Ad-hoc-Publizität*, Düsseldorf (IDW-Verlag) 1995, pp. 97–105.

SCHWEIKART, N.: "Der getriebene Chef. Shareholder value über all – das US-Modell setzt sich durch", *DIE ZEIT*, 20 (10 May 2001), p. 26.

SEN, A.: "Isolation, Assurance, and the Social Rate of Discount", *Quarterly Journal of Economics*, 81 (1967), pp. 112–124.

SEN, A.: "Money and Value. On the Ethics and Economics of Finance", *Economics and Philosophy*, 9 (1993), pp. 203–227.

SHILLER, R. J.: *Irrational Exuberance*, Princeton, NJ and Oxford (Princeton University Press) 6th edn. 2001.

SIEBERT, H.: "Ein Regelwerk für die Finanzmärkte", *Frankfurter Allgemeine Zeitung*, 250 (25 October 2008), p. 11.

SINN, H.-W.: *Kasino-Kapitalismus. Wie es zur Finanzkrise kam, und was jetzt zu tun ist*, Berlin (ECON) 1st edn. 2009, 2nd edn. 2009.

SOLOMON, R. C.: *Ethics and Excellence: Cooperation and Integrity in Business*, New York, NY (McGraw Hill) 1993.

SPIEGEL Magazine: "Der Pleite-König. Millarden-Versagen der Banken", *Der Spiegel*, 16, (18 April 1994), pp. 22–30.

STÄHELI, U.: *Spektakuläre Spekulation. Das Populäre der Ökonomie*, Frankfurt am Main (Suhrkamp) 2007.

STARBATTY, J.: "Warum die Ökonomen versagt haben", *Frankfurter Allgemeine Zeitung*, 258 (4 November 2008), p. 12.

STEIN, J.: *Das Bankwesen in Deutschland*, Cologne (Bank-Verlag) 1993.

STEINMANN, G.: *Theorie der Spekulation*, Tübingen (J.C.B. Mohr [P. Siebeck]) 1970.

STEINMANN, H. and A. LÖHR: "Einleitung: Grundfragen und Problembestände einer Unternehmensethik," in: HORST STEINMANN, ALBERT LÖHR (eds.): *Unternehmensethik*, Stuttgart (Poeschel) 2nd edn. 1991, pp. 3–32.

STEINMANN, H. and A. LÖHR: *Grundlagen der Unternehmensethik*. Stuttgart: (Poeschel) 1991, 2nd edn. 1994.

STERNBERG, E.: *Just Business: Business Ethics in Action*, Oxford (Oxford University Press) 2nd edn. 2000.

STEWART, J. B.: "The Omen. How an obscure Breton trader gamed oversight weaknesses in the banking system", *The New Yorker*, (October 20, 2008), pp. 54–65.

STOTZ, O.: "Germany's New Insider Law: The Empirical Evidence after the First Year," *German Economic Review*, 7 (2006), pp. 449–462.

STRIEDER, J.: *Studien zur Geschichte kapitalistischer Organisationsformen. Monopole, Kartelle und Aktiengesellschaften im Mittelalter und zu Beginn der Neuzeit*, Munich and Leipzig (Duncker & Humblot) 2nd edn. 1925.

STRUCK, E.: Article on "Börsenspiel", in: *Handwörterbuch der Staatswissenschaften*, Jena (Gustav Fischer) 1891, pp. 695–704.

STUDIENKOMMISSION GRUNDSATZFRAGEN DER KREDITWIRTSCHAFT (ed.).: *Bericht der Studienkommission Grundsatzfragen der Kreditwirtschaft*, Bonn (Studienkommission Grundsatzfragen der Kreditwirtschaft) 1979.

STULZ, R. M.: "Should We Fear Derivatives?", *Journal of Economic Perspectives*, 18 (2004), pp. 173–192.

SUMMERS, L. H.: "International Financial Crises: Causes, Prevention, and Cures", *American Economic Review*, 90 (2000), Issue 2, pp. 1–16.

SUROWIECKI, J.: "The Financial Page: The Trust Crunch", *The New Yorker*, October 20, 2008, p. 36.

SUROWIECKI, J.: "The Financial Page: Oil Check," *The New Yorker*, June 22, 2009, p. 30.

TANGNEY, J. P.: "Perfectionism and the Self-Conscious Emotions: Shame, Guilt, Embarrassment, and Pride", in: G. L. FLETT, P. L. HEWITT (eds.): *Perfectionism: Theory, Research, and Treatment*, Washington, DC (American Psychological Association) 2002, pp. 199–215.

TAVIS, L. A.: "The Moral Issue in Allocating Corporate Resources. Shareholders Versus Stakeholders," in: S. A. CORTRIGHT, M. J. NAUGHTON (eds.): *Rethinking the Purpose of Business. Interdisciplinary Essays from the Catholic Social Tradition*, Notre Dame and Indiana (University of Notre Dame Press) 2002, pp. 215–236.

TETT, G.: "How greed turned to panic", *Financial Times*, May 9/10, 2009, p. 17.

THALER, R. H.: *Quasi Rational Economics*, New York, NY (Russell Sage Foundation) Reprint 1994.

THALER, R. H. and C. R. SUNSTEIN: *Nudge: Improving Decisions About Health, Wealth and Happiness*, London (Penguin) paperback edition 2009.

THIEL, M.: *Eine Theorie der rationalen Finanzkrise*, Frankfurt/M. (Peter Lang) 1996.

THIELEMANN, U. and P. ULRICH: *Brennpunkt Bankenethik. Der Finanzplatz Schweiz in wirtschaftsethischer Perspektive*, Bern (Paul Haupt) 2003.

THOMAS AQUINAS.: *Summa theologiae* (1267–1273), Madrid (Biblioteca de Autores Cristianos) 1951.

TOOBIN, J.: "Barney's Great Adventure. The Most Outspoken Man in the House Gets Some Real Power", in: *The New Yorker*, January 12, 2009, pp. 37–47.

TRACY, J. L, R. W. ROBINS and J. P. TANGNEY (eds.).: *The Self-Conscious Emotions: Theory and Research*, New York, NY (Guilford) 2007.

TUCHTFELDT, E.: Article on "Kapitalmarkt", in: *Handwörterbuch der Wirtschaftswissenschaft*, Stuttgart, New York, NY (G. Fischer), Tübingen (Mohr Siebeck), Göttingen (Vandenhoeck & Ruprecht) 1978, Vol. 4, pp. 432–439.

VELASQUEZ, M. G.: *Business Ethics. Concepts and Cases*, Upper Saddle River, NJ (Prentice Hall) 6th edn. 2005.

WAGNER, A.: "Unternehmensethik: Ein Thema auch für Sparkassen und Banken? Teil 1", *Sparkasse*, 113 (1996), pp. 554–561.

WAGNER, A.: *Unternehmensethik in Banken*, Vienna (Bank-Verlag), Vienna (Orac) 1999.

WALDENFELS, B.: "Geschenkte und geschuldete Aufmerksamkeit", in: M. M. OLIVETTI (ed.): *Le don et la dette*, Padova (CEDAM e Biblioteca dell'«Archivio di filosofia») 2005, pp. 297–309.

WEBER, M.: *Die Börse, I. Zweck und äußere Organisation*, Göttingen (Vandenhoeck & Ruprecht) 1894 (= Göttinger Arbeiterbibliothek Vol. 1, No. 2/3, pp. 17–48).

WEBER, M.: *Die Börse, II. Der Börsenverkehr*, Göttingen (Vandenhoeck & Ruprecht) 1896 (= Göttinger Arbeiterbibliothek Vol. 2, No. 2/3, pp. 49–80).

WEBER, W.: *Wirtschaftsethik am Vorabend des Liberalismus. Höhepunkt und Abschluß der scholastischen Wirtschaftsbetrachtung durch Luis de Molina*, Münster (Aschendorff) 1959.

WEICKART, N.-J.: "Firmenübernahme: Festung Deutschland", in: *Manager Magazin*, April 19, 1989, pp. 128–139.

WENGER, E.: "Universalbankensystem und Depotstimmenrecht", in: H. GRÖNER (ed.): *Der Markt für Unternehmenskontrolle*, Berlin (Duncker & Humblot) 1992 (= Schriften des Vereins für Socialpolitik N.F. 214), p. 93f.

WESTMINSTER CONFESSION (1646), online edition: http://www.reformed.org/documents/westminster_conf_of_faith.html

WHITLEY, R.: "U.S. Capitalism: A Tarnished Model?," *The Academy of Management Perspectives*, 23 (2009), pp. 11–22.

WIELAND, J.: *WerteManagementSystem^{ZfW}. Prinzipien und Bausteine für Nachhaltigkeit in der Unternehmensführung* (Manuscript).

WILLIAMS, D.: *Japan: Beyond the End of History*, London and New York, NY (Routledge) 1994 (= The Nissan Institute/Routledge Japanese Studies Series).

WILLIAMSON, O. E.: "Firms and Markets", in: S. WEINTRAUB (ed.): *Modern Economic Thought*, Philadelphia, PA (University of Pennsylvania Press) 1977.

WILLIAMSON, O. E.: "The Modern Corporation: Origins, Evolution, Attributes", *Journal of Economic Literature*, 19 (1981), pp. 1537–1570.

WISSMANN, M., O. GRAF LAMBSDORFF, W. KARTTE, W. RÖLLER and F. NEUBER: "Die Macht der Banken", *Zeitschrift für das gesamte Kreditwesen*, 43 (1990), Issue 1, pp. 3–4, 10–22.

WOJTEK, R. J.: *Insider Trading im deutschen und amerikanischen Recht*, Berlin (Duncker & Humblot) 1978.

WOLFF, B.: *Banking Down Under: Differences between Australian and German Banking and some Conclusions for German Banks*, Working Paper, University of Witten/Herdecke, January 1990.

Name Index

Note: Page numbers in italics refer to quotations in footnotes or references